Group Captain John 'Joe' Collier
DSO DFC and Bar

Group Captain John 'Joe' Collier
DSO DFC and Bar

The Authorized Biography
of the Bomber Commander,
Air War and SOE Strategist
and Dambuster Planner

Simon Gooch

Pen & Sword
AVIATION

First published in 2015 by
Pen and Sword Aviation
an imprint of
Pen & Sword Books Ltd
47 Church Street
Barnsley
South Yorkshire
S70 2AS

ISBN 978 1 47382 751 6

A CIP catalogue record for this book is
available from the British Library.

Typeset by
Mac Style Ltd, Bridlington, East Yorkshire

Printed and bound in England
By CPI Group (UK) Ltd, Croydon, CR0 4YY

Pen & Sword Books Ltd incorporates the imprints of Pen & Sword
Aviation, Pen & Sword Family History, Pen & Sword Maritime, Pen &
Sword Military, Pen & Sword Discovery, Pen and Sword Fiction, Pen
and Sword History, Wharncliffe Local History, Wharncliffe True Crime,
Wharncliffe Transport, Pen & Sword Select, Pen & Sword Military
Classics, Leo Cooper, The Praetorian Press, Seaforth Publishing and
Frontline Publishing.

For a complete list of Pen & Sword titles please contact
PEN & SWORD BOOKS LIMITED
47 Church Street, Barnsley, South Yorkshire, S70 2AS, England
E-mail: enquiries@pen-and-sword.co.uk
Website: www.pen-and-sword.co.uk

Contents

Introduction

John Collier, always known in the Royal Air Force as 'Joe', led a very unusual and in some ways charmed life during the Second World War. Having joined up early, in 1936, he was actively engaged in hostilities from the first day, flying his Hampden bomber on a sweep of the North Sea looking for the *Admiral Scheer*. He went on to be one of the most decorated pilots of the early years of the war.

A wing commander at the age of 25 and having done much to smooth the introduction of the revolutionary new bomber, the Lancaster, into service with 97 Squadron, Collier was selected to perform a new role at the Air Ministry in the Directorate of Bomber Operations (B Ops 1). From early 1943 he was helping to plan the Combined Bomber Offensive, in co-operation with the rapidly-growing USAAF bomber force, devising the precision attacks of the next two years that did so much to help win the war. Perhaps surprisingly, despite the dramas of his sixty-three missions flown, John Collier's time spent in stuffy Whitehall offices – countering the V-weapon threat and planning the Dambusters Raid and much else – provided what he described as the real 'adventure' of his war.

While serving in the Far East just after the war ended, he wrote a typescript memoir of the Whitehall years and began with an 'Apology':

I fear that there will be many parts of this book that the technical experts and historians will not agree with. I ask their pardon for this book is in no way meant to be an historical record of events, but rather a general indication of the part played by one section of the vast Air Ministry organization during the War.

The book has been written largely from memory with a few 'official documents' for guidance – the temperature during authorship has been consistently over 90 degrees, and one of the original purposes was to find an occupation during the afternoons to keep myself awake, while the remainder of the Camp 'charped' (overseas language for slept). If there is anything you don't like about this book, please blame the temperature!

His own 'Introduction' stressed the greater significance he felt his work in Whitehall possessed:

During the War little was heard of the great Military Organisations which conducted and controlled the vast machinery of the War. The Air Ministry was one such of these. It is difficult to imagine that adventure can be found in a Ministry, surely the excitement and glory of War is on the Battlefield? For myself, I suppose it could be said that I had had my fair share of adventure during the four years I was on operations in Bomber Command. I refrain from writing about these adventures because they were in no way different from those experienced by so many airmen of that gallant Command, and further so many books have been written by real heroes, and my personal friends, such as Guy Gibson VC and Leonard Cheshire VC, both of whom are household names today. I found my adventure in this war in the Air Ministry. Not that I took more than a small part in the adventures, which may be a slight misnomer, but I was in a privileged position to watch the most interesting period of the war in Europe during the two most vital years. I had my senses of great thrill and disappointment, and occasionally of achievement, even though such achievements were initially on paper. You may agree with me that adventure can be found during War other than on the Battlefield itself. I hope so!

John Collier's modesty about his feats of airmanship and leadership in the front-line bomber squadrons, which saw him receive a DFC and Bar, a DSO, and to be Mentioned in Despatches three times, is admirable. However, perhaps the story now needs to be rebalanced somewhat, to give a full portrait of both John Collier the wartime pilot and the planner, as well as the young pre-war cadet and the post-war career RAF man who spent twenty-two years in total in the service.

This biography of John Collier is based on his log books, his record of service and squadron record books and combat reports. There are letters home to his parents, and some press reports. As well as including a large part of his own 1946 memoir of the Whitehall years and some of his first draft – with my own annotations, editorial comment and researches – there are also his shorter accounts (written much later) of active service in Britain and the Far East. 'Joe' Collier also features substantially in other wartime memoirs, notably his friend Guy Gibson's classic *Enemy Coast Ahead*.

Almost seventy years after the end of the war the sacrifice of the men of Bomber Command has finally been recognized at the heart of the capital with a grand monument at Hyde Park Corner, unveiled in the summer of 2012. Controversies remain over the prosecution of the air war, and in particular the role of Sir Arthur Harris, but the unimaginable bravery and dedication of RAF air crew cannot be denied, and likewise the intellectual achievement of its planners. I hope in particular that this expansion of John Collier's unique life story will add even more to the lustre of his and his remarkably youthful comrades' record of intense involvement in the epic struggle of 1939 to 1945.

Acknowledgements

Special thanks to Mark Collier for the inspiration for this biography of his father, based on John Collier's unpublished memoir and its first draft, and for access to the family archive of documents, letters and photographs; all of the illustrations included in this book come from the Collier family collection.

Many thanks to the wider Collier family for help and encouragement, especially John Collier's ex-RAF niece Maureen Hodgson.

I gratefully acknowledge Dr Carol Downer's permission to quote from the papers of her late father Air Vice Marshal Sydney Bufton CB, DFC, held by the Churchill Archives at Churchill College, Cambridge [correspondence with John Collier in BUFT/5/13; transcript of taped interview in BUFT/5/19]. Thanks also to the director and staff of the Churchill Archives Centre for their assistance.

I also gratefully acknowledge Alastair Reid's permission to quote from his late aunt Jean Barclay's privately-published book *The Brave Die Never*.

Simon Gooch, 2014

Official Recommendations

Squadron Leader John David Drought Collier, 83 Squadron:

Strongly recommended for the immediate award of the Distinguished Flying Cross, 20 August 1940.

'A fine type of leader who has done uniformly excellent work.'

A.T. Harris, Air Vice Marshal

Squadron Leader John David Drought Collier DFC, 44 Squadron:

Recognition for which recommended: Bar to Distinguished Flying Cross, 30 July 1941.

'This is a very gallant and consistently reliable Bomber pilot and a fine Flight Commander. He is very strongly recommended.'

J.C. Slessor, Air Vice Marshal

Wing Commander John David Drought Collier DFC and Bar, 97 Squadron:

Recognition for which recommended: Distinguished Service Order, 29 September 1942.

'This officer throughout his period of command has maintained his squadron in the very highest state of efficiency. His leadership and example have been exemplary.'

W.A. Coryton, Air Vice Marshal

Letter of Condolence to Mark Collier

Air Chief Marshal Sir Peter Squire KCB DFC AFC ADC FRAeS RAF

Chief of the Air Staff

Ministry of Defence
Main Building
Whitehall
London SW1A 2HB

27 November 2000

Dear Mr Collier,

I was immensely saddened to hear of the death of your father, and I write now on behalf of the Royal Air Force and my Air Force Board colleagues to express our sincere condolences at your very sad loss.

He will be remembered by the Royal Air Force for all his accomplishments, courage and bravery during World War II. He gave devoted and exemplary service in a variety of appointments, all of which he filled with great distinction. In particular, we remember your father's qualities of leadership and dedication, most evidently displayed both on the ground and in the air when serving with Bomber Command.

The Royal Air Force remains most grateful for his considerable contribution and he will be remembered with great esteem.

Sincerely
Peter Squire

Squadron Leader John Collier DFC and Bar in the winter of 1941/2.

On the London Underground, June 1944

Wing Commander John Collier was sitting on a crowded Tube train that was crawling towards the centre of the battered, blacked-out city. Soon he would be passing through the sandbagged entrance to his airless offices in Whitehall after enjoying a few minutes of fresh air in St James's Park. Yet even here in the half-light, faces around him were more animated than usual. The wartime mood had suddenly brightened. It was the second week of June 1944, and the war seemed to be going all our way... The Allied armies were ashore in Normandy, had survived the first difficult days and were preparing to push on from their beachhead. The newspapers being devoured enthusiastically by his fellow passengers were still glowing with the success of D-Day, and the public mood in London was buoyant.

However, John Collier was torn between a boyish enthusiasm for the Second Front, wishing he was back in the fray, and his well-informed misgivings about this illusory sense that it was all over bar the shouting. He knew that all sorts of 'unpleasant things' might arrive in London any day. What, he wondered, would be the reaction on that Underground train if he announced that there would soon be rockets raining down on the city...

For a year now Collier and his team in B Ops 1 – the Directorate of Bomber Operations at the Air Ministry – had been trying to understand the precise nature of Hitler's threatened 'retaliatory weapons', and in August 1943 John himself had drafted the plan of attack on the rocket research establishment at Peenemünde. Knowledge of the bigger rocket remained sketchy, but it was known that a trainload of 'pilotless aircraft' had been seen in the Pas-de-Calais in the last few days. The greatest and most worrying uncertainty was over the nature of the warheads carried by these revolutionary new weapons. Would they, perhaps, contain an atomic weapon, or anthrax?

The tension in the Directorate was palpable, and John was finding it very difficult to live with this inside knowledge. He had already moved his protesting wife and two small boys away from their 'ricketty' digs in Chelsea down to her parents in Sussex some weeks before, but then relented and brought them closer to home. He would join them at Farnborough most nights and attempt to sleep, without much success.

A few days later on the night of 13 June 1944 he was with them there again, lying in bed and thinking through some of the grislier possibilities for the coming onslaught. He also recalled some of the nights he had spent dodging searchlights and flak over German cities in his three years as a bomber pilot, knowing that if he did sleep, these memories would come back to him in unnervingly vivid dreams. Then suddenly a 'peculiar roar' sent him stumbling through the darkened room to the window.

Heading north-west, towards London, was 'a small aircraft with a long flame squirting from its tail. So it had come!'

Part I

Airfields

Chapter One

Wings

A Letter of Application

John Collier was only 18 in 1934 but already alert to a growing sense of danger in Europe after Hitler's election as Chancellor and his immediate suspension of democracy. Nazi aggression was increasing by the day and the young John Collier was sensible of this sobering new atmosphere, having 'seen earlier than most young men of his generation that war with Hitler's Germany was inevitable', according to *The Times*.

He had been working as a trainee land agent on Lord Leigh's estate near Leamington Spa and in January 1933 passed a preliminary examination for student membership of the Incorporated Society of Auctioneers and Landed Property Agents. He seemed to be settling down to a solid provincial career, but the times were not set fair for the social stability that underpinned such work, so in a rush of patriotic enthusiasm John Collier sent off a letter of application to join the Royal Air Force and waited for a reply.

His family background did not suggest such a path was to be predicted. Though subsequently known to his fellow airmen as 'Joe', John David Drought Collier was always plain John to his family. He was born in 1916 at Plympton in Devon; the youngest child of Claude Bertram Collier – 'Bertie' or, in later life, 'Bert' – and his wife Rose. The unusual third Christian name came from his mother's Irish background.

In an 'Appreciation' written for his father's funeral in 1953, John Collier lamented a lost family idyll, something he felt keenly all his life. He noted that at the end of the Victorian era the Colliers were 'comparatively very well off', having been in the wine trade in Plymouth since the seventeenth century – when for generations they were devout and peaceable Quakers – and in the navy's Victorian heyday (having drifted away from the Society of Friends) were supplying its ships' messes with Collier's Port. On the strength of this naval victualling, Bertie's father Mortimer, a partner with his elder brother

William in Collier & Co., built Foxhams, a twenty-three-room mansion at Horrabridge on the fringes of Dartmoor, where his children enjoyed 'a comfortable and enjoyable childhood' in glorious surroundings.

Bertie joined Collier & Co. in a junior capacity and 'was allowed to know little of the business. It was therefore a considerable shock to learn on the day of his wedding to my mother, Rose Mary Reeves, that the firm was financially in a very shaky condition and that he could be given no allowance.' The Collier family finances seem to have been weakened by some disastrous railway investments in America.

Not long after Mortimer's death in 1916, the wine business – dependent upon safe seas – was hit hard by the German U-boat blockade and even after the Great War, as the national economy faltered, things did not improve. Foxhams was put up for sale, but was rescued for Bertie's sister Dena by her husband Oscar Muntz. When John Collier was a very small boy his family moved out to the Plymouth suburbs and advertised a sale of household goods.

Bertie and his elder brother Morty split from the new Collier & Co. partnership with their cousin George in 1924, but a couple of years later their ambitiously-conceived emporium in Plymouth folded. In 1927 John's father moved to Leamington Spa where he managed a large department store for about ten years, but then problems arose with the owner and in the mid-1930s the Colliers moved to Stock, near Ingatestone in Essex, where the countryman-at-heart Claude Bertram Collier started a chicken farm.

These financial insecurities, combined with the knowledge of a comfortable existence in the recent past, powerfully shaped the young John Collier's attitude to education and career and may have had some influence in his choosing at first a very practical line of work. Economic stability became key in the light of his family's relative privations. In another era he would have been trained up, like his father, in the wine trade but also, in another era, there would not have been the existential threat to his country that was becoming increasingly apparent in the mid-1930s.

The reaction of most people in Britain was to cling desperately to any chance of peace, however illusory, and the National Government's policy of appeasement was highly popular. However, it was not an entirely myopic administration as the decision in July 1934 to double the number of squadrons in the RAF would appear to have been a rare moment of hard realism. Prime Minister Stanley Baldwin, who knew that the Germans were using the expansion of the civil airline Lufthansa to get around restrictions on manufacturing military aircraft, declared that the British frontier was no longer the white cliffs of Dover but the Rhine. A year later he admitted that he had underestimated the growing strength of the German Air Force and proposed an increase to 123 squadrons by March 1937 to maintain parity. Winston Churchill, who had no illusions about the Nazis, considered even this to be an underestimate.

It was during this period of rapid expansion of the service and the modernization of its fighters and bombers that John Collier applied to join the Royal Air Force, but his acceptance was delayed. He was not the only young man to be inspired to act decisively and the RAF – more glamorous than the navy, it seems – was inundated with applications.

While waiting for what he assumed would be an imminent call from the Ministry, Collier obtained a temporary job at Benedict House, Northiam, in Sussex, working on another chicken farm set up by a retired London architect John Bishop whose redoubtable wife Evelyn ran the house as an hotel. He arrived there in May 1934 and stayed for eighteen months – longer than anticipated – while he waited for his application to be processed, and though he was 'teased mercilessly' by the Bishop daughters, he fell for the eldest, Elizabeth, known to the family as Beth. However, it was not until Beth saw John Collier in uniform after he was finally taken on by the RAF on a short-service commission in 1936 that she began to think of their very youthful-looking poultry boy in a more romantic light.

Learning to Fly

In March 1936 John Collier wrote home from Benedict House:

Whooppee – I have passed. I heard on Saturday night, I have been provisionally accepted by the Air Council, and will be communicated with later on. Meanwhile, they tell me to learn up a long list of things with the help of a tutor if possible. The list is all more or less arithmetical mechanics, and pure arithmetic, so I am going to take lessons with a tutor in Hastings if I can find a reasonable one.

I shall not be called up until July at the earliest, so I propose, as the quantity of things I have to learn is very large and difficult, to come home for a month, so that I can give all my time to doing the job properly, as the more I learn the quicker I hope I shall get on once I am in...

The Bishops drank my health and luck with a bottle of Champagne last night...

From 1923 de Havilland, builders of the Tiger Moth, had been permitted to run an aviation school for the RAF at their Hatfield aerodrome in Hertfordshire. This was formally known as the No.1 Elementary and Reserve Flying Training School. Another ten civilian flying schools had been brought on board to help out with the sudden expansion of pilot numbers in the RAF by Air Commodore Tedder, Director of Training.

John Collier's Pilot's Log Book begins on 29/6/36 at the Civil Flying School, Hatfield, and the next day marks his first flight as the passenger in a Moth trainer, with F/O Mr Dault as instructor. He was soon learning 'Taxiing & Handling of Engine; Taking off into Wind; Medium Turns; Gliding; Landing & Judging Distances; Low Flying; Spinning' etc and on 21 July 1936 came his first solo flight in a Moth.

By 17 August he had completed fifty hours' flying time and on the 24th he received his Short Service Commission, with the rank of Acting Pilot Officer (Substantive Promotion), before moving up to Scotland and No.8 Flying Training School, Montrose.

He wrote to his parents on 16 September from Montrose, communicating his enthusiasm for every detail of planes and flying:

I have now gone solo in the Hart Trainer and managed quite OK – I went up again today for half an hour solo – and they really are a treat to fly. I went solo in three hours, which was not bad, as a lot of chaps take about 6.

The planes... are pretty large, full size in fact, same as you use in a fighter squadron. They have a 400hp Merlin Rolls-Royce engine – The dashboard of the cockpit is one mass of levers and knobs and instruments – on top of that you have four petrol tap controls, a radiator which has to be wound up & down, down when flying & up when taking off, also a wheel to adjust the tail planes – in fact you have quite a lot to remember, one way & another.

The throttle is 'gated' to prevent you going too fast. They have two tanks one of about 70 gals & the auxiliary of about 23 gals. They burn 30 gallons per hour, & also a lot of oil. They are nice to fly as they are very steady & you do not get bumped about…

If you look in today's *Times* you will see an announcement of our commissions.

By December he was sounding like an old hand:

We have nearly finished all our exams & only have two more – & those will be over by the end of next week, so the rest of the term will be filled up with drill & PT as they don't know quite how to fill in the time…

Luckily we have not been affected by the fog that has been everywhere else in England – but I went for a formation flight down to Edinborough [*sic*] & the fog was so thick there that we were not able to land, we had a hell of a job finding Edinborough… you could not see the Forth Bridge at all…

We had our morse exam & Aldis lamp test this week & I managed to cheat my way through the lamp, which is a load off my mind as I thought I could not pass – There is a devil of a lot of wangling in this racket, if you know how to do it.

John Collier was authorized to wear the RAF Flying Badge on 24/12/36. He sent a Christmas card from No.8 Flying Training School, with a photograph of a flight of Harts over Montrose; then on 23 March 1937 wrote home from No.1 Armament Training Camp, Royal Air Force, Catfoss, Hull where there were bombing ranges:

The countryside around here is most desolate – very flat – & we are seven miles from the nearest town [Hornsea], & there is no means of conveyance at all – no buses –

The aerodrome is in the most ghastly state – mud everywhere – you can only land in one very small corner & that is all ridges & if you are landing across them, as we were today, you bounce about 20′ in the air – the mud is really nearly knee deep in places & we will all wear gum boots most of the time –

Some of the chaps have been on the ranges today – firing Lewis guns from the a/c to the ground – We were taken over the ranges today & they are very complex & a good many men are employed on the job – The bombing targets are 1000 yds out to sea & the ground targets on the cliff edge…

83 Squadron and the Hawker Hind

Acting Pilot Officer John Collier was posted to the re-formed 83 (B) Squadron at RAF Turnhouse, Midlothian on 24 April 1937. He later wrote some 'Memories of Life in No.83 Squadron RAF' in which he waxed nostalgic about Turnhouse, with its plain facilities – 'a small wooden Mess, with a chilly walk to ablutions' – but delightful location, close to Edinburgh and surrounded by beautiful countryside. Among his mess-mates were Tony Bridgman, his future best man James Pitcairn-Hill, and the RAF legend-to-be Guy Gibson.

Life in the air force sounds pretty easy-going in these last years of peace: 'Our duties were not very arduous and were thoroughly enjoyable, with bombing practice in the Firth of Forth, with sunny days by the sea when one had the duty of Range Safety Officer, formation practice and cross country flights were routine.'

Collier was now flying the Hawker Hind, a two-seater biplane light bomber with an open cockpit and fixed undercarriage, but a machine that was rapidly becoming obsolete. He was learning dive-bombing and high-altitude bombing techniques.

He wrote later of the stable community that comprised the peacetime 83 Squadron with the hindsight of years of intense wartime experience and rapid changeover of personnel:

The real joy of Squadron life in those days was that apart from having your own aircraft, you constantly were with your own ground crew, and they formed a great part of one's life… they flew with you on occasions, and took a real pride in the aircraft. Then there were the air gunners and wireless operators who were your regular crew members, and in whom one had great reliance and confidence...

Soon after their arrival at Turnhouse the coronation of King George VI took place (on 12 May 1937), and John Collier and two RAF friends – Tony Bridgman and the raffish half-English, half-German Count Manfred Czernin – 'after obtaining permission from the CO... dashed off to London'. They arrived too late for the procession and, short of cash, called on the count's mother to obtain funds and found a coronation party in full swing with everyone in their regalia.

A month later Collier flew down again, this time to Farnborough for the Hendon Display Formation Practice, and wrote to his proud parents about the Great Fly Past that they would be attending: 'You wanted to know if you would be able to distinguish me out of the other hundreds – Well you may be able to as we are at the end & so low down – There will be a large 108 in red on the side of the plane.' He included a sketch diagram showing planes in five columns: 'A. – Single Seater Fighters / B. Single engine Hinds / C. Twin engine bombers / D. Single engine Hinds / E. Single seater fighters. I hope to be on the outside right in the second last row of Hinds in B line...'

From 29 June 1937 John Collier was a pilot officer (substantive promotion) and noted in a letter from Turnhouse that: 'We are I am sorry to say losing our CO [Dermot Boyle] and having a new one who is Sq Leader [Leonard] Snaith, who however sounds quite nice & is a Schneider Trophy pilot...'

His log book notes some more aggressive-sounding activities: '9th August 1937 – "Raid" on Tilbury Docks.' and '10th August 1937 – Low level attack on Worthy Down.'

From October 1937 John Collier was a flight commander with 83 (B) Squadron, and was able to borrow a plane for a trip home. On the way back, he wrote: 'I saw the "balloon barrage" at Cardington as I flew by & I must say it rather impressed me, I think it would be an excellent defence.'

In November and December 1937 Collier recorded several flights with P/O Gibson. In his book *Enemy Coast Ahead*, Guy Gibson described the carefree atmosphere of the pre-war 83 Squadron. He was in 'A' Flight at Scampton and 'Joe' Collier in 'B' Flight, and according to Gibson 'we were always putting it across B both in flying and drunken parties!' 'B' Flight were therefore, in the parlance, 'stooges'. This rather schoolboyish rivalry matured into a strong friendship between Collier and Gibson through the challenging times to come.

Gibson was, according to a biographer, an acquired taste; especially in his early, somewhat boastful incarnation when his own ground crew gave him the frankly unequivocal nickname of 'Bumptious Bastard'. Nevertheless he was, from the start, a brave and skilled flyer. Similar drive and leadership qualities in the two young men seem to have created both a bond and a certain detachment in their relationship, although none of this is actually spelled out in either man's written accounts of their RAF service. They were destined to fly together, command squadrons at the same base and collaborate on the most celebrated bombing raid of the war. By the time Gibson came to put his experiences down on paper in the winter of 1943/4, he and Joe Collier were two of the last survivors of the pre-war 83 Squadron.

* * *

Three letters home were sent from Air Service Training Mess, Hamble, Southampton – 'Britain's Air University' – which John Collier attended from March to May 1938. One announces 'just books for me for the next three weeks' and 'We are beginning on the final laps of the exams now – only ten more working days!!' He also bought a second-hand Triumph car.

Others, from May to July 1938, came from No.1 Flying Training School, Royal Air Force, Leuchars, Fife, for armament training and where:

> I went for a trip off the catapult that they have got here for launching airplanes straight into the air – a terrific woomph!! & lo & behold you are airborne – quite a queer sensation – your velocity increases from 0 to 60mph in 25 feet –
>
> …We have been carrying on with our gunning & bombing. The bombing is still good but the air firing is also very bad!!

In March 1938, 83 Squadron had moved from Turnhouse to RAF Scampton in Lincolnshire, while Collier was at Hamble. He recalled that they were sorry to leave 'our rather remote life' at Turnhouse, with its apparent 'lack of supervision from higher authority'. 'Sunny' Scampton, in what became classic wartime bomber country in the flatlands of Lincolnshire, was a large and modernized station with a second squadron based there – 49 – and 'Higher Authority' (the newly-created Bomber Command 5 Group's HQ) just down the road at Grantham.

Training continued, but then on 18 August 1938 the Munich Crisis, sparked by Hitler's demand that he should be permitted to annexe the Sudetenland border area of Czechoslovakia, brought the very real prospect of a new European war. Air-raid precautions were instigated in Britain's cities, slit trenches dug in parks, barrage balloons sent up aloft, gas masks issued and women and children evacuated.

While this drama was played out in the foreign ministries of Europe, on 15 September John Collier's log recorded 'Passenger in a Blenheim, Pilot F/O Lamb'. Then on 21 September came his first solo in a Blenheim; the first step in the conversion process for 83 Squadron from the outdated Hawker Hind to the new Handley Page Hampden.

John Collier wrote home from Scampton:

> The European Crisis certainly seems a bit tricky at the moment but it has been a state of emergency for so long now that I doubt very much if anything serious happens – however they are not taking chances & leave for more than 48 hours has been cancelled for a long time now, & everything is ready here in case of emergency, however otherwise things are all very normal.
>
> I have nearly finished my flying on Blenheims & will wait until we get Hampdens before I fly twins again...

The Munich Agreement was signed between Chamberlain, Daladier, Hitler and Mussolini on 29 September 1938, to end a crisis that had rumbled on through the summer. 'Peace for our time' was promised by Neville Chamberlain but at the price of the Sudetenland, and within a few months the Germans occupied the rest of the Czech half of Czechoslovakia.

Collier later recalled the Munich Crisis as:

…very long periods of 'standing by' in our cockpits, with the aircraft at dispersal points around the airfield at Scampton. This tended to be rather boring, and when the 'stand down' was finally announced, there was considerable relief and some bright spark declared that he would be first back to the hangars. This led quickly to us all taking up the challenge, and resulted in many aircraft taxying at high speed, with tails up, towards the hangar. Some had overlooked the problem of stopping and the likelihood of collision, and there were a number of accidents. We were very fortunate to have such a long-suffering CO.

The Flying Suitcase

From 31 October 1938 83 Squadron re-equipped with the Handley Page Hampden and had twelve aircraft – enough for two 'wings' – by 9 January 1939. John Collier's log book records: '4th November – Passenger in a Hampden', and '25th November – Hampden solo'. On 20 January 1939 the *London Gazette* confirmed that from 29 December 1938 Pilot Officer John David Drought Collier was promoted to Flying Officer.

While John Collier's RAF training progressed and with Europe teetering on the brink of disaster, 83 Squadron was modernizing, relegating the biplane Hawker Hind to history:

By the end of 1938, we were busy converting to Hampdens, first having had a conversion course on Blenheims. There was no possibility of dual instruction on the Hampdens, so most of us had to be content with an experienced officer just checking us out on our first flight… The checking out officer had to stand behind the pilot's seat throughout, and this must have been quite hair-raising, but the method worked and there were no casualties, and I soon had the pleasure of collecting our first Hampden from Radlett [the company's factory and airfield in Hertfordshire], destined for 'B' flight.

The Hampden, by repute, was designed by a German and built by Handley Page; it certainly looked Germanic, with a box for the body, a narrow boom for the tail and twin rudders. However, the aircraft was delightfully easy to fly and companionable for the crew.

The Hampden, or 'Flying Suitcase', was indeed designed by a German: Gustav Lachmann, a pilot in the First World War who came to England to work for Handley Page in 1929. He was interned on the Isle of Man at the outbreak of hostilities but was later released to resume work with the firm.

Space was very restricted inside the aircraft – hence the nickname – as the fuselage was at most 3 feet wide. The navigator/bomb-aimer was positioned in the Perspex nose cone; the cockpit was above that and behind it an upper compartment for the wireless operator/air-gunner; beneath him was the under-gunner. Both sets of machine guns faced backwards with limited traverse; the Hampden was therefore vulnerable to beam attack. Seemingly rather frail, when put to the test in the coming months the Hampden would prove able to take substantial flak damage. It was good to fly, handled like a fighter and had a longer range (though less bomb-carrying capacity) than the much sturdier Wellington.

John Collier was exclusively flying Hampdens from the beginning of 1939; 83 Squadron now had its full complement of sixteen front-line aircraft and five reserve. He recalled some time spent training at RAF Northolt:

Re-equipment rapidly took place and the Squadron learned its role with many air firing development exercises at Northolt by February 1939, when techniques were developed for defence against fighters.

The cosmopolitan life of London was a novelty for the bomber boys from the bleak lands of Lincolnshire and quite a number of unusual experiences resulted from mixing up the fighter and bomber boys together at Northolt mess.

During this period a set display of modern aircraft was given at Northolt to a delegation of Arab Sheikhs, including the late King Faisal. However, although the demonstration during the day went off smoothly, the day before had been disastrous with a number of accidents including a Hampden crashing on to the roadway at Northolt, a Lysander upside-down and various other mishaps due to very bad landing conditions. Even so, the bits and pieces were all swept away in time.

From 2 March 1939 John Collier was an acting flight lieutenant (non-substantive promotion), but his steady progress would soon be accelerated.

As 83 Squadron's complement increased, there was a feeling of impending doom as events in Europe moved fast towards catastrophe.

On 31 August 1939 telegrams were sent out: 'Return to unit immediately.' The next day Nazi Germany invaded Poland, and full mobilization was ordered in Britain.

Chapter Two

Bombers: 83 Squadron at War

Sweeping the North Sea

In *Enemy Coast Ahead* Guy Gibson described the 'tremendous flap' at Scampton in the days immediately before war was declared, with everyone standing by, waiting to see if Germany would respond to Britain and France's ultimatum and halt its invasion of Poland. They had entered 'a world about to go mad. For us a funny feeling that the next day we might not be in this world.' The deadline came and went, and on the radio a lugubrious Neville Chamberlain made his announcement that 'as a result this country is at war with Germany'.

The balloon having gone up, the War Office wanted to show the offensive spirit and so 83 Squadron went into action almost immediately. German warships had been spotted out in the Schillig Roads, off Wilhelmshaven. Gibson recorded Squadron Leader Snaith's portentous announcement:

> We are off on a raid. We have got to provide six aircraft – three from A Flight and three from B Flight. I don't know where the target is. I think it is against shipping – probably German battleships. We are carrying four 500-pounders each; they have all got a delay of 11½ seconds, so we can go in pretty low. F/Lt Collier is leading the three from B Flight. You two [Gibson and Ross] had better come with me. Take off will be at 15.30.

John Collier's log book described this, his first op, succinctly: '3rd Sept 1939 – war declared on Germany. Sweep for German Fleet in North Sea.' A little bit more informative, but decidedly morose, is 83 Squadron's Operations Record Book: '3/9/39 Formation of six aircraft ordered to locate and attack enemy fleet. Owing to bad weather and darkness aircraft returned to base having jettisoned their bombs.' Hampden L4054 was piloted by Flight

Lieutenant Collier, with crew Flight Officer Pitcairn-Hill, Sergeant Fitchen and Aircraftman Baxter.

Much later John Collier described this first, improvised, wartime sortie:

> The prime target was the German Fleet, then supposed to be sailing towards England at a high rate of knots... I was detailed to lead a flight of three behind S/Leader Snaith, and in company with Gibson and others, we set course with the sketchiest of information...
>
> We flew out into the gathering dusk as a formation of six Hampdens, in the rather vain hope that we would find our target, which was the German battleship the *Admiral Scheer* reported as sailing somewhere in the Heligoland Bight. Our briefing had been pretty sketchy, but we had had given to us a photo of the battleship which had been spotted by Coastal Command earlier that day... I still have that photo... I cannot recall exactly how we were expected to attack, but fortunately for us we never saw the battleship in spite of a search, and Snaith, much to our relief, decided the light was too poor and we headed for home.
>
> Our return to Scampton involved a night landing, for many for the first time. The whole station was there to welcome us home, but it was a complete anti-climax, for we hardly could be held as very heroic, without scar or blemish, and nothing to report.

In the briefing for the sweep, as reported by Gibson, the Group Captain in charge of Scampton had stressed: 'I must warn you that serious repercussions will follow, must you bomb civilian establishments, either houses or dockyards.' In the months ahead Bomber Command would be restricted to military targets (partly in response to President Roosevelt's appeal to both sides in the conflict to refrain from bombing civilians) and would remain so while Chamberlain was prime minister.

Gibson also recalled that this was the first time they had flown with a live bomb load on board, and that after various delays nerves were in shreds by the time they finally took off. At last they were away, setting course over Lincoln Cathedral, as they would do so many times in the year ahead, and out to sea over Butlins at Skegness, wondering if they would ever make it back...

Perhaps understandably Gibson did not mention one teasing comment aimed at him by Snaith that night, but John Collier recalled it in a short piece he later wrote on the process of awarding medals in the RAF:

Way back in 1938 – when we were mostly so-called 'PO Prunes' and newcomers to 83 Squadron – there we were standing outside the so-called Officers Mess at Turnhouse, on a summer's evening, having been surprisingly well-fed by the Italian mess steward… & in expansive mood… and Guy stating with conviction that should war come, he intended to win a VC – naturally we took no notice at the time, but obviously his intentions had been registered elsewhere, as later in 1939, when war was a fact, and we were all basking in the sunshine outside the hangar at Scampton, awaiting final instructions for our first sortie, I recall Leonard Snaith… turning to Guy and saying 'Well now Guy, here is the opportunity for you to win that VC'…

Nothing much happened for months after the damp squib of 3 September. Under the Bomber Command Scatter Scheme, on 6 September the squadron was temporarily dispersed to Ringway, which was still under construction, near Manchester. The RAF had in mind the Luftwaffe's destruction of most of the Polish Air Force on the ground a few days before.

Ten unreal days followed for 83 Squadron, geared up as they were for combat. They were billeted in a pub 'where many an evening sing-song was held' and raced requisitioned Manchester buses around the airfield. With a static situation along the Maginot Line and no offensive operations by either side, what soon became known as the Phoney War set in. This would prove a godsend for the under-trained men of Bomber Command, allowing them to improve their night-flying, bomb-aiming and navigation skills. Also in the coming months vital improvements would be made to the Hampden, adding armour and self-sealing fuel tanks.

After their return to Scampton, Guy Gibson described various planned operations against shipping being cancelled after hours of standing by with the aircraft bombed-up.

To coin a phrase, 83 Squadron were getting 'browned off'…

* * *

This inactivity allowed John Collier the opportunity to propose to Beth, and on 11 October 1939 *The Times* printed this notice: 'MR.J.D.COLLIER and MISS BISHOP – The engagement is announced between Flying Officer John Collier, son of Mr and Mrs Collier, of Woolpit, and Elizabeth, eldest daughter of Mr J. Bishop FRIBA and Mrs Bishop, of Northiam.' The peacetime RAF dissuaded air crew from marrying, but in war this paternalistic stricture was waived. (John's parents had recently moved up from Essex to Dale House, Woolpit, in Suffolk, where Bert continued to raise chickens, started a market garden and kept bees. It sounds idyllic, but while there he was once strafed by a passing Messerschmitt and forced to dive into a ditch.) Aged just 23, Flying Officer Collier now became Acting Squadron Leader.

Collier family matters also came up on 16 December 1939 when his log book records 'Lorenz practice, Waddington'. The Lorenz system used a VHF radio beam as a short-range aid to landing in fog. A pre-war German commercial invention (as was the Enigma encoding machine), it was used by both the Luftwaffe and RAF, but the Germans had developed a longer-range version, code-named *Knickebein* (literally, 'crooked leg') as a navigational aid with a 250-mile radius. The devastating raid on Coventry in November 1940 was accurately guided by this radio beam and the target-finding planes of *Kampfgruppe* 100, a specialist unit that preceded the RAF's Pathfinder Force and its own navigational aids by more than two years.

One of the 'what ifs' of the Allied bombing campaign was an initiative taken a decade earlier by John Collier's Anglo–Italian cousin Roberto Clemens Galletti di Cadilhac (whose mother was a Collier). He had been a radio pioneer since before the First World War, initially working for and then in competition with Marconi, and was developing a guidance system for Ferranti between 1928 and 1931. An aeroplane had been successfully flown from Manchester to Bristol and back following a radio beam, but with Roberto's early death in 1932 the project lapsed and the company concentrated on the development of radar with Robert Watson-Watt. If Galletti's work had been sustained and adopted by Bomber Command, it might have led to parity in navigational ability with the Luftwaffe's bomber force by 1940.

It was only on 21 December 1939, over three months after war broke out, that John Collier's second op was recorded in his log: 'Daylight Sweep of

North Sea to Norwegian Coast. Almost 8 hours.' Once again, 83 Squadron's Operations Record Book was flat in tone:

One section [including F/Lt Collier] took off to locate and destroy the battleship *DEUTSCHLAND* believed to be off the NORWEGIAN coast. This section proceeded in company with two sections of 49 Squadron… Owing to weather conditions the *Deutschland* not located and pilots were instructed to return to the nearest aerodrome before dark.

Collier's plane was part of a force of twenty-four Hampdens and eighteen Wellingtons hunting the pocket battleship *Deutschland* – renamed *Lutzow* to avoid a potential propaganda own goal for the Germans if it was sunk. This was a large formation for those days, with aircraft from several units – nine from 83 – and was led by Wing Commander Sheen of 49 Squadron. Guy Gibson recalled that 'the briefing did not take long; there was not time… At the last moment Joe Collier took my place and left me fuming on the ground. But he was to regret his keenness a few hours later…'

Collier described an operation that was 'a pretty good disaster from the start':

Navigation was, in the early days, a pretty chancy business, and if the weather was against you there was little expectation of the bombs being on the target. An early daylight raid… in which most of the Hampdens of the Group took part was an example of how wasteful a sortie could be because of bad navigation. The first sight of land was off Denmark – the loosely grouped aircraft then flew North to the coastline of Norway… Formation flying was very difficult, particularly when we got near Norway, for there were many snow showers. Fortunately for us again no surface ships were seen, and the formations were not intercepted by German fighters, or the results for us would have been dreadful probably…

On the trail home, to make matters worse, it was obvious that we were being led too far to the North, and on top of this the Leader [Sheen] kept losing his speed as his undercarriage tended to come down, with great changes on his airspeed every time it went up and down... It was obvious that we were way off track and confidence in the Leader deteriorated and plummeted by the hour and finally abated altogether when he was seen to circle a fishing boat vainly hoping, we supposed, that the crew would point towards land.

A dreadful situation and all the sub-formation leaders took the initiative and flew on to seek England. The first land we saw was the Farne Islands, near Newcastle, which we thought were the Orkneys... An argument ensued as to whether the colour of the sea was right for the Atlantic or not; however, the coast of England hove in sight and we landed safely at Acklington [Northumberland], nearly out of petrol. Others were not so lucky and ended up in the Firth of Forth, where they were treated as 'hostile' and one or two attacks took place... All this nearly led to a private war... We never heard the results of the Enquiry...

Two of the stray Hampdens (from 44 Squadron) were shot down by Spitfires of 602 Squadron, north of Berwick. That was, thankfully, the last excitement for some time. Gibson described Christmas Day at Scampton when, after an op was cancelled, 49 and 83 Squadrons let their hair down. In the RAF tradition the officers served dinner to the 'erks' [aircraftmen], who were free to verbally abuse their superiors. In response to the chanting of 49 Squadron, a drunken war-cry rang out: 'It's not 81, it's not 82. It's 83!'

Then on 30 December 1939 John David Drought Collier married Elizabeth Julia Bishop at Ewhurst, Sussex. His best man was James Pitcairn-Hill, from 83 Squadron.

On 17 January 1940, after leave, Collier's log book resumes but expresses only frustration. In the flat expanses of Lincolnshire heavy snow blocked the war effort for almost a month, until mid-February, but planes still had to be kept readied and bombed-up, outside the hangars. Beth visited her husband in late January at his digs in a private house near Scampton and John Collier wrote home on the 30th:

Beth got back to London yesterday after a 9 hour train journey – I expect you are completely snowed up as we are – no flying – no motoring... It must be 'hell' in the Observer Post [Bert Collier was serving with the Royal Observer Corps and the Home Guard in Woolpit] – I am glad I haven't got that job.

On 21 February 1940 nine aircraft from 83 Squadron moved up to Scotland, seconded to Coastal Command:

> …we were temporarily based at Lossiemouth, in order to carry out our so-called 'North Sea Sweeps'… we were armed with a strange device with which we were supposed to attack any enemy submarines which we might sight. The weapon, called the 'B' bomb, was to be dropped beside the enemy submarine, and one then hoped that it surfaced against the side of the submarine and blew up… The only attack made by the Squadron was unfortunately against one of our own submarines returning to base…

No harm was done in the incident, which took place on 27 February, but an irate admiral was waiting in the Ops Room when the planes returned. The splendidly-moustachioed Squadron Leader Sam Threapleton, who had led the attack on the friendly sub, got into a bit of trouble for this, and the fact that he had ignored another submarine that turned out to have been a genuine U-boat! Threapleton was posted elsewhere in May (though not, evidently, as a punishment; Gibson described him as a 'grand type') and John Collier then 'returned to my former position as Flight Commander "B" Flight'.

Two North Sea sweep exercises may have been organized in response to this confusion. On 3 March 1940 eight aircraft carried out an interception of an imaginary enemy fleet by homing on a shadowing flying boat: 'D/F [direction-finding] loops were used with excellent results.' Two days later this was repeated by nine aircraft and 'a successful interception was made'.

Gardening in the Baltic

On 19 March 1940 the nine 83 Squadron Hampdens returned to Scampton. Night-flying practice was reported at the end of March, and the squadron 'stood by for leaflet raids' [code-name NICKEL] which never happened. These night-time drills stood the inexperienced squadron in good stead when the Phoney War suddenly exploded into the real thing.

The surprise German invasion of Denmark and Norway on 9 April 1940 was followed by the Allied expedition to secure Narvik (and high-grade iron ore supplies from northern Sweden), and Chamberlain famously concluded that the Nazis had overreached themselves – 'Hitler has missed the bus' – but it was the Allies who were rapidly outmanoeuvred.

John Collier's log book records his first participation in the attempt to interrupt the progress of the German seaborne invasion of Norway, on 21 April 1940: 'Mining aka "Gardening Operations", Copenhagen.' Squadron Operations Record Book:

21/4/40 – Seven [aircraft] detailed for 'Gardening' off DROGDEN lighthouse. One returned with defective oil pressure after 45 minutes, the others all returned safely to base. / All these aircraft [including F/ Lt Collier in L4058] carried out 'Gardening' operations, four planted 'daffodils' successfully, the remaining two failed to find the target.

There were three channels for shipping passing through the Skagerrak and Kattegat, the sound between Denmark, Sweden and Norway, up which the German invasion force – which had been massing at Kiel, chivalrously unmolested by the RAF – had to pass. It was hoped that magnetic mines (a German invention, swiftly copied and improved upon by British 'boffins') would at least block supply lines to the forces already in Norway.

Each Hampden carried one 1,700lb mine that had to be dropped from very low altitude, using a parachute, and would often need several runs to get the correct spot for 'planting', thereby exposing planes and crews to anti-aircraft fire. If they failed to find the precise spot, the mine had to be brought home or dumped at sea in deep water; on no account were these weapons to fall into enemy hands. The whole business of sea-mining remained secret and all sinkings were unpublicized.

The mines themselves were known as 'vegetables', or whatever particular flower or vegetable variety matched the code-named sea area, and every mine laid was recorded on charts.

John Collier did not write about this first gardening sortie, but Guy Gibson did: 'The next night [21 April] we went to Oslo Fjord to lay mines in the harbour. I had a pretty easy trip myself, but Joe Collier had to plant his vegetables within a few yards of a battleship and said that he didn't enjoy the experience very much...'

Gibson may have been confusing Oslo with Copenhagen in his memory, as the Drogden lighthouse is in the middle of the Oresund, the body of water between Copenhagen and Malmo. Mining spread around the coasts of occupied Europe and on 2 May 1940 Flight Lieutenant Collier reported '"Nasturtium" successfully planted', but on the 6th, in the mouth of the Elbe: 'Target not identified. Returned with "Hollyhock".'

Such ventures were not in vain: the one Allied success in the whole Norway debacle was the heavy losses of German shipping, either in naval engagements or by hitting mines. This depletion of tonnage would assume great significance when the invasion of Britain was in prospect in a few months' time.

John Collier looked back to these early mine-laying operations when discussing his later proposal for a safer alternative – a high-level mining technique – in his 1946 memoir:

If I remember correctly it was the German invasion of Norway that really activated serious mine laying operations by air – then for security reasons code named 'Gardening Operations'. In April 1940 we were busy in No 83 Squadron, laying mines singly from our Hampden aircraft in the shipping lanes in the Baltic, leading to Norway. Then operations were relatively unopposed, and drops could be expected to be reasonably accurate, but as the war proceeded the mining became more widespread, the enemy placed 'flak ships' and used night fighters to oppose the mining – the opposition became more and more effective, and by June 1943 [when he presented his paper to Bomber Command] heavy losses of our mine-laying aircraft showed up how vulnerable our four-engined aircraft had become, and a change of tactics was an obvious necessity.

Planes had to fly low to locate a landmark from which to start a dropping run, which often put them in jeopardy:

> Fortunately in those days the opposition was quite light, and we had the benefit of the well-lit coastline of Sweden. We all had our 'regular' crews then and I was fortunate in having Pilot Officer Redmayne, who was an excellent Navigator, Sgt Johnson was our Wireless Operator [and air-gunner] and Sergeant Hayhurst was my more regular bottom gunner.
>
> In those days operations were an individual matter and the aircrew chose their own routes and time of take off. There was a delightful air of informality about the whole thing and the war was really quite pleasurable in some ways, except that every now and again the Germans used to object by letting fly from their flak-ships and the occasional night fighter would intercept.
>
> I recall one excitement when mining… The fact that we were being tracked by an enemy night fighter was announced by a stream of tracer bullets passing over our heads. This certainly woke us all up, for Johnson loudly announced over the intercom, 'Cor sir, they're shooting at you. What shall I do?' He was given a terse instruction: 'You bloody fool, I can see that – shoot the bugger…'
>
> But generally these operations were reasonably safe although it was always a tricky business coming down to low level to drop the mine as there was a danger you would fly into the sea itself.

The fiasco of the British intervention in Norway led directly to the fall of Chamberlain's government. Its conduct of the war was debated in the House of Commons and found wanting, and on 10 May 1940 Winston Churchill took office as prime minister. That same day the Germans invaded Holland, Belgium and France and all leave was cancelled; bomber crews had to be ready to take off at a half-hour's notice. On 13 May Guderian's Panzers broke through at Sedan and the rapid rout of the French armies by the blitzkrieg had begun. The British Expeditionary Force, over-extended in Belgium, was soon in headlong retreat.

For a few days, as the situation in France unravelled, 83 Squadron pressed on with 'Gardening'. On 13 May 1940 Collier logged 'Gardening/Mining Operations, Kiel area' and reported 'Attempted to plant a "lettuce", but could not locate target owing to bad weather.'

Guy Gibson described this dud sortie, which took place the day before Holland surrendered:

As we sat in the crew room we were told of the importance of the plan. How we might block all traffic if we were successful in doing our job thoroughly. We were also told the uncomfortable news that there were balloon cables every 300 metres along the [Kiel] Canal, and that all the bridges were very heavily defended with light cannon and flak. It looked like being a sticky target, and long were the faces of Oscar [Tony Bridgman], Joe [Collier], Pit [Pitcairn-Hill] and myself as we smoked our last cigarettes...

The trip was lousy. None of us got there and we all brought our bombs back. The weather was the trouble. Low cloud had been on the hills all the way and made it quite impossible to find a tree, let alone a canal.

Ploughing in the Ruhr

Three days later John Collier's log book marks a change of theatre of epic significance for Britain and Germany, modest though its immediate aims were: '16th May 1940 – "Ploughing" in the Ruhr area.' Squadron Operations: '16/5/40 – Six aircraft carried out "Ploughing" operations. All were successful, though two were hit by A/A fire. / [Flight Lieutenant Collier's report] Electricity works attacked and bombed at DUISBURG.'

Ploughing – that is, bombing – Germany itself had finally begun in earnest: 83's Hampdens were part of a loose force of almost 100 bombers sent to attack oil depots and railways in the rear of the invading forces. Chamberlain's government had not permitted attacks within Germany, even military targets, for fear of hitting private property (a euphemism for killing civilians). However, once Churchill became prime minister and as Holland, Belgium and France were overwhelmed, everything changed, although a caveat was issued by the Air Ministry: 'In no circumstances should night bombing be allowed to degenerate into merely indiscriminate action, which is contrary to the policy of His Majesty's Government.'

The first RAF bombing raid on a German town had taken place on 11/12 May, its target Mönchengladbach, but this attack on the Ruhr on the 16th that involved 83 Squadron – a direct response to the Luftwaffe's terror bombing of Rotterdam on 14 May – was the first of any size and the first allowed to go east of the Rhine.

May/June 1940 became a frenetic time for 83 Squadron, with the RAF desperate to take the pressure off the retreating BEF with 'nuisance raids' on the German railway system. The bombers were up against considerable anti-aircraft defences in and around the Ruhr Valley, but they were nowhere near as lethally-organized as they became a couple of years later:

At this time German flak was not too tricky and you could see the tracer bullets had a limited height, so air crew used to fly around in relative safety at the top of the trajectory of the light flak, while the heavy guns were unable to pick you up… but they were developing a pretty nasty technique with their searchlights.

Bombing accuracy and effectiveness were hampered by problems of visibility and the reliability of the weapons themselves:

Often the target was covered in cloud and bombing blind was the only possibility. So much was wasted, one wondered if anything was being achieved… And again in the early days the bombs just did not 'go off'. We were doing low-level bombing at night and could definitely report when they did for the crunch of the bomb would shake the aircraft and duds were often the order of the day…

Then there were the land mines adapted from our sea mines: the armourers tried to copy the Germans in this, the only difference being that the safety pins were sheared by the shock of the parachute opening – often aircraft of ours failed to return when carrying this load, to the extent that a special trial was eventually carried out and the truth was discovered. How many aircraft did we lose?

How glad we were that the English coast ran roughly North and South, so a return safely to base was not too difficult from Germany – when in doubt fly due West and you will meet the coast somewhere!

Guy Gibson saw a silver lining to those encounters of the summer of 1940, when German fighter superiority east of the Channel forced Bomber Command to operate under cover of darkness: 'Those grim days and nights were the playing fields of Eton to the would-be night-flying pilot. We learned the hard way, but we learned every day.'

Not every target was in Germany. On 20 May John Collier bombed a road bridge at D'Origney, over the Oise, and reported: 'Direct hit scored on target which collapsed.' Two days later Squadron Operations reported: 'Six detailed for "Ploughing". Railways, [rolling] stock and roads as objectives. Four were successful. One crashed near HUDDERSFIELD on return (Sgt Jenkins) and was destroyed, all the crew being killed. / [Flight Lieutenant Collier's report] Bomb dropped on aerodrome at UPENBURG [Ypenburg, near The Hague]. Train attacked near EMMERICH [in the Rhineland, on the Dutch border]. Landed at STRADISHALL [in Suffolk].'

On 27 May the king visited RAF Scampton to decorate officers and men of 5 Group. The Operations Book notes 'several officers were presented to the King in the Mess after tea', but then on 30 May it was back into the fray, aiming at Hamburg. Flight Lieutenant Collier reported: 'Oil tanks at A7 not located owing to bad weather. Flare path bombed.' Another attack (possibly that of 5 June) on oil tanks in the Hamburg docks was mentioned by Gibson, who wrote of the casual-sounding briefing by 'Willie' Snaith: 'Fly to the target whichever route you wish and bomb at any time between 1200 hours and 0400 hours', the normal practice at the time. Crews were still required to be absolutely sure they would hit the target, or else bring their bombs home with them, which made landings even more dangerous than usual.

This improvised bombing campaign against the German rear had no serious effect on their army's rapid progress, and from 27 May to 4 June the bulk of the British Expeditionary Force and a considerable part of the French army were being taken off from the beaches of Dunkirk in Operation DYNAMO.

Nevertheless, 83 Squadron pressed on with attacks on the German supply lines and on 5 June, the day after the evacuation was completed, John Collier was again bombing Hamburg. Squadron Operations: '5/6/40 – Bombing of oil refinery at HAMBURG carried out by twelve aircraft. S/Ldr Field and crew missing, believed shot down over target. / [Flight Lieutenant Collier's report] A20 attacked. Believed successfully.'

Squadron Leader Dennis Field had taken over 'B' Flight from John Collier, but not for long, as Collier recalled with regret:

He was by our standards an older officer, but was extremely 'press on'. He already had a fine reputation as a member of the British Bobsleigh team. Amongst ourselves we were rather worried about his extreme enthusiasm, which we feared might be shortlived. Sad to relate Squadron Leader Field went missing after only a few sorties, and once more (I think for the third time) I assumed the duties of Flight Commander 'B' Flight.

Two days after Hamburg, the target in Collier's log book was an oil refinery at Misburg, near Hanover, that was said to be owned by Reichsmarshall Göring himself. Its destruction by 83 Squadron was described with great relish by Guy Gibson: 'There was a woomph! and every tank blew up. The most wonderful sight that any man could hope to see, especially when you are responsible for it, and even more especially when they belong to Hermann Goering.'

This virtually non-stop raiding – acts of defiance rather than a real offensive – continued through that anxious summer. On 9 June 1940 John Collier was '"Gardening" Mining, Little Belt, Denmark', planting a 'wallflower', and on the 11th bombing Flushing aerodrome in occupied Holland. On 14 June the target was Dortmund, when 'Railway at SOEST attacked. Bombs overshot into town, causing fires.'

Railway marshalling yards became prime targets, as at Euskirchen on the 17th, then on 21 June another strategic priority: 'Aircraft factory at KASSEL attacked by twelve aircraft. All however not successful owing to thick haze. Secondary targets bombed. / [Squadron Leader Collier's report] Failed to identify F19. Bombed yards at Diepholz [near Osnabrück].'

An armistice was signed in France on 22 June 1940, and Britain (and her intact Empire) stood alone. Perhaps in order to bolster morale, the *Sunday Dispatch*, dated 23 June 1940, printed a photograph showing bomber crews 'receiving detailed target instructions before setting off from a bomber station in England to carry out raids on enemy troop concentrations and lines of communication'. The unnamed officer briefing the carefree-looking men of this anonymous squadron was Acting Squadron Leader John Collier.

On 27 June he was bombing Wismar, far off on the Baltic coast of Germany, where there was a big Dornier factory situated at an aerodrome. Gibson was awarded the Distinguished Flying Cross for this operation, after which his badly-holed plane was unserviceable for a week. He described a 'great argument in the briefing room when we got back as to who had started the only fire on the aerodrome...'

June 1940 had been a desperate month and crews were 'all-in', but the schedule continued remorselessly. On 7 July John Collier's twenty-fifth op was against Frankfurt, then on the 11th Strasbourg (though the primary target had been Ludwigshafen, on the Rhine). A raid on 15 July was aimed at Hamm, north-east of the Ruhr, and Collier later wrote: '...we had several dive bombing attacks on the marshalling yards at Hamm, for in those days we were full of enthusiasm and belief that every bomb counted and must where possible be delivered individually (our opinions changed considerably as the war progressed)...'

On 21 July 83 Squadron returned to the Dornier aircraft factory at Wismar. Press reports exulted that 'explosions were seen to break out within the target area and of the many fires started one great blaze was visible from 50 miles away...'

This repeat of the raid of 27 June involved John Collier on a long flight into the Baltic:

In the early days of the war navigation largely relied on visual recognition of 'landfalls', particularly such relatively good identifications as the coastline... We endeavoured to locate our position over Denmark and were flying rather low, when inadvertently we passed directly over Kiel. We were way off course, and were the only aircraft there at the time, and all was quite quiet until every gun in the neighbourhood informed us of our error and let us know in no uncertain terms where we were. We were well and truly 'coned' by the searchlights and it was obvious that it was only a question of time before we got hit…

Our technique at the time to get out of trouble was to dive the aircraft towards the 'deck', and at the same time to drop one of our flares in the hopes that it blinded the anti-aircraft gunners. So I put the Hampden into a steep curving dive, and at the same time instructed the rear gunner, Pilot Officer Bowman, to drop out flares… I can't remember getting any acknowledgment of these urgent instructions, but I do remember shouting 'Get the damn things out' or something to that effect. Meanwhile, amidst much banging and bumping, we dived down over Kiel, finally getting so low that we could distinctly see docks, water and shipping in reflected light.

Heading out and fortunately quite unscathed from that affair, we had an aircrew check to see that everyone was quite OK, but as to our rear gunner there was no reply.

'Get down there Sergeant Johnson, will you, and find out what has happened to P/O Bowman…'

After a moment or two came the reply, 'He's gone…'

It was Spring 1942 when I received a card from Bowman, sent from Oflag VIB and dated January 1942 expressing regret at leaving us 'so suddenly'. He had suffered only a broken leg on landing by parachute in Kiel. He added: 'I hope it was not too draughty going home after we had parted company… Don't interrupt the good work…'

On 26 July John Collier and his colleagues were bombing an oil depot at Nantes. Gibson described the plant all lit up, and the planes circling to warn the French workers to leave, which they did in a panic, '…then the boys proceeded to knock it flat'.

On 2 August Collier was again mine-laying in Lübeck Bay, planting a 'hollyhock'. Eighteen of these florally-named magnetic mines blew up at the Scampton bomb dump in August. Gibson described it as the biggest explosion he'd ever heard, accompanied by a column of black smoke rising 3,000 feet into the sky.

Mentioned in Despatches and DFC

These operations in the summer of 1940 appear to have been of an almost haphazard nature, but on 12 August Squadron Leader John Collier played a key part in the first properly-planned and rehearsed attack of the air campaign, involving Hampdens of 83 and 49 Squadrons. Despite its desperately dangerous, almost suicidal action, it was something of a portent for precision bombing raids to come.

The target was an aqueduct carrying the Dortmund Canal over the River Ems, which formed a key link (especially through the Dortmund-Ems Canal's intersection elsewhere with the east-to-west running Mittelland Canal) in the strategic German waterways network. Both squadrons trained very carefully for this mission, practising at night over fenland canals and drains at low level, and studying scale models of the target.

The Squadron Operations Record Book reported the bare facts of the raid from 83's perspective:

12/8/40 – Five aircraft detailed for bombing and special gardening operations on M25 [Dortmund-Ems Canal]. Two aircraft (F/Lt Mulligan and F/O Ross DFC) failed to return. Sgt Stubbings (Navigator [in John Collier's plane]) and Sgt Roscoe (W/Opr) were slightly injured as a result of intense flak fire. / [Squadron Leader Collier's report] Hampden P1355: S/Ldr Collier, Sgt Stubbings, Sgt Johnson, Sgt Threlfall. Time up: 2050 12.8.40 Time down: 0805 13.8.40. Diversion successful – a/c twice hit, Navigator injured slightly. 2 bombs dropped near lock gates and 4 bombs near flak battery – results not observed.

Guy Gibson, who did not participate but would go on to execute the most celebrated precision raid of all, described Dortmund-Ems in *Enemy Coast Ahead* as: 'One of the first attacks of its kind during the war. A special attack trained for by crack crews; a completely successful attack planned by men who flew. It was the first of many.'

Collier's diversionary force, consisting of three Hampdens, attacked a nearby canal lock at Münster, while other planes from 83 and 49 Squadrons attacked the aqueduct itself. His aircraft was hit before it reached the target, but somehow he managed to nurse it home.

He later recalled his part in the raid:

> ...I had acted as a 'decoy' to distract the enemy gunners as our crews
> went in to drop their mines. I fear we were little help, but we did get a
> direct hit from a 20mm shell. 'Hell,' my navigator said, 'I have been hit
> in the bottom, and am bleeding – what shall I do?' Sit on it, I said, until
> we're out of this. And sit on it he did, without murmur of complaint,
> until we could give him some first aid some twenty minutes later.

Gibson described the dramatic main attack:

> Pitcairn went in first, dropped his bomb in the right spot and got shot
> up very, very badly by the light flak defences. Next came Rossy. He
> went in low, and the next they saw of him was a flaming mass on the
> ground. Poor old Rossy was killed. Then came Mull. His port engine
> was set on fire, but he managed to climb up to 2000 and was able to bale
> the whole of his crew out. Then came Matthews and he too bombed
> accurately, but had to return on one engine. Lastly came Learoyd; in
> the face of blinding searchlights his bomb-aimer managed to put his
> bombs in the right spot.

For this much-publicized raid Squadron Leader J.D.D. Collier was
Mentioned in Despatches and is said to have been recommended for a
Victoria Cross. Flight Lieutenant Roderick Learoyd of 49 Squadron, whose
plane was repeatedly hit, did win the VC (there seems to have been a rule of
only one per op), and John's great friend James Pitcairn-Hill was awarded
the Distinguished Service Order for his coolness under heavy fire. Their
popular Australian comrades Mulligan and Ross would be much missed:
Ross's blazing plane had narrowly missed Collier's, but 'Mull' survived and
was awarded the DFC while in captivity.

The canal was breached and the raid did much to hold up the movement
of a fleet of big Rhine barges to the North Sea coast, but a parallel waterway
– cropped from the photograph published with press reports – had come
through the attack unscathed, so some traffic continued. The Dortmund-Ems
Canal was repaired and operational after ten days, but Hitler was forced by

this setback and the continuing air-raids on barges in the Channel ports to delay the planned invasion of Britain, Operation SEALION, by a week to 21 September 1940. His schedule for a rapid victory was getting tighter by the day and he raised the stakes three days after Dortmund-Ems: on 13 August 1940 the Luftwaffe launched Operation EAGLE, the Battle of Britain.

While Spitfires and Hurricanes were defending the south of England, 83 Squadron continued to target vital industrial plant and military supplies. On 17 August John Collier took part in an attack on an aircraft factory at Emmerich in the Ruhr, and two days later oil tanks at Bordeaux. That summer he was no longer living in a 'dispersed billet' but like the rest of the air crew was back on the station at Scampton, with the perk of having his own batman:

Batmen… were very keen supporters of their particular officer. My batman was quite disappointed in me for he could not say that 'his officer' had any medals… He expressed his disappointment to me. The situation was that we had already been briefed for our target for the night, which was the oil tanks at Bordeaux, which sounded reasonably easy… so I gave my batman an assurance that I would do my best to see that he was no longer disappointed.

We set off on the 19th August for the long haul to Bordeaux. It was a moonlit night, and navigation was particularly easy and the target area stood out clearly alongside the Gironde river. We had made sure we were first in the target area and our Navigator and Bomb Aimer Pilot Officer Turner did an excellent piece of bomb aiming, and the result was more dramatic than we expected, with a large fire resulting which we could see for miles on the return journey. The whole crew was most enthusiastic, Sgt Johnson and L.A.C. Hemmingway being the rear gunners and best able to report on the success. They were confident that some acknowledgment must result, and in fact it did, for the next day I was able to tell my batman that I had been given an immediate award of the DFC. Really it was to Turner that most of the credit should have been given… however I did then have a satisfied batman.

The recommendation for a Distinguished Flying Cross made it clear that this was a composite award for Bordeaux and Dortmund-Ems:

PARTICULARS OF MERITORIOUS SERVICE

On the night of August 19/20th this Officer was the leader of a successful attack on an enemy oil refinery and storage tanks.

After locating and identifying the target Squadron Leader Collier carried out a low level attack from 100 feet, obtaining direct hits which set the target ablaze. Intense fire from local defences was experienced, but these were eventually silenced by the explosion of the tanks and the gun positions themselves becoming enveloped in flames.

As a result of his action the remainder of the aircraft found little difficulty in locating the target and completing its destruction.

On the night of August 12/13th this officer was the leader of the diversionary aircraft which carried out attacks with bombs and machine-gun fire from low altitudes on M25 [Münster canal lock, i.e. the Dortmund-Ems Canal raid] and the defences in the immediate vicinity. In spite of his aircraft being hit in many places, this Officer continued these attacks at a very low altitude until the main attack was completed.

In these and other operations, Squadron Leader Collier has displayed outstanding qualities of leadership, skill, courage and devotion to duty. He has carried out a total of 31 operations against the enemy in the course of which he has completed 178 hours flying as a first pilot.

RECOGNITION RECOMMENDED: Strongly recommended for the immediate award of the DFC.

APPOINTMENT HELD: O.C. 'B' Flight, No.83 Squadron, RAF Station Scampton

Signature of Commanding Officer: H.S.B. Walmsley, Group Captain.

COVERING REMARKS BY AIR OFFICER COMMANDING No.5 GROUP
A fine type of Leader who has done uniformly excellent work

A.T. Harris, Air V Marshal, 21.8.40

There was no resting on laurels. John Collier's log book notes the next sortie on 25 August 1940: 'Bombing aerodrome east of Berlin. 9 hours 40 mins. Landed North Coates.' The Hampdens of 83 Squadron were part of an improvised raid, aiming at Berlin itself for the first time, carried out by a force of eighty-one bombers. Churchill had personally ordered this retaliation after the bombing of London by Luftwaffe planes (which are thought to have been aiming for the Short aircraft factory at Rochester) the night before. It meant a 1,200-mile round trip:

> We were detailed to attack targets in Berlin… The whole route was overcast and there was no sign of Berlin at our estimated time of arrival, so having gone so far we were not prepared to waste our bomb load, so all agreed to get below cloud level to locate some target… We broke cover right over an active enemy airfield, where night flying was in full progress. We reckoned we should join in too, and dropped our load on what we thought were lighted hangars. We did not wait to see results, but hurried home. However, there was a strong headwind and we were just about out of fuel when we arrived over the Humber. We were sending out SOSs… but we were told we were about sixth in the queue. [The crew] had been told to prepare for ditching when fortunately we saw North Coates airfield coming up in the morning gloom and we landed there on one engine and the other engine stopped on landing, dead out of petrol… We landed so quietly that we had to hammer on the armoured cars of the Army to let them know.

Squadron Operations reported on a wild night:

> 25/8/40 – Eleven aircraft detailed for bombing B57. Three aircraft identified and attacked target, one of which [Pitcairn-Hill] landed in the sea east of Grimsby, all the crew being rescued after 7 hours in a dinghy. Of the other aircraft, one attacked aerodrome at FURSTENWALD 2. attacked railway line South of target and landed at North Coates 3. Brought bombs back, landed in the sea off the Wash and crew were rescued 4. Bombed viaduct near WESTERHAUSEN 5. Returned with engine trouble 6. Crashed at Usworth with one serious injury 7.

Returned with wireless trouble. / [Squadron Leader Collier DFC's report] Furstenwalde aerodrome attacked from 200 feet. Bombs burst on buildings adjoining large hangar and large fire was started. Landed at North Coates.

Gibson was dismissive of this 'lousy' raid, on a night with 'as good a head wind as any'. Because of the thick cloud 'I don't suppose more than ten bombs actually landed on Berlin.' However, the psychological blow to Berliners and the Nazi leadership was substantial. This brazen defiance by the RAF of Göring's pledge that no enemy plane would ever get through to the German capital is seen as a crucial moment in the air war, and more immediately the Battle of Britain. It is said to have prompted the Germans to divert their bombers from attacking fighter bases in southern England to target London.

Certainly Hitler's rhetoric became more shrill: '...when they say that they will attack our cities, then we will wipe out their cities...', he ranted at a Sportpalast rally in Berlin in late August. However, the first Luftwaffe bombing raid aimed at London was not until 7 September, so the attack on Berlin was only an element in the fateful change of tactic, which was at least in part dictated by German losses in daytime dogfights with the RAF. Hitler was always seeking the line of least resistance, and the blitz on London may have been a calculation that attacks on civilian targets would undermine morale to such an extent that a risky seaborne invasion might be rendered unnecessary: a shocked nation would sue for peace and the war would be over.

Whatever might be in the offing for a beleaguered Great Britain, John Collier would be watching from the sidelines for several months.

His log book was, of necessity, written up some time after the night of 30 August 1940: 'Bombing Magdeburg. Returned with engine trouble. Crashed on landing!' Squadron Operations: '30/8/40 – Returned owing to engine trouble. Crashed on landing at Base. S/Ldr Collier slightly injured.'

Collier looked back on his potentially fatal thirty-fifth op:

Four days after our attack on Berlin, with my usual crew consisting of P/O Turner as Navigator, Sgt Johnson as W/Operator, and P/O de

Bressey as under gunner, we set off to the Target for that night, which was to be Magdeburg. De Bressey should have a special mention for he was a considerable character, reputed to have driven a side car outfit at a circus complete with a lion in the passenger seat… He certainly was a courageous fellow and good to have with one as crew. He did me a very good turn that night when we had to return shortly after take off with a faulty engine.

…we found that one engine was over-heating and obviously was running rough and so returned to Scampton immediately because we did not think we would make the coast to drop the bombs in the sea…

Arriving back at Base we were refused permission to land because of a local 'red alert' [enemy aircraft in the area, meaning the flare-path lights were off], and I judged that we just could not wait about under the difficult circumstances, and opted for a landing without help… I judged a low approach necessary but overdid this and our undercarriage got tangled up with some wires [at the bomb dump] on the approach, and although we did end up on the airfield it was in a very broken state. I had received a considerable blow on the head and was unconscious, and as I learned later… de Bressey had most unselfishly dragged me from the aircraft, at considerable risk to himself, seeing that there was a full bomb load still on board and a high risk of fire.

Snapshots of the wrecked Hampden were preserved in a family album as some sort of talisman. The same day as the crash, Collier's DFC was officially authorized and published that morning in *The Times*. He would have known of it before leaving for Magdeburg. After the crash a telegram was sent from the Air Ministry to his father at Dale Farm, Woolpit, in Suffolk: '1/9/40 regret to inform you that your son Squadron Leader John David Drought Collier DFC has been admitted to station sick quarters at Scampton suffering injuries…'

In a letter home from RAF Hospital, Rauceby, Sleaford, Lincolnshire, he dismissed the incident as '…a bit of an argument with the windshield of a Hampden when I did a very bad landing & I bumped my head fairly hard – I am enjoying my holiday & feel fine…'

In *Enemy Coast Ahead* Guy Gibson acknowledged that this was a significant, even a portentous moment for the core membership of 83 Squadron: 'Some nights later Joe Collier undershot when landing and crashed, giving himself very severe concussion... Gradually our numbers were dwindling, and out of the great bunch of boys who had started to fight a war against Germany, only Pitcairn, Oscar and I were left.'

After a spell in hospital, John Collier was grounded for six months. In later years, looking back on the crash, he saw that it had perhaps preserved his life:

> That event put an end to my service with 83 Squadron, probably very fortunately for me, for the next six months proved a very difficult time for the Squadron and many crews were lost, amongst whom were all my very best pals... I was reminded of this at the 83 Squadron reunion many years after the war, which took place at Scampton. I can only recall some three or four of the original crowd being there...

While John Collier was convalescing, his usual plane P1355 – or 'Bet', named after his wife – was hit by flak over Antwerp when bombing the German invasion fleet in the crucial 'Battle of the Barges'. The rear gunner and navigator baled out, and despite ammunition bursting all around him and the aluminium floor melting, the fire was put out by the heroic efforts of Flight Sergeant John Hannah, the 18-year-old wireless operator and air-gunner. The pilot nursed Bet home and Hannah was awarded the VC; the youngest recipient of the whole war.

The strain of constant flying and danger was starting to tell on even such an enthusiast for aerial action as Guy Gibson, who admitted to '...getting nervy, there was no doubt about it; this bombing was beginning to get me down'. He was either suffering sleepless nights or nightmares and shouting out in panic in his sleep. 'If ever there was such a thing as a war of nerves, then some of us in 83 Squadron were certainly beginning to get affected...'

The worst thing was the loss of old and close friends, whose numbers were dwindling night by night. Gibson's stark words in *Enemy Coast Ahead* still send a chill down the spine:

Two nights later we went against Antwerp, and this city, with its heavy flak defences, shot down one of the few left. I saw him flying straight and level over one of the basins, taking his time about his run, making sure that all his bombs went in the right spot. Then he blew up – and Pitcairn-Hill had gone to join his fore-fathers.

John Collier kept a cutting from *The Times*: 'Obituary of Flight Lieutenant James Anderson Pitcairn-Hill DSO DFC.' He was described as a 'natural leader and went "full out"'. 'A correspondent' wrote: 'It is a fine thing to have known such a man, even for a short time.'

He was shot down on 18 September 1940 and was buried in the churchyard at Luc-sur-Mer. A portrait drawing by William Rothenstein shows 'Pit' in his flying suit and helmet. James Pitcairn-Hill was described by Gibson as 'as straight-laced and true a Scotsman as any'. Many years later John Collier was still mourning 'the kindest and dearest of fellows'.

Such desperate sacrifice was not in vain: 15 September 1940 had seen the last German bombing raid of the Battle of Britain 'Blitz'. Having failed to defeat the RAF or break the spirit of Londoners, having suffered aircraft losses twice those of their opponents, and with the fleet of invasion barges battered at their moorings, on 17 September Hitler had quietly postponed Operation SEALION 'until further notice'.

John Collier's other great friend from 83 Squadron, Tony Bridgman DFC (always referred to by Guy Gibson in his book as 'Oscar', his middle name), was an acting squadron leader when he was brought down by flak on 23/24 September 1940. He was the pilot of Hampden L4049 and on his way to attack Berlin as part of Bomber Command's biggest operation to date, involving a force of 200 aircraft. Bridgman baled out over Bremen and was the only survivor from his plane, becoming a prisoner of war for the duration.

Collier and Gibson would not have been aware at the time that their mutual friend was still alive, and Gibson's stunned account in *Enemy Coast Ahead* suggests this: 'We waited all night; we waited till the grey darkness of the early hours became purple, then blue as the sun rose in the East over Lincoln Wolds and it became daylight. But Oscar never came back.'

He recorded the reading of Bridgman's will in the mess at Scampton and concluded dolefully: 'I was the last one left... all my friends had gone now...'

From Stalag Luft III Tony Bridgman corresponded with John Collier's sister-in-law Virginia Bishop, with whom he had become close, throughout the rest of the war.

In October 1940 Guy Gibson transferred from the husk of 83 Squadron to 29 Squadron, flying Bristol Beaufighters as night-fighters. The 'old crowd' was no more.

* * *

From September 1940, during the most intense phase of the blitz, a divergence of philosophy was emerging in the Air Staff and the Cabinet. The RAF was still concentrating on specific targets but Churchill, needing to placate public opinion, wanted retaliatory attacks on German cities, whose chief object was what was then called enemy 'moral', or morale. Sir Charles Portal, made Chief of the Air Staff in October, took the prime minister's side – a pragmatic decision because of the inaccuracy of most bombing, as revealed by reconnaissance flights – and a directive was sent out from the Air Ministry to Bomber Command that has been described as prioritizing 'profitable targets in profitable surroundings'.

The devastation of Coventry on 14 November 1940 by a Luftwaffe force of 449 aircraft tipped the balance of the argument strongly in favour of Churchill and Portal's new harder-headed strategy. As a Coventry survivor said at the time, 'We've been gentlemen too long...'

However, for the time being such 'big picture' considerations passed John Collier by and for several months he was in limbo. From 20 October 1940 he was at RAF Waddington in Lincolnshire, listed as 'SN' – supernumerary – unattached to a squadron; then from January to March 1941 he was doing some light training there, when his log book notes half a dozen local flights in Ansons and Magisters.

On 15 February 1941 Squadron Leader J.D.D. Collier attended an investiture by King George VI at Buckingham Palace, at which he received the Distingushed Flying Cross for the Bordeaux raid of 19 August 1940.

Then on 11 March 1941 he formally moved onto the strength of 44 Squadron, based at RAF Waddington.

Chapter Three

Bombers: 44 and 420 Squadrons

Salmon and Gluckstein

From 14 March 1941 a fully-recovered Squadron Leader John Collier was flying Hampdens again with 44 (Rhodesia) Squadron at RAF Waddington in Lincolnshire, and was a flight commander under Wing Commander Misselbrook.

Keeping Watch: A WAAF in Bomber Command is a nostalgic memoir of life at 'Waddo' in the Misselbrook era written by Pip Beck, who found the Rhodesians of 44 Squadron had an informality and self-reliance that made them stand out from the RAF crowd. Their language was peppered with Afrikaans and colonialisms: the English were 'rooineks' or rednecks; crew transport vehicles were 'gharries'.

In contrast to these free-ranging characters, John Collier was living – on one level – the conventional existence of a married man, staying with Beth in digs near to the airfield; and in March 1941 she gave birth to a son, John Mark Bishop Collier, at Lincoln. He was known as 'Joey' as a baby and small child, in acknowledgement of his father – who was always 'Joe' to fellow airmen – and later as Mark. Tony Bridgman, unavoidably absent in Stalag Luft III, was his godfather.

Yet of course this could not be normal married life. At the end of March 1941, her husband was back in operational flying and Beth's composure would be tested with every sortie. He took one of her opal earrings with him as a good luck charm.

The first op of this new era for John Collier came on 29 March: 'Mine laying, Brest.' Squadron Operations Record Book:

29/3/41 – Eight aircraft took off… for mine-laying operations near BREST where, it is known, the German Pocket Battleships *SCHARNHORST* and *GNEISENAU* are docked. Seven mines were dropped in allotted positions whilst the eighth was brought back to Base as position could not be accurately located owing to thick cloud. One aircraft (Captain – Sgt Atkins) bombed a 'FLAK' SHIP, dropping 2 x 250lb bombs. Results, however, were not observed. / [Squadron Leader Collier DFC's report] Target: GARDENING 'JELLYFISH'. One ordinary vegetable successfully planted in allotted position at 04.08 hours from 500 feet. Two 250lb wing bombs brought back to base as no target was found for them.

'Gardening' might sound routine almost two years into the war but it remained a hazardous business. Against the heavily-defended port of Brest and its two significant threats to Allied shipping, *Scharnhorst* and *Gneisenau* – codenamed 'Salmon' and 'Gluckstein' (after a chain of tobacconists' shops) – it was carried out in a cauldron of flak, searchlights and smoke.

John Collier and 44 Squadron returned to the fray on 5 April, logged as 'Day operations to Brest', in which three aircraft directly attacked the *Scharnhorst*, although without effect.

On 15 April the squadron bombed Kiel, another notoriously heavily-defended target, and Squadron Leader Collier reported: 'Bombs were seen to burst in the North part of the town on the East bank of the river. No further results observed. Main target not attacked owing to [failure] to recognise correct area until after bombs were dropped.'

On 26 April it was the turn of Hamburg, and this time Collier noted: 'Following fall of bombs a medium sized fire broke out yellow in colour, which is thought to have gone out soon.' On 3 May, 'Operations Cologne', Collier: 'Bombs (1 x 1900, 2 x 250) dropped through 10/10th cloud on COLOGNE which was identified by flak fire and ETA. The three bombs were seen to burst through the cloud but could not be pinpointed. About half a minute later a large fire was seen in the position where the bomb had burst.'

None of these raids by Hampdens can have caused the enemy serious concern, though no doubt the civilian populations were discomfited. The mass raids with heavy bombers that laid waste to Germany from 1942 onwards were still only a gleam in Bomber Command's eye.

The Cologne raid was John Collier's fortieth operation and later in the war this would have marked the end of a tour, a feat achieved on average by just 35 per cent of airmen. Pilots were then officially 'tour expired' or 'screened', and sent off for six months as instructors. Their second tour would consist of twenty operations, and if they survived that they could volunteer to carry on or return to instructing or go on to higher things. Collier was typically laconic about all this: 'In those days there was no such thing as a "Tour", so we assumed that one went on flying on operations indefinitely, and one just hoped to stay out of trouble... We all of us had plenty of adventures and lucky escapes.'

Arriving back in one piece from a raid he and his crew would sometimes wind down by not going to bed at all: '...we preferred to find our way to Lincoln swimming pool and rest there after an early morning swim.'

John Collier and 44 Squadron pressed on, returning on 8 May 1941 to Hamburg as part of a force of 170 aircraft. Squadron Operations: 'Judging from reports submitted, this operation was very successful, as large fires were burning when aircraft left the target area, in fact, one Air Gunner states he counted fifty large fires in the town.'

In June the focus returned to the German capital ships at Brest. Squadron Operations:

10/6/41 – A force comprising 38 Wellingtons from No.3 Group with 28 Whitleys and 39 Hampdens set out to attack the enemy battleships *SCHARNHORST, GNEISENAU & PRINCE EUGEN* at BREST. Thirteen Hampdens from this Squadron were engaged in this operation, and commenced to take off at 2310 hours. All reached their objective and found the enemy had again made use of an effective smoke screen. Early in this operation, aircraft crews were able to pinpoint the various docks and jetties through the smoke, and were thus able to bomb with a fair degree of accuracy. Several large fires were started, and one particularly large fire was observed between Docks Nos 1 & 2... Pilots report a fair amount of searchlight and A/A activity. / [Squadron Leader Collier DFC's report] Target attacked – Battlecruisers at CC49. Time 01.41 hrs. Height – 12,000 ft. 1 x 2000 & 2 x 500 [bombs]. Target attacked from NW to SE and identified by the river. Visibility extremely bad owing to smoke screen. Bombs dropped in stick within target area and seen to burst. Accurate pinpointing impossible.

Three days later they went back in force. Squadron Operations:

13/6/41 – BREST… 23 Wellingtons from 1 Group, 48 Wellingtons & 5 Stirlings from 3 Group, 37 Hampdens of 5 Group including 13 from this Squadron. There was practically no low cloud, and only thin layers between 14,000 & 16,000 feet. Ground haze, however, coupled with the enemy's smoke screen made observation difficult. Although the target was not completely obscured, no direct hits are claimed, but the majority of bursts were seen within the target area. / [Squadron Leader Collier DFC's report] Target – Battle Cruisers at BREST. Target area identified and bombs dropped in stick to the West of the target area. Two smaller bombs seen to burst. Accurate observation difficult owing to weather conditions.

It was a frustrating business, but the Germans had to be commended for arranging their defences, decoys and deceptions so well. *Scharnhorst* and *Gneisenau* had been sheltering in Brest and undergoing repairs since March 1941, after two months spent attacking Atlantic convoys at random, and had remained unscathed ever since. On 1 June 1941 they were joined by the *Prinz Eugen* after she and the *Bismarck* had sunk the battleship HMS *Hood* and damaged HMS *Prince of Wales* off the North Cape.

There was more confusion on raids over Germany itself. On 15 June, with poor visibility, the main target was the marshalling yards at Düsseldorf with Cologne the alternative, but Squadron Leader Collier hit 'Estimated ESSEN District. Bombs not seen to burst or results observed owing to 10/10ths cloud. Bombs were dropped on concentration of flak and searchlight, and flak greatly increased in intensity afterwards.'

Kiel was one of Collier's least favourite destinations. Squadron Operations:

25/6/41 – Shipyards at KIEL attacked by seven Hampdens, two of which were of this Squadron (S/Ldr Collier DFC & P/O Biggane) … several very large fires resulted. Both our aircraft appear to have had a very warm reception from flak which necessitated violent evasive action, during which the bombs dropped off of their own accord.

This could be the same occasion that he recalled when illustrating the Hampden's ability to be 'easily handled and thrown about like a fighter if necessary':

> I think one night over Brunsbuttl [at the far end of the canal from Kiel itself] in dire exertions to avoid the searchlights and the flak, we actually ended upside down in cloud... Anyway, the crew maintained this and cash out of my pocket fell on my head when opening the cockpit hood on landing – however else did it get up there?

In a letter home sent in July from RAF Waddington, he made no fuss about these travails:

> The Squadron has been fairly busy, and doing very well really, but there is little of interest I can tell you. I personally have <u>not been doing much flying as I am not allowed to fly too often</u> [his father underlined this sentence and noted 'Good' in the margin]. I hope to have some leave at end of August...

Frustration at the poor results of bombing to date had registered at the highest levels. Portal's 9 July 1941 Directive to Bomber Command ignored evidence of the durability of morale in blitzed London. Inspired by a new sense of urgency that Britain should do something to counteract the rapid collapse of the Red Army after Germany invaded the USSR on 22 June, it promoted '...destroying the morale of the civil population as a whole and of the industrial workers in particular'. Bombers should now aim for large cities, considered impossible to miss, largely because of the lack of accuracy in night-time bombing of more specific targets. In May 1941 Sir John Slessor, CO of 5 Group, had reported crews 'failing to find and hit any but the most obvious targets on the clearest moonlight nights'.

This Directive became, in effect, Bomber Command orthodoxy for the remainder of the war – the rationale for area-bombing – and was set in stone by a plan produced by the Directorate of Bomber Operations in September 1941. However, some specific targets remained almost an obsession, and a major effort was made to destroy the battleships at Brest, after careful rehearsals, with a massed daylight attack on 24 July 1941 that turned into an epic aerial battle. From 44 Squadron Operations:

24/7/41 – Six Hampdens left Waddington on 23rd July for Coningsby piloted by S/Ldr Collier DFC [and others]. Their purpose was to be briefed at Coningsby with other crews for a daylight operation projected over BREST where the enemy warships *GNEISENAU* and *PRINCE EUGEN* were docked. It is recorded that formation flying has been practiced by these pilots for four weeks for this operation. / 24th July. The six Hampdens took off from Coningsby at 11.00 hrs to form part of the strong force of 149 aircraft detailed for the daylight attack on the *GNEISENAU* and *PRINCE EUGEN* at BREST and the *SCHARNHORST* at LA PALLICE with Blenheims acting as a diversion at Cherbourg.

Extract from Bomber Command HQ report:

3 Boeings [RAF B-17 Flying Fortresses] of 2 Group, 14 Wellingtons of 1 Group, 31 of 3 Group, 11 of 4 Group, and 18 Hampdens reached BREST and attacked the German warships. The Boeings opened the attack in ideal weather soon after 1400 hrs and were followed by the main body, escorted by Spitfires, in a sustained attack lasting until 1545 hrs. Enemy fighters and A/A put up a strong defence but it had not any effect upon the tactics planned by the bombing force, which carried out its task with great success. 7 direct hits were registered on the *GNEISENAU*, and *PRINCE EUGEN* and the tanker were both straddled and in all probability damaged. Apart from these hits, many bursts were observed on and around the docks in which the warships are berthed and severe damage was inflicted upon barracks and dock buildings adjacent to the targets. Owing to evasive action after dropping their bombs, several crews were unable to observe the results of their attack. The *SCHARNHORST* recently left BREST for a quieter life

at LA PALLICE. Her departure did not pass unnoticed, and, after receiving a direct hit from a Stirling of 3 Group on the evening of July 23rd, her new home was well plastered during the same night. Today, whilst the attack was developing at BREST, 15 Halifaxes of 4 Group attacked her again and at least one direct hit is claimed. Final figures of enemy aircraft destroyed by our escorting fighters are not yet available, but it is certain that the bombing force accounted for 12 enemy fighters.

John Collier's plane, Hampden A0795, was in the thick of it, and he filed a Combat Report on his return:

After attacking and apparently destroying machine on port (P/O Clayton) an Me109 came in to attack from port quarter. Upper gunner had swung his gun round to endeavour to support Clayton's machine, but attack came straight on and F/Sgt Williams opened fire at point blank range 50 yds, port quarter on same level, joined by under gunner both firing 200 rounds each. The Hun was seen to turn over and dive vertically into the ground where it burst into flames. Claimed as 'Destroyed'.

The Times of 25 July 1941 made much of this drama:

SCHARNHORST HIT AGAIN / GNEISENAU BOMBED AT BREST / 'FLYING FORTRESS' IN ACTION / [The Fortresses dropped bombs] from a fantastic height, scarcely visible and certainly inaudible to anyone on the ground... Thousands of feet below the Fortresses the crews saw a tight formation of many Hampdens sweeping in over the target and they could also see a star cluster of flames where bombs from the Hampdens had ringed the German warships. The Hampdens had come in with a guard of fighters, and after they had finished their work it was the turn of the Wellingtons to continue the battle.

German fighters which went up to intercept our bombers were unable to check the ferocity of the attacks. The bombers approached their targets, bombed, and darted away again to leave room for the procession that followed.

Each attack was timed to the minute. There was no confusion, and, as a pilot said 'It was a marvellous sight to see in the sunshine bombers ahead of us and bombers behind us with the fighters weaving overhead. All the little ships in the harbour scuttled out to sea, as we came in, with frightened trails of white foam behind them'...

[A wing commander confirmed a hit on the *Gneisenau*:] 'The ship was perfectly plain,' he said, 'and one of our bombs hit it. All the guns seemed to be going at once. We went straight through it all.'

The next day *The Times* made even more of the 'greatest daylight operation against enemy warships', claiming in its headline 'RAF CRIPPLE WARSHIPS' and describing the 'fierce battle' that John Collier took part in: '...Messerschmitt 109s attacked the Hampdens which came in in tight formation, while the Fortresses were still overhead. Though combats seemed to follow one another in an unending succession, nothing could check the drive and impetus of the assault.'

The *Scharnhorst* did suffer several direct hits that day at La Pallice, but she made it back to Brest on 25 July and repairs began again. Despite the boldness and drama of the RAF raid, neither *Gneisenau* nor *Prinz Eugen* – thanks to the distraction of decoy ships – were damaged.

The elder John Collier had a veteran airman's ironic perspective on the whole operation:

After a spell in hospital and grounded, March 1941 saw me back flying with 44 Squadron as a Flight Commander and back on the old roles of mine laying, bombing etc. One operation was of interest and this was a daylight attack on Brest where the *Scharnhorst* and *Gneisenau* were waiting to steam up the Channel. We came back with some nice photographs showing we had passed slap over the target – goodness knows where the bombs ended because shortly after that [February 1942] the ships sailed quite unharmed up the Channel – much to the consternation of all concerned.

During this daylight attack we were able to practice some good defensive measures and believe we gave as good as we got from the German fighters. We lost one aircraft out of my Flight, but we reckon we shot down two or three of the Germans – whether this was so is impossible to say.

One thing we proved and this was that the Hampden was very good for defence and manoeuvre provided the 'box' formation was closely kept. The aircraft we lost unfortunately did not keep position and therefore was quickly picked on.

At the time of the attack he was more exuberant, writing home on 27 July:

...we have been busy. You may have read in the News in Telegraph about the huge daylight attack on Brest – I was leading our Squadron – it was quite exciting and we were very pleased because our squadron boys shot down four & possibly five ME109s right over the target and we lost one.

Although he was not immediately aware of it, Squadron Leader J.D.D. Collier would be awarded a Bar to his DFC for his 'outstanding courage and airmanship' on this operation. The recommendation read:

This officer was the leader of the sub-formation of six aircraft which carried out a daylight raid on Brest on the 24th July 1941.

Squadron Leader Collier has worked exceedingly hard and taken an immense amount of care in training the formation for this raid. It was mainly due to his fine leadership and example that the formation succeeded in its task and allowed the other members of his formation to destroy four enemy aircraft and damage one.

30th July 1941. Signature of Officer Commanding: J. Boothman Rank: Group Captain

Remarks by Air or other Officer Commanding: This is a very gallant and consistently reliable Bomber pilot, and a fine Flight Commander. He is very strongly recommended.

J.C. Slessor Rank: AVM 5 Group Date: 2 August

On 4 August it was back to business. Collier's log book notes 'Bombing Hanover (not on one engine).' Somehow he managed to bring the plane home:

> The Hampden had proved a remarkably versatile aircraft but one of the snags was that the bombs were not really designed for the aircraft and they would insist on us flying with a 1950lb bomb, which meant that we could not close the bomb doors and the aircraft had a terrible job to fly... During one of these flights over Hanover one of our engines stopped and we had to fly back on one engine all that long way with the Navigator clutching the rudder bar to keep the aircraft straight. We proceeded home on a series of half-loops, having assumed that the engine had been knocked out by flak; however, all that had happened was that all the petrol had been drained from one side of the aircraft to the other, thanks to a new modification which had been introduced to enable petrol to be transferred from one side to the other and about which we had no knowledge. Therefore when the left-hand tank read 'No Petrol', the engine naturally stopped and we assumed that we had lost all our fuel...

A crisis of confidence in Bomber Command was impending. In August 1941 the secret Butt Report concluded that on moonlit nights only two out of every five crews bombed within 5 miles of the target; on moonless nights this dropped to one in fifteen. Doubts were raised as to the efficacy even of bombing cities, but Churchill had no alternative to the air campaign at this point in the war and Portal argued that the full potential of Bomber Command was yet to be realized, although Stirling and Halifax heavy bombers had been introduced in mid-1941 with 5-ton bombloads.

Nevertheless, whatever the shortcomings of the aircraft and their guidance systems, the RAF pressed on. On 5 August 1941 forty Hampdens of 5 Group (of which eleven were from 44 Squadron) attacked railway workshops at Karlsruhe. On 19 August over Kiel the bomb doors on Collier's Hampden did not open and the 1,900lb bomb was brought back to base.

Then on 6 September, when mine-laying in Oslo harbour, John Collier had a close shave. Squadron Operations: '6/9/41 – Ten aircraft took off to proceed to Lossiemouth from which base they would carry out mine-laying operations in the Oslo Fjord…. S/Ldr Collier DFC in Hampden AD930 received direct hit from HE [flak] and although his aircraft was damaged he returned safely.'

His fifty-fourth op on 12 September 1941 was similarly nerve-racking, though the Hampden returned unscathed. Squadron Operations:

12/9/41 – Nine Hampdens from this Squadron among 37 aircraft from 5 Group to attack railway marshalling yards FRANKFURT but only six actually took off owing to an enemy air attack on the Station during take-off. All six reached and bombed objective. Weather conditions over Frankfurt were not good as 8/10 to 10/10 and intense darkness made pin-pointing difficult. Results were not observed. / [Squadron Leader Collier DFC's report] Main target not attacked owing to aircraft being caught in cone of searchlights, making identification of marshalling yards impossible. Target attacked – FRANKFURT TOWN. Two photographs attempted – both unsuccessfully.

A week later John Collier had his first intimation of a new era in Bomber Command, when he encountered the Avro Lancaster for the first time, flying as 2nd pilot/passenger with Squadron Leader Peter Burton Gyles. However, for the time being the Hampden remained the workhorse of 5 Group, and on 12 October he was off on a raid on Bremen. Squadron Operations:

12/10/41 – HULS CHEMICAL WORKS attack by 90 aircraft of 5 Group, including eight from this Squadron. [Same night] attack on the Deutsche Schiff Shipbuilding Yards at BREMEN. S/Ldr Collier was unable to identify the target, but attacked… the town of BREMEN, during which his rear gunner Sgt Bott received a minor injury when he was hit by shrapnel in the left arm causing medium flesh wounds.

However, with the revolutionary four-engine Lancaster now waiting to be deployed, 44 Squadron's Hampdens were nearing the end of active service. Elsewhere in Bomber Command the need for a fresh start was becoming painfully obvious. A disastrous raid on Berlin in bad weather on 7/8

November 1941 caused 12.5 per cent casualties among the bombers and eighty-eight crew were lost. Even heavier losses would be sustained towards the end of the year, bringing a desperate Directive from the Air Ministry ordering a cutback on sorties to Germany. This crisis eventually cost Sir Richard Peirse his job as C-in-C Bomber Command, opening the way for his successor Sir Arthur Harris in early 1942, and for all his inflexibility it would be 'Butcher' Harris who took the bomber force to new heights of destructive power.

On 25 November 1941 John Collier was at Buckingham Palace to receive his medal from King George VI. A press photo was headlined 'RAF HERO AND HIS BABY SON', with the caption 'Squadron-Leader Collier, who received a Bar to his DFC at a recent investiture, was carrying his baby son, John Mark, aged 8 months, when he left the Palace.'

Though he probably did not yet know it, this in effect marked the end of John Collier's association with 44 Squadron, who were scheduled to be the first to convert to fly the new Lancaster in December '41. The Hampden, although John was still quite happy to fly it, was 'becoming rapidly obsolescent, with its short range, low service ceiling and small bombload'. In other words, it had no place in the coming era of the heavy bomber.

On the verge of this transformation came a disaster for 44 Squadron on 13 December 1941, when the Waddington station commander Wing Commander Misselbrook and his crew, flying a Hampden, were lost while on mine-laying operations at Brest.

Almost a week later, on 19 December, John Collier was promoted to acting wing commander. He remained at Waddington but transferred to the newly-formed 420 (RCAF) [Royal Canadian Air Force] Squadron, his first squadron command.

The Hampden's Last Hurrah

The Hampdens of 44 Squadron were replaced by Lancasters on Christmas Eve 1941, and the older aircraft were handed over to John Collier's nascent 420 (RCAF) Squadron, which shared Waddington with 44. Numerous 44 Squadron personnel, air and ground crews, crossed over to 420 with their familiar planes.

Collier was the youngest wing commander in the Group, and applied himself 'with immense enthusiasm and energy, determined to make 420 as good as 44'. This was not an easy task, as John Collier himself put it in blunt terms:

> Forming a new Squadron is quite a problem because you get posted to you all the misfits and the weaker members of Society, and it was only after vigorous protests to Group that a few really reliable NCOs and men were fed in and the Squadron became operational within three months.

Jean Barclay was a WAAF intelligence officer stationed at Waddington at this time and a shrewd but not dispassionate observer of her Bomber Command colleagues. While there she wrote a personal account (published posthumously and privately in 1993 as *The Brave Die Never*) of life on a bomber base, which began with the shock of losing 44 Squadron's popular CO Wing Commander Misselbrook.

Her spirits were raised after a Christmas of drowning sorrows by the arrival of 'a brave new squadron' – 420 (RCAF) – at Waddington in the New Year:

> Joe Collier, a young and very keen flight commander of 44 Squadron, had been made Wing Commander as 1942 came in and it was into his super capable and enthusiastic hands that the launching of the new Canadian squadron fell. He put heart and soul into it, worried himself sick about it, his keenness and anxiety to make a success of it seemed to galvanise us all into excitement and enthusiasm. The most junior commander in the Group, he was so anxious to compete successfully with his old squadron, from which he had emerged with a DFC and Bar. An alarmingly high standard to set but one which was to prove [420 (RCAF) Squadron] not unworthy.

Looking back from 1943 she reflected on the glory days of 44 Squadron, its 'valiant leader' Misselbrook and of Joe Collier, one of its 'great' flight commanders. However, in the winter of 1941/2 RAF Waddington and

44 Squadron in particular were still under a cloud, following the loss of their CO, struggling with the Lancaster's teething troubles and, wrote Barclay, greatly missing Misselbrook's

incredible vitality and cool, devastating common sense… it almost seemed as if the spirit of his squadron had died with him. As it turned out later, it had been only sleeping…

The station needed a tonic, an eye-opener, and it soon came. Wing Commander Collier provided it and swept 420 onwards to its 'maiden voyage'. He also had every known difficulty to contend with and overcame them by sheer determination and hard work. Many of his ground crews were some 'not required' by 44, tools failed to arrive, some of the Hampdens handed over by 44 were alarmingly ancient, all sorts of hitches occurred. But Joe Collier was undaunted and on 21 January 1942, 420 operated for the first time, its squadron commander in a fever of anxiety. It began inauspiciously, its aircraft were late taking off due to a hitch in petrol loads, this being the one and only matter he had not investigated personally. However, they got away, their target being Emden, and we settled down to the trying business of waiting. Misfortune was to haunt that first trip of 420. Their 'B' flight commander, Squadron Leader Wood, was outstanding as the others came back and as the night progressed the Wing Commander and I looked at each other and knew he would not come back with them. To lose a flight commander on your first operation would be a bitter discouragement to any squadron commander, but Joe was still disbelieving as he drove me back to the mess. We had stood by the plotting table, he muttering 'Come on, Woody' as the tracks became fewer and fewer. Then the board was empty and we left it, telling each other that the morning might bring news. Of course we knew it wouldn't, it never does.

Winter weather interrupted operations in February, first with heavy snow, then a thaw that created 'swampy' conditions on the grass airfield. This may have been a relief for Collier and his crews, who could collect themselves after this ill-starred beginning.

Meanwhile at Bomber Command HQ a new spirit was stirring in this bleak month. Arthur Harris had left 5 Group, was knighted and made commander-in-chief to replace Peirse. The Air Ministry plan, agreed in principle in late 1941 and communicated to Bomber Command in a Directive dated 14 February 1942, was now to attack the main industrial cities of Germany principally using incendiaries. In effect, the intention was to destroy housing as well as industrial plant, with civilian morale the explicit 'primary object'. The winter restrictions on sorties to Germany after the heavy losses of late 1941 ended, and Bomber Command was encouraged to 'employ your forces without restriction'. The new radio guidance system GEE would be used to improve accuracy and it was estimated that it would take six months for the Germans to find a way to jam it. Essen, home of the mighty steel and armaments producer Krupps, would be the first target on the list.

Preparations for this new phase of the bombing campaign were suddenly derailed when the *Scharnhorst*, *Gneisenau* and *Prinz Eugen* broke out of Brest on 12 February 1942 in an attempt to reach their home ports. Eluding Coastal Command's spotter planes, the three great ships had followed a route north that had been swept through minefields. They benefited from a continual fighter escort and radar jamming, which meant they were not observed until almost through the Channel. Confusion reigned as the RAF improvised from very meagre local resources, and all six Swordfish biplane torpedo-bombers sent to attack them were shot down.

Bombers converged from their northern bases but low cloud, poor visibility and the heavily-armoured decks of the ships frustrated them. Squadron Leader Harris – Wood's replacement as 'B' Flight Commander – was the pilot of one of two Hampdens from 420 Squadron lost in this 'forlorn chase in the Channel'. Mines were hurriedly laid in the Elbe estuary and *Scharnhorst* was hit twice, slowing her down, but she finally limped into Wilhelmshaven.

The 'Dash up the Channel' enraged British public opinion and the press. *The Times* thundered: 'Nothing more mortifying to the pride of the sea power in Home Waters has happened since the 17th century.'

After embarrassment came the flush of success. On 3/4 March 1942 John Collier and three other Hampdens from 420 Squadron joined forty-four others (in a total force of 235 aircraft) in a bombing raid on the Renault works at Billancourt, near Paris, which was 'virtually obliterated'. It was claimed that 300 bombs hit the factory, which normally turned out 18,000 lorries a year and was now making tanks for the Germans, and put it out of action for four weeks. The real point of this raid, however, was to try out the new and much-debated idea of target-marking with greater numbers of flares and incendiaries dropped by a lead group of planes. Success at Billancourt helped promote Collier's future boss Sydney Bufton's inspired idea to create 'daylight bombing by night', using a specialist unit in every Group, which eventually came into being as the Pathfinder Force.

John Collier had initial reservations about the technique. Squadron Operations:

3/3/42 – Hampden 298D. W/C Collier – Captain. Renault... BILLANCOURT. Bomb load 1,900lb GP. One burst seen and felt. One fire already burning in NW corner of area. Bomb thought to burst in centre of area – large fire started. Visibility good but smoke from flares made things difficult. Target identified by island, bridge and bend in river. Target definitely identified ¼ hour before time but on returning smoke from flares made definite identification difficult and a further 50 minutes was spent going up and down the river before dropping bombs on target. Pilot's report: 'The flares when too numerous are a hindrance as the smoke blots out details of target and necessitated nearly an hour being spent in area before dropping bombs.'

Jean Barclay described the scene at Waddington that afternoon when the Hampdens left for Paris; a day that also marked the historic transition of one era of Bomber Command to another with the debut of the Lancasters of 44 Squadron and a new dimension of air power:

The take-off was in daylight and was unforgettable. It seemed as if half the station had turned out to wish them luck. Betty Davies and I went to the head of the flarepath and with many others watched the aircraft emerge from their dispersals. First to go were the four Hampdens, they were on the famous Renault works raid that made such headlines in the papers. I was sorry, in a way, that it had to be on the same night, it rather overshadowed the Lancasters' 'premiere'. Over the airfield streaked Wing Commander Collier's machine, then followed Squadron Leader Campbell's. F/Sergeant Pinney followed and a fourth Hampden was soon in the air and fading into the distance. Then there was a pause before the first Lancaster came with a deafening roar of engines to the taxying post. On to the flarepath it came and stood still, vast and towering, the four motors turning over. Then came the revving up and the ground trembled under our feet. One's heart seemed to beat faster as the speed increased and the sound grew in an overwhelming crescendo. It seems the very embodiment of power, this colossal aircraft, as it stood quivering and straining at the brakes.

Often when I was watching Hampdens revving up, Shakespeare's lines would come into my mind:

'I see you stand like greyhounds in the slips,

Straining upon the start.'

But this was no greyhound, it was more like a giant lion or tiger about to spring. At last when it seemed that one's head would burst with the sound and one's nerves snap with anxiety and excitement the vast machine began to move. Slowly it passed us, the crew waving and smiling at us and we waved back and prayed for their good fortune as it shot down the runway. God, would it never leave the ground? But there it was, safely in the air and the next Lancaster had come up to take off.

Barclay had an anxious wait that night for the Hampdens and the Lancasters to return:

The Hampden crews came in first. Cheerful and grinning all over their faces, their's had been a sensational raid and they knew it. 'Bags of fires', 'No flak – wizard!', 'Never saw anything like it, Blackpool on Saturday night', 'Renaults have had it, don't worry'. These were no 'line-shoots', as the photographs proved. Joe Collier laughed when he pulled out a cigarette and I lit it with a match from a folder marked 'Prunier, Avenue Victor Hugo'. I had had it for a long time before the war but I asked him if he had brought it back this evening!

The four Lancaster crews followed and they too were smiling. The great strain over and a job well done. There had been no hitches and they were loud in praise of their machines… Squadron Leader Nettleton arrived in the ops room, grinning and excited. 'Marvellous', said JD happily 'I came screeching in at well over 200!'

Spirits were high that night, everything had gone well, the AOC was pleased, the station commander justly proud…

So once more we had at Waddington two first-rate operational squadrons and as the spring came to our bleak countryside both of them began to add splendid pages to their squadron records.

Over the next three days *The Times* stressed the raid's cautionary example to French industrialists:

PARIS WORKS BOMBED / The company is known to have been engaged in making and repairing transport vehicles, tanks and aero engines for Germany / BIG DAMAGE AT PARIS WORKS / Aided by a full moon and clear sky, and with the Seine as a guide, the RAF crews had no difficulty in finding their targets. Much of the Renault works is situated on the Ile Seguin, in the middle of the river, and can be seen for miles… / The cooperation of the Renault factory in the enemy's war effort has long been notorious, and, despite British warnings as to the consequences, that collaboration has increased recently in response to the German call for greater output…

John Collier had a pithier view of the Renault raid, which was officially described as 'the most outstanding success of Bomber Command so far in the war', when writing in later life:

During this period we were sent to bomb the Renault works, Paris, and spent what seemed HOURS over the target to make sure that we didn't kill any Frenchmen unnecessarily. The briefing story is that the number of each aircraft had been put on to the tail of [its] bomb and if this was found outside the target area the crew would be court martialled.

Needless to say, at the time Collier was rather more jubilant in a letter home:

> I had an interesting flight the other night. I took part in the raid on the
> Renault works at Paris. The Air Force put up a good show. Knocked
> the place nearly flat, and hardly a bomb went on French houses... [The
> letter is illustrated with sketches of Admiral Darlan (CO of Vichy forces
> in North Africa, who was known to be visiting Paris at the time), hiding
> behind the Eiffel Tower and quoting ITMA's 'I think I go home'; and
> an aerial view of the Renault works, by the Seine, ablaze – 'The last
> time I saw Paris'.]

The Renault raid was almost the last hurrah of the Handley Page Hampden.
Jean Barclay, looking back from 1943 when the mighty Lancaster was the
dominant presence in Bomber Command, recorded her feelings about the
end of an era:

> By the autumn of 1942 gradually the old Hampdens had disappeared
> off the station, the last of them. For the first time for... how long? there
> would be no war-worn familiar shape within the bounds of Waddington.
> There was a sadness about it, in spite of the relief at operating so much
> better an aircraft. For a chapter of history was closed, which it would
> be hard to equal.

John Collier later gave his own verdict on the plane, which he did not fly in
anger again:

> My experience with the Hampden had started at the end of 1938 and
> finished in March 1942, and during this period one had grown quite
> fond of the beast which had proved a most versatile aircraft, easy to
> manoeuvre and thoroughly reliable, and certainly it had seen us through
> the early days of the war when many hard lessons had to be learned and
> many air crew had to thank the sturdiness of this aircraft for the fact
> that they survived at all.

To the layman perhaps the Hampden did look peculiar and had a 'broken back' appearance when flying, but the air crew generally thought they were very lucky to have this aircraft to see them through.

...The two Bristol Pegasus engines seldom gave trouble although they could 'oil up' if kept idling before take-off and caused heart failure when clearing themselves under full load. But both engines and airframe could take a great deal of punishment... The slim silhouette of the airframe was a great help by day and night and the defence from the rear was reasonably good, but the Hampden could be easily shot down if attacked from the front by a rear-firing fighter. The pilot had a fixed front gun, usually incorrectly sighted... I believe Gibson did shoot down an enemy aircraft over Holland [using the front gun] – I tried the same night tactic but only succeeded in a near collision with all concerned thoroughly shaken by the experience...

...Crew comfort was very poor, the pilot being strapped in position with no opportunity of moving for up to nine hours, and he invariably suffered from cramp; the rest of the crew also had poor accommodation. However, luxuries were not expected and the deficiencies were more than accepted with good grace.

...the role of the Hampden bomber was soon forgotten; this was clearly illustrated at the 5 Group reunion at Brize Norton in October 1975 when... the whole evening appeared to be devoted to the glory of the Lancaster and the role the air crew played. As one old Hampden pilot mentioned at the dinner 'We seem to have been forgotten – what about the Hampden?'

In March and April 1942, before being posted to 97 Squadron at Woodhall Spa, Wing Commander Collier did not fly himself but oversaw a series of attacks by 420's Hampdens on the Krupp factory at Essen (using the GEE navigation system), and one on the Humboldt Works at Cologne as part of a force of 263 aircraft. At Cologne it was observed that no bombs fell within 5 miles of the works; at Essen less than a third of the planes bombed the primary target.

Chapter Four

Bombers: 97 Squadron

Lancasters at Woodhall Spa

Wing Commander John Collier took command of 97 (Straits Settlements) Squadron – sponsored by donations from Singapore, which had not yet fallen to the Japanese – at RAF Woodhall Spa in Lincolnshire on 30 March 1942 as both squadron commander and station commander, it being a one-squadron base instead of the usual two. The squadron had recently been re-equipped with Lancasters, replacing their unreliable two-engine predecessor the Avro Manchester, and had moved to Woodhall Spa from Waddington on 1 March 1942. The four-engine Lancaster had a huge 14,000lb bomb-load capacity, yet could fly at 290mph and was very manoeuvrable. Once its early flaws – which bedevilled the pioneer 44 and 97 Squadrons for a while – were corrected, this would prove the culmination of bomber design in the wartime RAF.

Back at Waddington, Jean Barclay – and 420 (RCAF) Squadron – regretted his moving on so soon after setting them up:

At the beginning of April we lost, to our sorrow, Wing Commander Collier – to another squadron. He went to command 97, the second Lancaster squadron in the Group which, of course, was no more than he deserved. The squadron seemed stunned by his sudden departure and I think he too was sorry to break with 420, which he had made himself.

John Collier described the way this sudden change was announced to him by his formidable boss (just before he, too, moved on):

It was April 1942 and I had been for two months happily settled with No.420 Royal Canadian Air Force Squadron at Waddington,

Lincolnshire. We had formed this Squadron with a small nucleus of Canadians and had just got operational. It was, therefore, a considerable worry to receive a peremptory summons to report to Group headquarters at Grantham to the Air Officer Commanding there, who was then Air Vice-Marshal Harris, a man of some repute whom junior officers held in great regard and some fear.

However, the interview was not at all as expected, and my instructions were to take over command of No. 97 Squadron at Woodhall Spa immediately. The instructions of the Air Vice-Marshal were very explicit – that the Squadron was to be pulled together and got operational as soon as possible as things had not gone too well recently. I think I must have looked somewhat unhappy, and on being questioned as to 'why I was not pleased at receiving such a "bouquet"', I replied to the effect that this bouquet had a large brick in it, as having just got 420 Squadron operational I was now going to be faced with many difficult problems and separated from my new Canadian friends.

A few days later, at lunchtime, I found myself at the Officers' Mess at Woodhall Spa where, to make matters worse, I had to take over the Squadron from a very old friend of mine, Jack Kynoch. Fortunately, he seemed quite relieved to see me, and met me with 'Well, I am glad you have arrived to take me out of my misery.'

Wing Commander Kynoch had had to deal with the teething troubles of the Lancaster, notably a lack of strength in the wing tips which tended to break off or bend badly when the plane was fully laden with petrol and bombs. Half a dozen or so Lancasters had been damaged or wrecked before this problem (as well as 'skin-wrinkling') had been overcome by improved riveting. An entry in 97 Squadron's Operations Record Book for 17/3/42 states baldly: '18 Lancasters, 9 serviceable.'

Nevertheless, John Collier settled in to pretty familiar surroundings:

Woodhall Spa was a typical wartime airfield, stretching over miles of fertile Lincolnshire countryside; very flat and with the wartime collection of Nissens hidden among the trees and spreadeagled around the airfield. One could travel many miles contacting various sections…

Living in Nissen huts in damp woods has been experienced by many, and was never the happiest of environments. Even so, the good spirits of the NCOs and men was very noticeable, and the complaints were very few and far between. When an offer came from Group HQ to move the officers' quarters to the large and luxurious Petwood House at Woodhall Spa, we felt this would be a mistake, as it seemed hardly fair to the NCOs and men who would be left in uncomfortable quarters.

We were very fortunate in one respect in that as we were away on our own, being a satellite station several miles from the Parent Station at Coningsby, then commanded by Group Captain Rowe, we suffered few visits and little interference... One of the few occasions we met up with the Base Commander was when there was a gas alert, when all should have been wearing gas masks – we had not taken the exercise seriously, but Group Captain Rowe appeared in the Officers' Mess, complete with his gas mask, and being entirely unrecognisable did not get the respect he was due and naturally got rather annoyed at our seeming lack of discipline.

At about the same time that Collier assumed command at Woodhall Spa, his friend Guy Gibson was promoted wing commander, at the age of 23, and took over 106 Squadron at Coningsby. The latter was still flying the unhappy Manchester, but would soon convert to Lancasters. Gibson described his arrival back in Lincolnshire in *Enemy Coast Ahead*, and a conversation in the mess:

The other squadron in the Station was already equipped, and was very proud of the fact, as it was the second in the Group to have them [after 44 Squadron]. The CO of this outfit was W/Cdr Joe Collier, who used to be in 83 Squadron with me. After his crash in September 1940, he had come back to bombers again, and had done about sixty sorties to date. He went on talking for a while and as I listened I realised that Daddy Rowe was commanding a happy station, even though there was a certain amount of rivalry between the two squadrons. But still, there always is...

For the first week of April, 97's planes had all been grounded while the problems were sorted out, then on the 8th were cleared for operational flying.

John Collier's takeover at 97 Squadron was briskly achieved, but there was one little detail that could have proved embarrassing:

> I had not even been converted to Lancasters, having come straight from a Hampden squadron, and again an old friend of mine, Squadron Leader Dugdale, had to teach me to fly the aircraft. It would probably horrify most pilots today to consider that a few hours sitting beside a fellow-officer and just watching was adequate to pass oneself out as competent…

Collier later admitted that his initial reception at Woodhall Spa had been a bit hostile, as 97 Squadron had been very fond of their departing CO, Jack Kynoch. As a result he was appreciative of the friendly welcome he received from Flying Officer 'Darkie' Hallows. He felt the tide of opinion was turning in his favour when he accidentally overheard a conversation about 'the new CO' in the officers' ablutions, when a fellow officer had opined 'Well, you must agree he means what he says.' Collier concluded: 'It seems the message had been received and understood.' Before long the fresh-faced wing commander (aged 25) was enjoying his fellow officers' affectionate nickname of 'Boy'.

He also came to appreciate the 'great support and encouragement' shown to him and other squadron commanders by the new commander of 5 Group, Air Vice-Marshal Coryton, who had replaced the promoted Harris. Coryton seemed omniscient, capable of running 5 Group while at the same time devising new navigational aids. Gibson thought him the best Group CO he ever encountered, a father-figure to his crews. Coryton, wrote Collier, 'would never wish the loss of an aircraft incurred unnecessarily.'

An example of his direct support came in the early days of John Collier's command of 97:

> The Squadron at Coningsby [106] and our Squadron had been selected also for a special role, and this was to deal with the *Tirpitz*, the threat from which had haunted the Admiralty throughout the war. About half the Squadron's aircraft had been specially modified and equipped with

a very special bomb which was specifically designed for attack of capital ships. In theory the bomb operated at low level by driving a heavy lump of steel straight through the battleship. However, the delivery of the bomb as envisaged called for extremely accurate flying and at low level …we considered there was little or no prospect of delivery as the aircraft would be destroyed well before the bomb could be released. The *Tirpitz* and other capital ships seemed to be permanently 'in dock' and extremely heavily defended. On top of all this, the *Tirpitz…* was at that time safely tucked away in a Norwegian fjord with precipitous mountains all around.

I expressed this point of view to the Senior Air Staff officer from the Air Ministry who came to inspect our capability. Fortunately he was accompanied by Air Vice-Marshal Coryton. The Air Staff Officer took the criticism badly and retaliated by inferring that it was probably lack of moral fibre that was the trouble. Air Vice-Marshal Coryton took exception to this and strongly supported our view.

…later we were greatly relieved to hear that the modified aircraft were taken out of service and converted back to their normal bombing role with the Main Force. …Gibson, in fact, was one of the very few people who had actually dropped one of these weapons (from a high altitude), achieving a large splash in one of the Baltic ports!

Seven Lancasters from 97 Squadron did in fact attack *Tirpitz* from Lossiemouth on 27/28 and 28/29 April 1942, while Collier was on leave and temporarily replaced by Wing Commander Leonard Slee. Instead of the contentious capital ship bomb, they dropped more conventional 4,000lb bombs, while Halifaxes simultaneously came in at low level and laid special mines that were supposed to hit the ship below the waterline. As predicted, the difficult terrain, smokescreens and heavy flak meant that no damage was done to *Tirpitz*.

The Augsburg Raid

A healthy rivalry developed between 106 Squadron at Coningsby and 97 Squadron at Woodhall Spa. Guy Gibson now had a DFC and Bar and a growing reputation – like John Collier – as one of the most experienced and decorated pilots in the RAF. Both were now developing into formidable leaders of men. Gibson had always been the more driven of the two and Collier noted that he 'was in his usual "press on" form' with 106, even when hampered by its troublesome Manchesters; 97, by contrast, had been 'in the doldrums' after the earlier accidents with the Lancasters and the fact that it was not yet operational 'weighed heavily on us all'.

...It was, therefore, with some excitement that the first operation instructions were received: to carry out no less than a daylight raid on South Germany – quite a stiff introduction to the war...

The Augsburg Raid deserved special mention – first of all because it was quite novel, involving heavy bombers roaring at a very low level over enemy-occupied France, and Germany itself. Special problems were involved in navigation and attack – the front guns were a problem as the hot cartridge cases would distract the bomb aimer, so they were not used in the final run-in to silence the enemy flak, and this fact probably cost us at least one of our aircraft.

We had selected our six most experienced crews [led by Squadron Leader John 'Flap' Sherwood] and were given some freedom in planning the flight, and were fortunate to avoid the enemy fighters. This was not the case with Nettleton's Squadron [44] who encountered stiff opposition near Paris and had to fight its way through. All our six arrived on time and as planned at the target [the MAN factory in Augsburg, making diesel engines for U-boats] and carried out their attack – also on time. The flak shot down two over the target, but W/O Mycock continued his run on into the target and dropped the bombs although on fire all the way in. This was a very heroic action, as the crew put duty before their safety – ending up a mass of flames past the target.

The attack, now considered a success, came in for considerable publicity, and the question of suitable rewards was a real problem. I heard mention of a recommendation for a VC for the other Squadron Leader [Nettleton] and considered that as our Squadron had the major role in the success, if an award of that nature were being considered then it should come our way – after all, W/O Mycock was a justifiable case for consideration [and Collier did recommend Sherwood for a VC, seconded by Arthur Harris]. However, in the end the Squadron achieved a DSO [for Sherwood], several DFCs, DFMs and a shower of MiDs, and later a posthumous [MiD] for W/O Mycock – so we were content. The Squadron had proved itself, and earned the respect it had hoped for.

Preparation for Operation MARLIN, as the Augsburg Raid was code-named, had been meticulous, and security the tightest possible. There had been low-level training in V-formation, including a simulated attack on Inverness that had gone to Scotland by way of Selsey Bill in order to simulate (to some degree) the extremely long flying time required to reach Bavaria, a round trip of 1,500 miles. Wing Commander Collier flew on this particular practice run to assess the crews' abilities. The 44 Squadron planes had failed to rendezvous with 97 Squadron at Selsey Bill, and this was to happen at the same spot on the actual raid, beginning the slight divergence of flight path that was to lead 44 into serious trouble over France.

The six 97 crews (and two reserve) gathered to hear their fate at Woodhall Spa on the morning of 17 April 1942. A route map marked with a long line of tape stretching to Augsburg had been met at first with laughter – it had to be a joke – but then 'Boy' Collier entered and announced: 'Well, gentlemen, now you know what the target is.'

He went on to relay Bomber Command's daring, perhaps suicidal, plan with a 'studied gaiety' that persuaded his men that this was no hoax. Much of the briefing by Wing Commander Collier – received in stunned silence – is quoted verbatim in a classic account of the war in the air, Ralph Barker's *Strike Hard, Strike Sure*, and reading it in full conveys something of the increasing chill that his audience must have felt:

The vital area of the target covers some 600 by 300 yards and comprises the main diesel-engine shop, cylinder machinery plant, crankshaft turning and grinding equipment and the main testing and assembly shops.

Aircraft from each squadron are to fly in two sections of three, keeping within supporting distance. If touch is lost between sections or squadrons they are to proceed independently. If one aircraft is forced to turn back in the early stages of the flight, the whole section of the three will return to base.

To ensure as far as possible that all four sections are within supporting distance in case of fighter interception during the flight across the Channel and to the South of Paris, a time of departure for Selsey Bill will be given to all aircraft.

The period immediately after the crossing of the French coast presents the greatest danger from fighters, and to counteract this a massive diversionary operation is being mounted, involving 30 Boston bombers and some 800 fighters. They will attack airfields and other targets in the Pas de Calais, Rouen and Cherbourg areas 10 minutes before you cross the coast. This should take care of the German fighters. And once you've penetrated 100 miles into France you can expect a clear run at the target.

Your route is from here to Selsey Bill, then to Dives-sur-Mer, where you cross the French coast, and on through Sens and Ludwigshaven to the north end of the Ammer See [just west of Munich], where you will make a wide left-hand turn and head straight for the target. The latter part of the route, as far as the Ammer See, is pointed at Munich with the object of deceiving the enemy into thinking that the attack is aimed at that city.

The route crosses some high ground between Sens and Ludwigshaven and section leaders are to use their own discretion in making short detours to avoid the highest points, following the general run of the valleys where practicable. Towns and defended areas are deliberately avoided by this route.

Sections should be opened out to about 3 miles between each section before reaching the Ammer See. After the wide left-hand turn you will cross a light railway, and later a main railway line and a river will give you an easily recognisable lead into the target. Attacks are to be made by individual sections in formation, from as low a level as possible consistent with accurate navigation, each aircraft dropping four 1000lb bombs in salvo with eleven-second delays.

Take-off will be at 15.00 hours, and times of setting course from Selsey Bill have been calculated so that the first wave will reach the target at about 20.15, or shortly before dusk. The return route will be direct from the target to base unless the remaining daylight necessitates a withdrawal to the South-West.

Navigation, signals, intelligence and met. briefing follow. But first I want to repeat what I said at the beginning. [Pause] I can't emphasise too strongly the vital importance of destroying this target. It's literally a matter of life and death in our struggle against the U–Boats. That's all.

The crews' first impulse had been to go to the armoury to beg odd bits of armour plate to sit on to protect their vital parts on this low-level ride across enemy territory.

The Augsburg Raid made world headlines as a spectacular and daring 'hedge-hopping' debut for the Lancaster bomber, and was lauded by Winston Churchill in the Commons: 'We must plainly regard the attack of the Lancasters on the U-boat engine factory at Augsburg as an outstanding achievement of the Royal Air Force. Undeterred by heavy losses at the outset, 44 and 97 Squadrons pierced and struck a vital point with deadly precision in broad daylight.'

Harris, too, was jubilant that his plan to announce the arrival of the Lancaster, and thereby promote and glamorize his strategic bombing campaign, had succeeded. He wrote:

The resounding blow which has been struck at the enemy's submarine and tank building programme will echo round the world... The gallant adventure penetrating deep into the heart of Germany in daylight and pressed home with outstanding determination in the face of bitter and unforeseen opposition, takes its place amongst the most courageous operations of the war.

However, closer to home, Jean Barclay – still at RAF Waddington and reflecting the mixed feelings of 44 Squadron after its catastrophic losses

– thought the raid 'both bitter and glorious'. John Nettleton was indeed awarded the VC, but his was the only one of his flight of six to make it back. A defective gyrocompass meant that he returned to base via the Irish Sea and an overnight stop at Blackpool. Yet the real problem for his contingent had been the too-early deployment and breaking off of the diversionary attack, which meant that German fighters returning from that engagement chanced upon the six 44 Squadron Lancasters. Having drifted slightly off course, they were passing right over the German fighters' base at Beaumont-le-Roger. The Messerschmitts, in the process of landing, took off again immediately and four bombers were shot down there and then.

The 97 Squadron Lancasters all arrived safely at the target but – as planned – just after Nettleton and his fellow survivor of the ambush (who crash-landed after dropping his bombs on the MAN plant). This meant that 97's planes took the full force of the alerted flak batteries. Sherwood's aircraft and Mycock's aircraft were downed, but four (including 'Darkie' Hallows') made it back to Woodhall Spa.

John Collier had the unenviable task of visiting Sherwood's wife in Woodhall Spa the next day and informing her that 'Flap' was missing. She took it calmly, quite convinced that he was alive. Two months later news came via the International Red Cross that he had been the only survivor of his crash, thrown clear by the impact, and was now a prisoner of war.

This was the first time since the early harum-scarum days of the war that a low-level daylight attack had been launched by Bomber Command, and having made its dramatic entry onto the stage the Lancaster prudently reverted to a night-time role. Despite the rhetoric of Churchill and Harris and the considerable damage to buildings at the giant MAN plant, it was later estimated that only 3 per cent of the machine tools had been put out of action.

The Lancasters were soon busy again and 97 Squadron's Operations Record Book lists a wave of sorties aimed at the Heinkel Aero Works at Rostock in late April, in what was a calculated combination of a precision attack on the aircraft factory and an incendiary raid on the highly-combustible houses of this ancient Hanseatic town. Goebbels denounced the burning of Rostock and the bombing that had wrecked historic Lübeck on 28 March 1942 – which involved 420's Hampdens – as *Terrorangriff* (terror attacks), and retaliated with the 'Baedeker Raids' on historic English cities such as Norwich, Exeter and Bath.

Operation MILLENNIUM

Arthur Harris was even more ambitious than Joseph Goebbels in his vision of a vengeful destruction from the air. He had another spectacular in mind, with the Lancasters to the fore: an attack on Cologne, scheduled for 30/31 May 1942, that would be the first 1,000-bomber raid on Germany, to signal to the Nazi authorities 'the growing might of Bomber Command'.

Operation MILLENNIUM was planned for maximum psychological effect on the German population, and as a morale boost for the British in a bad year. Before the attack Harris sent a portentous message to the crews:

The force of which you form a part tonight is at least twice the size and has at least four times the carrying capacity of the largest air force ever before concentrated on one objective. You have an opportunity therefore to strike a blow at the enemy which will resound, not only throughout Germany, but throughout the world…

He added, in a more blunt, if anatomically vague style: 'If you succeed… the most shattering and devastating blow will have been delivered against the very vitals of the enemy. Let him have it – right on the chin.'

To make up the round number of 1,000 aircraft, Bomber Command used up virtually its entire strength and included hundreds of planes from operational training units. Some 400 of the bombers were Wellingtons and only 73 Lancasters. Sixteen of these were from 97 Squadron and they flew in the third wave of the bomber stream, guided by the red glow as Germany's oldest city burned. Wing Commander Collier, with a scratch crew, led the 97 Squadron contingent. He later described it, in brief, as '…a very awe-inspiring raid for those taking part. Now we did feel that Bomber Command was really making Germany reel under our attack, and we were proud to know our Squadron was well near "the top of the league" for total bombing tonnage.'

Cologne was undoubtedly very badly hit: 1,455 tons of bombs were dropped, two-thirds of them incendiaries; over 3,000 buildings were destroyed and many more damaged; and seventeen ancient, mostly Romanesque, churches were destroyed or partially destroyed (although the great Gothic cathedral survived). A relatively small number of people – 469 – were killed; a testament to German air-raid precautions and shelters. All services – gas, electricity and water – were cut, and key bridges over the Rhine were hit. The fires were visible to aircraft from 150 miles away on the Dutch coast.

The 97 Squadron Operations Record Book included Wing Commander Collier's report:

Bomb load 1 x 4000lb HC [the new High Capacity 'cookie'], 8 X SBC 4lb [incendiary]. Lancaster R5552P W/C Collier – Captain; F/O Hooey – 2nd Pilot; F/O Ifould – Nav; F/S Turner – W/Op; Sgt Brummitt – F/G; Sgt Martin M/G; P/S Jones R/G. Up 0008 Down 0455. Bombed town from 15,000 ft. No cloud & visibility good. Bombs dropped on West bank of river. Bursts not observed owing to many fires. Rows of buildings seen on fire. Trip amazingly uneventful.

By contrast, *The Times* of 1 June 1942 pulled out all the stops, reporting 'OVER 1,000 BOMBERS RAID COLOGNE / BIGGEST AIR ATTACK OF THE WAR / 2,000 TONS OF BOMBS IN 90 MINUTES' and making much of the ominous tone of comments by the prime minister, who growled: 'This proof of the growing power of the British bomber force is also the herald of what Germany will receive, city by city, from now on.'

Harris exulted: 'We are going to scourge the Third Reich from end to end. We are bombing Germany city by city and ever more terribly in order to make it impossible for her to go on with the war.' However, he had also created something of a hostage to fortune, as *The Times* observed later in the year: 'It is interesting to recall that Air Marshal Harris, C-in-C, Bomber Command, said recently that if he could send 1,000 bombers a night to Germany, the war would be over by the autumn.'

Despite the devastation in Cologne, the official German assessment was that 'within two weeks the life of the city was functioning almost normally'.

On 11 June 1942 Acting Wing Commander J.D.D. Collier DFC received a certificate to mark being Mentioned in Despatches 'for distinguished service' which, though it was unstated, seems to have covered both the Augsburg Raid and Cologne, and may have been an indication that a DSO was in the offing.

Collier was certainly busy organizing 97 Squadron in the summer of 1942. Operations continued thick and fast in June, against Essen (no less than seven times), Bremen, Dieppe and Emden, although John Collier only participated in one sortie (his sixtieth) on 25 June: 'Bombing Bremen'. He led sixteen of 97's Lancasters in what was a 900–bomber raid (one of four major attacks on the city in this period). In theory the target was the Focke-Wulf aircraft factory, but thick cloud meant that it was the rest of Bremen that was hit.

Squadron Operations:

25&26/6/42 – BREMEN... / [Wing Commander Collier DFC's report] Load 1 x 4000lb bomb & 8 x SBC 4lb. Lancaster R5512C W/C J.D.D.Collier; Sgt J.Forsyth; F/O F.L.Ifould; Sgt N.L.Smith; P/O J.N.Eslick; F/S A.Nickeson; F/S R.A.Westgate. Up 2337 Down 0407. Attacked primary target on TR fix. 10/10ths cloud at 5000 feet. Bombs believed to have fallen on eastern end of town. Nothing of interest on way out. Red glow under cloud near Bremen. On way out saw what was thought to be fighter go down in flames. Lots of friendly aircraft in target area with navigation lights on.

Technically, this sixtieth op would have been the end of a second tour for an RAF pilot. John Collier does not seem to have anticipated taking a break but higher up in 5 Group, Bomber Command and the Air Ministry, his competence and attention to detail had been noted and plans were being made for him.

He was well aware that a confident spirit had grown up in 97 Squadron since the spring of 1942:

The Summer saw the Squadron going from strength to strength... with a very high morale. Losses had been low and the aircraft were the first of their type to be put into the air battle, and could fly higher and faster than the Halifaxes and Stirlings which had a rough time and suffered casualties. We were given the particular honour of being supplied with a Lancaster ['A for Queenie'] which was actually signed by Queen Elizabeth when she had visited the factory. Naturally we made a big fuss of this aircraft, which was fitted with a carpet to fly on special occasions.

It must be appreciated that one's life completely centred on the airfield and one hardly even thought of going off, night or day. The Squadron meant everything and it was with the greatest pride that we were able to make our daily return to Group of the highest serviceability, more often up to the maximum possible. We really felt we were a strength to Bomber Command.

It was not all high efficiency and operational discipline in this elite squadron:

We did manage to talk the Group into providing us with a spare aircraft for local flying so as to save the Lancasters and, at last, they delivered an ancient Whitley (in which we actually found grass growing inside the fuselage – a unique feat for any aircraft) which Hallows and I took up for the first time together. It proceeded to belch forth smoke and vibrate badly, and practically caught fire with clouds of smoke from the batteries. After flying this around for a short while, we decided it was quite unfit for anybody to fly again and finally it was designated for the dump...

At the end of another non-stop month in July, with raids on Bremen, Wilhelmshaven, Danzig, multiple attacks on Duisburg, as well as Saarbrücken and Düsseldorf, Wing Commander Collier went aloft once more on 26/27 July: 'Bombing Hamburg. 1 x 4000lb 10 SBC (1000 A/C) GOOD SHOW.' Squadron Operations included his report:

Visibility very good. Target clearly identified and bombed East of lake in endeavour to fan up two large fires. Little opposition. On way out saw flash in sky and what appeared to be an aircraft burning in sea.

Again on way home saw flash in sky and an aircraft crash in sea. Crew worked very well and altogether a very enjoyable trip.

A signal was received from AOC Bomber Command, Arthur Harris:

Congratulations on last night's magnificent effort against Hamburg. One of the outstanding successful attacks of the whole war. This operation together with the three highly effective Duisburg-Ruhr attacks completes a week's work in the face of the most difficult weather which the German enemy will long have cause to remember. You will eventually get the Boche down for the count. It is but a question of time and numbers. You may as yet be too few but you are damned good.

Harris was pumping up the morale of one of his crack squadrons, excited by the destructive power that his new planes were unleashing. He also broadcast to the enemy, looking back to the blitz and forward to a greater ordeal, as quoted in *The Times* of 29 July 1942:

'YOU HAVE NO CHANCE' / WARNING TO GERMAN PEOPLE / REICH TO BE BOMBED FROM END TO END / 'You thought, and Goering promised you, that you would be safe from bombs. And indeed during all that time we could only send over a small number of aircraft in return. But now it is just the other way. Now you send only a few aircraft against us, and we are bombing Germany heavily.

Why are we doing so? It is not revenge – though we do not forget Warsaw, Belgrade, Rotterdam, London, Plymouth and Coventry. We are bombing Germany, city by city, and ever more terribly, in order to make it impossible for you to go on with the war. That is our object. We shall pursue it remorselessly... Let the Nazis drag you down to disaster with them if you will. That is for you to decide.'

Wing Commander John Collier was again Mentioned in Despatches, his third oak leaf. Nevertheless, he had caveats about the RAF's performance in this 'fire raid':

...although it was claimed to be very successful, one was amazed to see aircraft releasing their bomb loads some 50 miles short of the target on the run-in. This disturbed a number of our crews who did their duty and continued right over the target. It seemed to us that there was no excuse for this bombing short... at Hamburg as the docks stood out like fingers in the moonlight for many miles leading up to the target.

A letter home from Woodhall Spa, 28 July 1942, was more positive:

I had a very good trip the night before last on Hamburg. I think we really gave the Jerry something to think about, the fires were almost as large as the ones at Cologne, and the visibility was much better, we knew exactly where we had placed our incendiary bombs which was very satisfactory.

He was now 'living out' with Beth and young Mark at High Park, a farmhouse that was only about 100 yards from Woodhall Spa's officers' mess. Despite an edict from Command that wives were not allowed around the base and that officers were expected to live in the mess, the CO felt he could not in fairness enforce the rule:

I found the arrangement excellent for me as my wife had always continued to give me support, never asking any questions and always seeing that I was well fed and not worried about domestic matters. My young son Mark, aged one, proved quite a popular mascot among the officers who were always ready to entertain him on the billiards table with billiard balls.

Operations continued remorselessly through August 1942 and on the 27/28th six Lancasters from 97 Squadron bombed the port of Gdynia, downriver from Danzig, which involved a 1,800-mile round trip; they were aiming yet again for the *Scharnhorst* and *Gneisenau*, which may have been hit but not mortally. Meanwhile Guy Gibson's 106 Squadron were trying to drop 5,600lb armour-piercing capital ship bombs (the ones intended for the

Tirpitz) on the unfinished German aircraft carrier *Graf Zeppelin* at Gdynia but were frustrated by poor visibility.

The Pathfinder Force was inaugurated in August 1942, after dogged resistance from Harris, and bombing accuracy was thereby much improved. Guy Gibson recalled a discussion in the mess at Coningsby that had concluded that Joe Collier's 97 Squadron was Bomber Command's best and should be selected as the Pathfinder Squadron for 5 Group, but instead that honour went to their old mutual alma mater, 83 Squadron.

While Collier was in charge of 97 Squadron a major advance in bombing technique was introduced. An accurate guidance system – GEE – had been fitted to Lancasters from March 1942, using a triangulation of radio pulses broadcast from three stations. Measuring the time differences between pulses gave navigators accuracy to within 5 miles. However, GEE's range was limited by the curvature of the earth, and the Germans (who had used a radio beam for guidance since the outbreak of war) learned how to jam it, but jamming only worked after a plane had passed the continental coast and was already on its true course.

Further refinements came later in December 1942 with OBOE, which was an audible pulse that altered when a plane deviated from the correct route. On approaching the target a signal of dashes, then dots, was broadcast by the OBOE transmitters. When the dots stopped, the bomb-aimer pressed the release button.

Other innovations in 1942 included target-indicating markers, consisting of hundreds of small coloured incendiary balls (released from a single bomb) that burned for five minutes, long enough to guide in a considerable number of bombers. As the selected colours changed night by night, it was harder for the Germans to create dummy versions to lure the bombers from the target. According to Guy Gibson: 'These were the bombs that put night bombing on the map.'

A Nearby Cloud

John Collier's log book records an abortive sixty-second op on 16 August 1942: 'Mine laying, Stettin. Returned early engine seized.' His sixty-third came on 28 August: 'Bombing Augsburg [in fact the target was nearby

Nuremberg, as stated in 97 Squadron's Operations Record Book]. 1 x 8000lb.' Eleven planes from 97 Squadron took part, guided by Pathfinders. To accommodate its giant bomb, Collier's Lancaster had to be adapted in an ad hoc way, with a larger 'belly' and an arrangement of heavy-duty elastic to hold the bomb doors together, on the correct assumption that the weight of dropping the bomb would snap the elastic and open the doors...

Squadron Operations:

28&29/8/42 – NURNBERG... / [Wing Commander Collier DFC's report] R56095 W/C J.D.D.Collier, Capt; Sgt A.H.Airy, 2nd pilot; F/L R.A.Boddington, Nav; Sgt M.H.Middleton, Bomb; Sgt A.O.Stafford, W Op; Sgt C.L.Johnson, M/gun; Sgt J.McMahon, R/gun. Up 2113 Down 0326. Primary visually pinpointed on river, bombed from 13,000 feet. Enormous column of smoke & debris flew into air as bomb burst. Many searchlights over target area.

John Collier did not know then that this would be his last sortie and that – remarkably – luck was to remain on his side to the very end:

Superstition plays a large part in one's life when flying. In the early days many crews flew with 'lucky charms'. These, of course, usually got lost, and it was therefore with some seriousness that I listened to the warning by a member of the ground staff that I should not fly my aircraft because it had an 8,000lb bomb on board, as this was considered to be 'unlucky'; influenced, perhaps, by the fact that the last time one was carried the crew did not return. However, I am glad to say we came safely through this raid which was to be on Augsburg Marine Works again [memory confusion about the target arises from the MAN company name, an acronym for Maschinenfabrik Augsburg-Nürnberg] – this time by night, of course. Due to the bad weather conditions we had serious doubts whether our bomb had actually landed in Germany, and so had some difficulty when our AOC Air Marshal Coryton, who had come down to welcome us back, cross-questioned us about the raid. However, we felt pretty sure the bomb had landed somewhere near the target area, although successful raids in those days were still very dependent on weather conditions as we had no real [electronic] aids. There was no doubt that most of the bombing still went very much adrift...

Perhaps a mid-air encounter with the Luftwaffe on the way to the MAN works gave a strong hint to John Collier that his luck was finally in danger of running out:

COMBAT REPORT by W/C Collier, 97 Squadron, 28/29 Aug 1942. Lancaster 'S' R5609. Operation: Individual night bombing attack on the town of NURNBERG. Disposition: On crossing the French coast at CHARELOI, flying at 12,000 ft, time 23.33 hrs, the R/G of above aircraft sighted an Me109 flying in the opposite direction on the starboard beam at a distance of approx 400 yards. The recognition was apparently mutual as the Me turned to starboard in the dead astern position and at a distance of between 700 and 800 yards where he continued to maintain that range for the duration of combat. A few seconds after the sighting of the Me109 the nose gunner spotted a second aircraft which was single engined but unidentified at a range of 600 yards crossing from port to starboard bow, following round to attack on the starboard beam. On reaching this position the enemy aircraft developed the attack, lessening range continuously on the starboard beam. The pilot at this critical stage turned to starboard with a slight dive at a speed of 320mph and was enveloped in a nearby cloud which completely lost the two enemy aircraft. (The moon ahead of Lancaster.) Result of combat: No rounds fired from Lancaster. The E/A attacking on the beam was presumed to have fired his guns as the perspex on the Astro hatch was damaged with a hole approx 3" in diameter through it. Actually no rounds were observed to have been fired from either.

A week or so after returning safe and sound from this close shave, John Collier was replaced as CO by Wing Commander Graham Jones DFC. After 'sterling work' with 97 Squadron, he had been provisionally selected – perhaps on the personal recommendation of 5 Groups's AVM Coryton – to join the Air Staff. Collier was subsequently awarded the Distinguished

Service Order for maintaining 97 Squadron 'in the highest state of efficiency' and for his 'exemplary conduct':

28/9/42 <u>CONFIDENTIAL</u>:

<u>RECOMMENDATION FOR A NON-IMMEDIATE AWARD</u>
Christian Names: JOHN DAVID Surname: COLLIER DFC & BAR
Rank: S/Ldr (A/W/Cmdr) Official Number: 39037
Command or Group: 5 Group, Bomber Command Unit: No.97 Squadron

Total hours flown on operations: 370 hours 30 minutes
Number of sorties carried out: 63
Recognition for which recommended: D.S.O.
Appointment held: Squadron Commander

Particulars of meritorious service for which the recommendation is made:

Acting Wing Commander Collier has commanded No.97 (Straits Settlement) Squadron from the 30th March 1942.

He already holds the D.F.C. and Bar to D.F.C., which decorations were awarded before he took command of the above Squadron. The D.F.C. was granted as an immediate award for his part in the bombing of Bordeaux on the 19th August 1940; that trip was his 34th sortie and he had completed by that date 197 hours 35 minutes operational flying. On the 24th July 1941, Wing Commander Collier took part in a daylight raid on Brest. For his gallantry on this, his 48th sortie, he was awarded a Bar to the D.F.C., and this raid marked the completion of 283 hours 40 minutes operational flying.

Wing Commander Collier after having formed No.420 Squadron was posted to command No.97 Squadron to improve the operational efficiency of this Squadron. The records of 97 Squadron during the past six months are very creditable and prove that this Officer, by his untiring devotion to duty and his leadership has accomplished the task assigned to him. His long operational tour of 63 sorties against all types of targets merits, I consider, the award of the Distinguished Service Order.

Date: 28.9.42 Signature of Commanding Officer H.G.Rowe Rank: G/ Capt

Remarks by Air or other Officer Commanding:
This officer throughout his period of command has maintained his squadron in the very highest state of efficiency. His leadership and example have been exemplary.

Date: 30/9/42
W.A.Coryton
Rank: AVM

Much later John Collier looked back on his short but productive final command of a bomber squadron in 1942:

My period with the Squadron and real knowledge of it was limited to only the Spring and Summer, and although this saw the Squadron fully operational and playing a major role, nevertheless I was quite grateful to be told that I had been posted to the Staff College Course because one felt one could push one's luck a bit too far – my first operational flight started on September 3rd 1939, and I was rather relieved to step out of the arena three years later, in September 1942. Even so, saying goodbye is always a moment of some emotion and it was very decent of the men to whip together to present me a watch which still goes and is a proud possession today. This, of course, should not have been accepted as it was against all Command's Regulations and Air Council's instructions!

Some late summer leave followed with Beth in the West Country, though he was still not quite sure what the next move would be, according to a letter home from Woodhall Spa: 'When you next write please address all letters to Benedict House… I have got a fortnights holiday – will probably go to Group for a fortnight & then I hope London!! This is all supposition as I don't know yet whether I am on the Staff college course or not!!'

On 26 October the next phase of John Collier's war began, when he was posted to No.7 Staff College War Course, Bulstrode Park in Buckinghamshire. Then on 6 November 1942 his Royal Warrant of appointment to the Distinguished Service Order was signed by Archibald Sinclair, Secretary of State for Air, on behalf of the king.

Part II

War Room

Chapter Five

B Ops 1

Small Wars on Paper

As a highly-experienced and highly-decorated officer and one of the 'great survivors' of Bomber Command – though still only in his mid-twenties – John Collier's practical knowledge of how to conduct bombing operations was now needed at the highest level. The Air Ministry wanted one of the best serving pilots and squadron commanders to join the Directorate of Bombing Operations in Whitehall to 'help run the war'. Apparently both he and Guy Gibson were singled out by Bomber Command and the Ministry as potential staff officers, but Gibson wanted to continue flying (he was still 'determined to get a VC') so only 'Joe' Collier moved to London.

As Collier stated himself, he was starting to feel that his luck might soon run out. He could sense that the air campaign over Germany was becoming more and more risky, despite the innovations in aircraft design and navigational aids. The problem was that the Germans were innovating too, improving the effectiveness of their night–fighters with co–ordinated radio and radar control, and making their flak and searchlight defences ever more formidable.

The odds were shortening – Bomber Command's losses rose to 6.7 per cent in the autumn of 1942 – and it was really something of a miracle that he had survived sixty-three operations. Jean Barclay's account of life at RAF Waddington is mostly about the death of friends, and like John Collier she lost so many, month by month, but somehow kept going through this routine of constant emotional uncertainty and sudden devastation. Too often planes full of her comrades went 'speeding down the flarepath and fading away towards the horizon and into eternity'.

Collier was no longer risking his life negotiating the German defences or dealing with the vagaries of the weather and the weight of direct responsibility for his crews, but he had to make some adjustment before moving to Whitehall, via a period of technical and theoretical training. The rarified atmosphere of the RAF Staff College at Bulstrode Park in Buckinghamshire in the autumn of 1942 was a new challenge for a man who had spent three years immersed in the pragmatic business of flying bombers and directing front-line squadrons.

He now found himself in the tranquil surroundings of the former country estate of the Dukes of Somerset and its rather forbidding Victorian Gothic pile of a mansion, from which he wrote home on 8 November 1942:

> I am enjoying it here very much indeed. The place is run as a University, and although we do fairly long hours we have the weekend free, and the work is so interesting that the time goes quickly. We start off by trying to improve our writing and spelling of English. We then learn all the organisations of the RAF, the backbone of Policies etc, and the High Strategy etc, and then we run our own small wars on paper… I only hope that I make the grade OK. It is not too easy for someone straight from squadrons as there is so much knowledge in Service writing procedure needed, which I lack, however we hope for the best.

One of his Staff College essays on 'Air Strategy' has survived, dateable to this period by a mention of the recent Allied landings in North Africa that had taken place on 8 November 1942.

When he wrote to his parents again, presumably not long after Christmas, from Benedict House, Northiam, Sussex, he was preparing for life in the capital with Beth and Mark.

An Office in Whitehall

A week or so after New Year 1943, with some trepidation, Wing Commander John Collier joined a team of specialist mission planners, the Directorate of Bomber Operations 1 – 'B Ops 1' – at the Air Ministry in London. Sitting typing at another desk in tropical Ceylon in 1946 he began his war memoir, to which he gave the provisional title *Adventure in the Air Ministry*, at this precise moment:

It is 0845 hours on the morning of January 12th 1943. I am hurrying towards Whitehall to take up my new appointment at the Air Ministry. Will you take a walk with me and capture some of the atmosphere and thoughts which oppress me?

We have left the Tube at Trafalgar Square and are now in wartime Whitehall. Whitehall has all the sombre dignity of British Officialdom. War has caused few changes. You are shaken out of the depression that pervades by the rather startling sight of large photographic displays of feminine beauty and nudity outside the Whitehall Theatre. What a daring trespass into the land of Officialdom! I recognise the charming person of Phyllis Dixey in 'Stardom'. My thoughts fly back many years earlier when Phyllis was performing at Lincoln. How well I remember enjoying her show during which she sang a song about 'The Show the Lord Mayor Banned'... Her black night dress worn during the performance was a terrific hit with the Boys, many of whom rushed off to see if they could not buy similar ones, presumably to glamourize their wives or girl friends!

Feeling unreasonably cheered, my thoughts return to matters on hand... Yes, I am nervous. It is a bit of an ordeal to face a new job of a nature entirely different to anything I have done before in the Air Force... I am really very vague as to what my work will be, and after many years of freedom of the Squadron, how will I stand the restrictions of a 'desk life'. Will I ever cope with the long appreciations that I have been taught to write at Staff College. The thought appals me, because I was really so bad at them. Oh dear, I never could spell... will that matter? And so I gradually work myself up into a state of nervous apprehension.

We are past the Horse Guards Parade and the Old Admiralty buildings. Poor old Admiralty – it has been severely shaken by bombings and looks thoroughly unsafe. I believe it was condemned before the War, but will of course have to carry on for many years – there has been a new addition, however [the 'Citadel'] a monstrosity that mars the Mall irrevocably! It may be bomb, blast and fire proof, but did it have to look like some kid's fort?

The War Office is untouched by war, but just looks slightly dirtier and dustier than usual. The bricked up windows do not help its appearance. However, what do looks matter in war time?

The Cenotaph alone appears as a shining example in all this dreariness, but even then the flags are in sore need of repair.

There is little traffic, for all who can have evacuated to avoid the air raids. Whitehall has the appearance of a ship cleared for action, and the battle ahead is likely to be long and costly for there are few bright spots on the Allied horizon. Germany stands almost supreme, and only is worried by the nightly bombing raids of our Bomber Command, and here I am about to join the Air Staff to try and help in the direction of that force. My head lifts slightly higher. How lovely those balloons look floating majestically in the early morning breeze, and there is Big Ben shining gloriously above the haze of the River Thames. The sight of Big Ben always stirs some deep feeling in me. As long as He stands, I am sure, so will England.

I steal a glance down that murky little Downing Street, where, in the gloom in the far end of the street such great decisions are being taken by the greatest of all statesmen, Winston Churchill. To think of Winston is a good thing for it puts me in my right perspective and I realize what a really small cog I am in the vast machine of War.

I enter King Charles Street, and am swept 'willy nilly' with the tide of many hundreds of civil servants and Air Force officers, who are hurrying to work in that vast monstrosity of a building, which is now termed Air Ministry, Whitehall. The building appears to my overwrought imagination much like a medieval fort into which little light or air can possibly enter. I am not impressed with this 'nerve centre of the air war' for there is no gleam of bayonets, no shining brasswork, no polished marble. Only a rather elderly doorkeeper in a dusty blue uniform, and small piles of leaves and litter mark the entrance. I cannot but recall Marshal of the Royal Air Force Lord Trenchard's description of Goering's Luftwaffe Headquarters in Berlin, with all its pomp and ceremony, where Trenchard told us he was asked to take off his shoes before entering for fear of marking the highly polished floors. How well I remembered his visits to our Squadron, how delighted we were, and how we loved him for he was the founder and champion of the Air Force. I could not help but smile because on both his visits he had told this same story... and how he had told Goering that he certainly was not going to take his shoes off, but would make as much mess as he liked. Trenchard had also told us that when the war was won we should all also stamp around Goering's headquarters and mess up his floors! In January 1943 that prospect seemed to be a long way off!

And so I found my way to my new job in the office of Bomber Operations 1 and awaited the arrival of Wing Commander Ken Smith whom I was taking over from...

The Air Ministry was in the Victorian building known as 'GOGGS' – Government Offices Great George Street – or the New Public Offices, which also housed the Cabinet War Rooms in a specially-strengthened basement. The entrance to the Air Ministry was in King Charles Street. The GOGGS building is now the Treasury, and the War Rooms a highly evocative museum. In his memoir John Collier modestly neglects to mention his investiture with the DSO on 9 February 1943 at Buckingham Palace, just across the park from his new place of work.

During the next few weeks Ken Smith patiently explained to me the various aspects and problems of my new job. It seemed to me that the aspect was delightfully wide, as it covered responsibilities for long-term planning of Bomber Operations, selection of vital targets, general conduct of Bomber Operations, and liaison with the Admiralty and War Office. Close co-operations with the American Eighth Air Force was one of the principal tasks, as at that time the over-all direction of their ever increasing forces lay with our Air Staff.

Knowing Air Chief Marshal Harris's strength of character and individualistic tendencies, I asked Ken as to the relations between our Department and Bomber Command, for I was very surprised to learn that the control of the Bomber Forces lay with Bomber Operations, Air Ministry. The general belief amongst aircrew was that Bert Harris alone said what and where was done with the Force. 'Oh not bad, [replied Ken] but they resent very much being told what to do, you have to be very tactful!' The Americans, he said, on the other hand, could not possibly be more co-operative and considering we were playing about with their forces, to some extent, were amazingly helpful.

Ken showed me around the labyrinth of passages, into which daylight never penetrated. It was much the same in our office where powerful electric lights had to burn all day – one could not read a letter five feet from the window! I suggested that the windows might be cleaned. Ken laughed and said it would be another six months before the window cleaners came around, it took them just one year to complete the whole building. Well, couldn't we get the women who cleaned the office to do the windows? 'Good heavens man, that would be breaking their union rules' – I was incredulous at the time, but how true I found his remarks to be!

My amazement never ceased at the lack of facilities for personnel serving in the Ministry – the 'Coffee Room' was a masterpiece of discomfort – situated three floors underground, you had to pass through more dusty doorkeepers who demanded your pass... you negotiated finally a narrow winding staircase, ducked under a door and you were in a room some sixteen feet square, interspersed with massive supporting pillars, which was always so crowded that it was almost impossible to force your way in. Maisie was the heroine who slaved day after day to serve us with refreshment – they gave her little pay, no running water and poor stocks, but she always remained cheerful... serving many hundreds of 'coffee & buns' during the morning.

Not far from the 'Coffee Room' was the 'War Room'. This place fascinated me for the two years I was in the Air Ministry. You needed a special pass to enter, but once in all possible information about disposition of our and the enemy's forces were available to you at a glance. The walls were covered with large scale maps of all theatres of war, and covered with flags and pins denoting different divisions, targets, shipping, submarines etc etc. For the amateur tactician here was the perfect set-up. I often used to think how easy it should be for the enemy to penetrate into this 'treasure house of intelligence' for we often got past the doorkeeper by displaying our Southern Railway tickets which were a similar green to the official pass!

The House of Shame

John Collier described himself as a 'small cog' in the Air Staff machine, but he was also part of a true team effort in B Ops 1, where most matters were discussed and agreed in a collegiate fashion before a decision was committed to paper and thence to action. Heated and lengthy arguments were an inevitable part of this process: '…but out of the fire came a tempered weapon, fashioned by us all – to this method of approach to the problems I attribute the [fact that] so many correct decisions were taken, when a mistake could have cost so dear.'

His ultimate boss in the Ministry – an edifice known to a sceptical RAF as 'The House of Shame' – was Air Chief Marshal Sir Charles Portal, Chief of the Air Staff, a remote though polite and sympathetic figure: 'passing him on the stairs was the nearest I got to personal contact with my Master…' However, Collier was very much closer in his day-to-day work to Air Commodore Sydney Bufton DFC, Director of Bomber Operations (promoted from deputy director on 10 March 1943, taking over from Air Commodore J.W. Baker). Known as 'Syd' or 'Buf', he was a tenacious and deeply-admired Welshman who 'would always pursue a point, however small, to its logical conclusion. Even though, at times, this appeared to be a maddening characteristic, one had to admit in the end that he was always right.' Bufton coped with a phenomenal workload with great composure, although Collier knew there were limits: 'I have never seen Syd excited by anything, and very seldom angry, but occasionally, when I trespassed too far on his good nature, I used to see a warning flush coming to his neck, at which I hastily retreated.'

Having served as a bomber pilot and a squadron and station commander in the current conflict (unlike many of his colleagues), Bufton would have appreciated the value of having someone of Collier's experience on board with ideas fresh from the front line. Bufton was very much a direct and hands-on staff officer himself, nothing like the cliché of the paper-pusher or desk-flyer, and he seems to have found a kindred spirit in Joe Collier.

Bufton had joined B Ops in November 1941 in the wake of the Butt Report into bomber inaccuracy. As an inventive electrical engineer, Bufton focused on the problem from a technical as well as an organizational standpoint, devising an improved barometrically-fused flare to illuminate targets. His inspired idea of the Pathfinder Force, an advance party of planes setting coloured flares to guide in the main bomber stream, had been stubbornly resisted by Harris (as was almost any innovation, especially if proposed by a junior officer). However, it was strongly backed by Harris's superior Portal, and so had become a reality from August 1942.

The role of Bufton and his staff at B Ops 1 was as a sort of 'think tank' with a degree of power, studying all manner of problems concerning targets, tactics, armaments, equipment, etc and ultimately preparing papers for Portal to present at chiefs-of-staff meetings. On his behalf they would also draft directives for Bomber Command concerning target selection, assisted at a higher level by Air Intelligence, ULTRA decrypts (derived from the German Enigma machine) and Ministry of Economic Warfare assessments of industrial targets. B Ops 1 therefore had substantial if indirect authority, but did not issue specific orders; that was up to Bomber Command HQ itself, and Harris had a genius for ignoring or subverting any directive to which he took exception.

The Directorate of Bomber Operations was divided into three parts:

- B Ops 1 concerned operational planning, target selection and liaison with Air Intelligence and the Ministry of Economic Warfare. (Once the Americans joined the war, liaison was extended to the USAAF and their Economic Warfare Division.)
- B Ops 2 (a) covered analysis of operations, the organization and composition of Bomber Command and navigational aids.
- B Ops 2 (b) was involved in weapons development: bombs, mines, etc.

Ironically, in view of the battles that raged between B Ops and Bomber Command, the whole idea for a dedicated Directorate of Bomber Operations (as distinct from Home Ops) had originated with Arthur Harris when he had served at the Air Ministry in 1940 as Deputy Chief of Air Staff. However, from when he took over as C-in-C Bomber Command in the spring of 1942, the 'Three Bs' of B Ops – Bottomley, Baker and Bufton (and their respective staffs) – went to the top of Harris's personal hate list.

John Collier was still a very young man when he joined the Air Ministry, and he found himself in the company of mostly older military men (although

Bufton was only 35). His years with bomber squadrons would not have prepared him as such for this new milieu, but it was his very freshness, allied with shrewd intelligence and substantial practical experience with the bomber force, that would make his input valuable in the discussions and analyses of B Ops 1. This was appreciated by his boss, as Sydney Bufton's widow Sue confirmed when writing to 'Joe' after Syd's death in 1993: 'Buf always had the greatest admiration for your ability & personality.'

In September 1942, at about the time Collier was whisked away from 97 Squadron to Staff College, Bufton had written a paper on 'Night Bombing – Tactics and Tactical Development' that envisaged a modernization of technical/scientific planning in a new Bomber Development Unit, but his words may equally have been aimed at B Ops and much of the 'House of Shame':

A special tactical development section is essential, with a staff large enough to deal with a number of projects simultaneously. It must work on 'fire-brigade' lines. It should be able not only to meet, but to anticipate requirements. Until this is provided we cannot hope to keep our tactics in phase with enemy developments.

As well as internal Air Ministry meetings, John Collier was regularly in attendance at chiefs-of-staff committees in the underground Cabinet War Rooms, which were usually presided over by Hastings Ismay, Churchill's Chief Staff Officer, if not by the prime minister himself. It seems that Collier could hold his own in these discussions, even at the highest level, and was famous for his ability 'to make Admirals so hopping mad that they lost the argument in committee', according to George (later Lord) Mackie, who composed a doggerel poem about B Ops 1 and its denizens that included this verse:

Joe is large and sprayed with gongs
To B Ops One
This brute belongs
He often is extremely rude
And would be ruder if he could

Seated at the desk opposite Collier for the next two years was a man who would set a high intellectual standard for him to aspire to, and a colleague for whom he developed the greatest respect. Wing Commander Arthur Morley was a successful industrialist who had applied his formidable energies to the prosecution of the war. He was

> very thick set with a bullet head and the determination of the devil. Many considered him a fanatic and certainly when he turned those steely blue eyes on you and thumped the table you were inclined to agree... He had no time for those who took the war easily or put personal considerations first, and he was prepared to say so.

It was Morley who had proposed a much greater use of incendiaries in bombing raids.

Assisting Bufton, Morley and Collier in the early days of 1943 were just two secretaries: Daphne Pegram, daughter of an admiral, and Joan Strattan. Squadron Leader Robert Whitehead, a lawyer in peacetime who 'had a very quick brain when he wanted to use it' then joined the group. Help was needed in drafting and presentation of plans, so Morley suggested bringing in John Strachey, a squadron leader working in the Public Relations Department. Strachey's skills helped oil the machinery of B Ops 1, and he later gave a series of graphic and highly popular BBC radio talks – his 'War Commentaries' – focusing on the Bomber Offensive.

Strachey had been a member of the Communist Party until 1940, when he quit on the issue of supporting the war, and this may have put anyone who associated with him under a certain amount of suspicion. Harris apparently tried to get Strachey removed from B Ops 1, but by the end of the war Strachey was in the Cabinet – after the Labour landslide victory of July 1945 – as Under Secretary of State for Air, and it was Harris who was out in the cold.

Chapter Six

Round-the-Clock War

Combined Bomber Offensive

Whe Wing Commander John Collier joined the Air Ministry in January 1943 the war was finely balanced: Montgomery's Eighth Army had won a decisive victory at El Alamein the preceding autumn and the Red Army had humiliated the Wehrmacht at Stalingrad, but Britain could only directly attack Germany through Bomber Command. However, the immediate priority was the mortal threat to shipping in the Atlantic posed by U-boat wolf packs; this meant a major diversion of aircraft to bomb the submarine bases in France and the German shipyards.

The build-up of the USAAF in Britain after the United States entered the war in December 1941 was beginning to alter the pattern of the air campaign. Whereas the RAF, after experiencing heavy losses in daytime raids, had become largely nocturnal in its operations, American planes were to fly exclusively in daylight. Mass-produced B-24 Liberator and B-17 Flying Fortress bombers had extra armour, and were equipped with the Norden bomb-sight that (in clear skies, not guaranteed in northern Europe) assisted precision bombing.

Thus an 'around the clock' air offensive evolved after discussions between Churchill and Roosevelt at the Casablanca Conference in January 1943, in the wake of the Allied landings in North Africa. The 'Casablanca Directive' had been issued by the Combined Chiefs of Staff, creating a Combined Bomber Offensive. It emphasized that: 'Your primary object will be the progressive destruction and dislocation of the German military, industrial and economic system, and the undermining of morale of the German people to a point where their capacity for determined resistance is fatally weakened.' It went on to list primary objectives 'within that general concept': '(a) German submarine construction yards. (b) The German aircraft industry. (c) Transportation. (d) Oil plants.' Other high-priority targets were the U-boat bases on the Biscay coast, Berlin, northern Italy, German capital ships and, in the not-too-distant future, targets associated with the invasion of Europe.

The Directive's generalized tone – despite the clear target list – gave enough leeway for Harris (indulged to a certain extent by Churchill) to use it to legitimize his remorseless campaign against the German civilian population. This was now, admittedly, total war, without much distinction between military and civilian targets, but Harris seems to have seriously underestimated the resilience of German morale.

The submarine pens at Brest, Lorient and Saint-Nazaire, with their massively thick reinforced concrete construction, proved impervious to attack, although some USAAF precision bombing was effective. Losses were high, and the top-priority plan to limit the effectiveness of the U-boats needed rethinking. John Collier came up with an idea that his boss in B Ops 1, Syd Bufton, approved:

At this time I thought that a sea mining campaign might be more successful than bombing to close the French Ports, and I put up a suggestion for high level mining attacks from the air, with mines densely laid in all approach channels, which at present were unapproachable from a low level due to defences, as a means of effectively retarding the movement of submarines. [His 'High Level Mining Technique' text is dated 25 June 1943, see Appendix.] Syd Bufton thought that there was something in my idea, and told me to raise it at a meeting to be held shortly with Admiralty and Bomber Command representatives. Perhaps I put the idea over badly, but it was heavily trampled on by the Admiralty representative, who stated in a lordly tone that the mines could not possibly be dropped safely from any height above 500 feet, and the idea of haphazard mining seemed preposterous! I got no backing and retired, very red in the face, to abandon the idea for some time. Time was to show just how possible the suggestion was…

He later wrote that:

This paper was only produced after careful consultations with the Admiralty Mine Design Dept, who supported the proposal, and said as far as they were concerned the ideas were practical. Further research indicated that any 'scatter' would not be detrimental to the technique [as shown on diagrams of distribution of mines around a target point, dated 21/4/43].

The essence of Collier's idea was that mines dropped from 10,000 to 15,000 feet could not be tracked and plotted by enemy observers, and would therefore make the task of mine-sweeping harder, using up time, men and resources and delaying U-boat sailings for longer. It would also make operations safer for aircraft and could take place under the cover of co-ordinated bombing raids against the ports.

The disadvantage of a greater degree of inaccuracy would be countered by using a new water/land mine – the Mark VIA – that would detonate on hitting solid ground. However, a reasonable degree of accuracy was to be expected by employing Pathfinders using OBOE or the new H2S guidance system and floating sea markers – Marine Marker Mk II – that would burn for two hours and be visible for 10 to 20 miles. The principle of high-level mining could also be used against other heavily-defended ports such as Kiel or Hamburg.

Collier had happier experiences liaising with the American Air Staff, notably Chief Intelligence Officer Colonel Hughes and the piano-playing Wal Rostow, a regular dining companion at the Churchill Club, which had been set up in the evacuated premises of Westminster School for the use of Allied servicemen. Rostow was a major in the Office of Strategic Services or OSS (forerunner of the CIA) and a selector of bombing targets, so was John Collier's rough equivalent in the USAAF; much later he had an impressive career advising JFK and LBJ. However, these were early, naive days for the unblooded American Air Force and the sometimes cavalier approach of their planners in Washington was about to be brutally exposed:

The 'Ploestie Affair' we called it. It came as rather a bolt from the blue to us. A youthful American Colonel Smart turned up in the office one day. He explained that he had come over from America specially to arrange an attack on the Ploestie oil fields. As the Ploestie oil fields lie in Roumania, and neither we or the Americans had forces in the Mediterranean available, and further as we were not on an 'Oil Directive' – we were more than surprised. However, it seemed that this was to be a very special show that had been thought out and 'cooked' in America, and nothing to do with us or the American Air Staff on this side, except – the Eighth Air Force would have to undertake the attack! I shuddered as the broad details were unfurled, and thanked my stars that we were to have little to do with it. Smart explained that he had been told he might use our office as a 'base' – certainly, we would give him all the help we could, but didn't he think it would be best really if the whole thing was called off!!

Smart seems to have been rather carried away with the significance of his role. According to Collier's first draft of his memoir: 'Colonel Smart was considered a very important fellow, and soon informed me how important he was, and how he had had dinner with Winston Churchill the previous evening.' His plan, however, looked more and more like a high-stakes gamble:

Ploestie, as is well known, is a great oil refining centre, and at that time was capable of supplying approximately half of Germany's requirements. Smart explained a sudden blow at this target would achieve surprise, and shake German morale and deprive her of large supplies of oil. This all sounded very well, but when one considered that it meant taking away a large part of the Eighth Air Force striking force in our theatre, after it had been so carefully built up, surprise might not be achieved, losses would be heavy, and we considered it doubtful if more than a third of the force would find its way back to England again. And anyway an attack of this nature had to be repeated to be effective. However, we had no right to interfere, but we knew the American Air Staff in England were not at all keen on the idea, so we could but hope that they would manage to get the scheme cancelled.

The 'Ploestie Affair' progressed. A speciality of the 'affair' was the special briefing film that was to be produced at Elstree Studios. This film would be complete in its briefing even to the extent of maintaining the morale of the aircrews concerned. Lord Forbes, then a Wing

Commander in the RAF, played a large part in the production of this film, which in its way was a masterpiece.

I witnessed a private showing of the film in the little Air Ministry cinema. The film commenced with pictures of President Roosevelt making one of his finer speeches about the rights of free men and finished with pictures of vast oil fires. In between this stirring propaganda came the briefing details with excellent photographs of models of the route and targets, and an amusing sketch depicting a lovely naked lady with Joe Stalin gazing on her with a look of lust, with the caption 'This is a virgin target and only Joe has had a stab at it!' I glanced at some of my Senior Officers – a look of horror was on their faces – well, anyway, it would give the aircrew boys a laugh!

...A force of some sixty Liberators flew to Libya, where they carried out special training against dummy targets in the desert, and then prepared themselves for the attack from Tripoli to Ploestie and return. Many thousands of miles... The attack was a do or die effort – at low level – regardless of cost. The element of surprise was a vital factor. Was that really possible? Maybe it was one Flight getting over the target area early that put the enemy on the alert, but the main force was met with a murderous hail of anti-aircraft fire and fighters. The attack was pressed home by all with incredible gallantry, and considerable damage was caused to the refineries and spectacular fires resulted – but what a terrifying cost, only half the force returned to base! Can anyone say the losses were justified?

Undeterred, the US Eighth Air Force was rapidly gathering strength in the spring of 1943. The Germans attempted to counter this new threat by transferring planes from the Eastern Front and massively increasing the production of fighter aircraft. Collier quotes figures of 38 per cent of the total number of German fighters operating against the Western Allies in 1942, rising to 50 per cent in April 1943 and 65 per cent in November 1943.

Aircraft production was organized with 'the usual teutonic thoroughness', with vast assembly plants sited deep inside Germany and Austria, and many smaller units feeding into the system. What the Germans did not yet realize was that the USAAF now had the ability to reach these targets in daylight.

An initiative of Brigadier General Ira C. Eaker, CO of the Eighth Air Force, resulted in the POINTBLANK Directive of 3 June 1943, according to which these aircraft factories and related suppliers were now the prime target of the Combined Bomber Offensive (though in effect Harris abstained, and continued with his area bombing campaign).

John Collier described the initial backroom planning stage of POINTBLANK:

By June all was set for this Offensive, and new Directives had been issued for the RAF and American bomber forces. By now the Americans had built up a very useful heavy bomber force in the Mediterranean theatre [the Allied invasion of Sicily began on 10 July 1943], and they were to operate against the more Southern targets, normally out of range from England. The broad principle of the Offensive was that RAF Bomber Command should obliterate by night the German cities and towns associated with the German aircraft industry, while the Americans would undertake the destruction of the factories, by daylight. Both forces had tasks most suited to their own bombing techniques and equipment, and we set high hopes on the results.

British and American Intelligence had searched every avenue in order to compile an accurate list of enemy targets. With the able assistance of Oliver Lawrence of the Ministry of Economic Warfare, and Charles Verity, then Squadron Leader, who was in charge of the Department for Preparation of Target Dossiers [in the Air Ministry], a really fine folder was produced detailing all the targets to be attacked to destroy the enemy fighter organisation. Goering himself later paid tribute to the excellence of Allied Intelligence, and it must have caused him considerable irritation when his aircraft factories, so carefully hidden away deep in the forests of central Germany were sought out and destroyed monotonously!

One of the most controversial points in the selection of targets for attack... was that of the enemy ball-bearing industry. Arthur [Morley] was a firm believer that if the enemy ball-bearing industry could be destroyed that his fighter aircraft construction would be seriously delayed and the whole of the enemy war potential affected. In the early days of the War the enemy ball-bearing industry was particularly vulnerable as it was concentrated mainly at one centre, Schweinfurt. Arthur's advice in those days fell on stony ground, for there were few that could believe that there was any easy way of winning the war or that Germany was vulnerable in any one point. However, Arthur had made a particular study of the industry, and knew from experience. The English ball-bearing industry at that time was in a similar position, and if the Germans had attacked seriously the very vulnerable [Hoffmann] factory at Chelmsford, we would not have been able to put new aircraft in the air, for we were living in a 'hand to mouth' existence in the supply of these vital components.

In the first draft of his memoir Collier wrote in praise of Arthur Morley's vision:

Almost from the day of entering Bomber Operations he had continued to press for the attack of this very small but so vital industry. In the early days Germany was producing the vast majority of her ball bearings from some 4 factories, the major of which was set at Schweinfurt, in Central Germany. Arthur contended that with the destruction of this factory and that of the Eckmer ball bearing works in Berlin and in Friedrichshaven, combined with economic pressure to prevent Swedish ball bearings from reaching Germany, it would be all that was necessary... Ball bearings were vital to every war machine. Their production was a very specialised business which had largely been invented in Sweden and of which few were expert. They could not be mass produced, nor could substitutes be found.

Several years on, Morley revived the plan to concentrate on ball-bearing production and now he was backed by the American Air Staffs and the Joint Economic Staffs. Schweinfurt was made the number one priority, but by now its anti-aircraft and smokescreen defences were formidable. As an equal matter of urgency the US Eighth Air Force also needed to concentrate on the three major Me109 fighter assembly plants at Regensburg, Wiener Neustadt and Leipzig:

It was on August 17th [1943] that we heard the news that both Schweinfurt and Regensburg were to be attacked by the largest force yet despatched by the Eighth Air Force. Here was a real start in the attack of the Luftwaffe, and if successful the attack would mean an immediate and large drop in the enemy fighter production. This was the real test of strength. There was little prospect of work in the office, for we were too excited and rushed about trying to gather news how [preparation for] the raid was progressing.

The plan of action was that one force of approximately 180 aircraft would attack Schweinfurt and about 130 attack Regensburg. Aircraft attacking Schweinfurt would return to England, while those attacking Regensburg would continue on and land at North African bases. A bold plan indeed.

With ample radar warning the enemy were soon hot on the trail of the Americans, and it was a continual battle from the moment the enemy coast was passed. Little assistance could be given by our fighters as they were suitable for short range operations only. The bombers had to fend for themselves. The enemy brought in fighters from North Germany and France, and gave the Americans hell, but they never wavered or turned, and in spite of the intense opposition some 87% of the forces reached and attacked their targets with deadly accuracy. A total of some sixty bombers were lost, a terrible price, but the Americans had proved that they could fight their way to deep targets and attack with excellent results – but the need for fighter support was only too apparent.

The Germans responded to the Schweinfurt Raid by dispersing production. A large quantity of ball-bearings had already been stockpiled, though a secret Allied flight to Stockholm had bought off the Swedish manufacturers from continuing to supply Germany. Britain had also been procuring them from Sweden throughout the war and 'smuggling' them by fast motorboats and Mosquito aircraft.

A second attack on Schweinfurt some two months later found the enemy even better prepared – this time with rocket firing twin-engined fighters [Me110], which could stay out of range of the bombers' guns.

Again the losses were very heavy. If only the Americans could be given fighter support it would be easy, but without, we all had to admit, the prospect was a bit grim! All the antagonists of daylight bombing raised their voices in a loud cry 'Ah, we told you so, daylight bombing can never survive'.

An additional worry was that the American public were becoming critical and restless about the losses in the European theatre. There were many who considered that Japan was the first enemy of America and that all American bombers could be best employed in the Pacific area.

In November '43 a 'Combined Bomber Offensive Progress Report' was produced by our Directorate in conjunction with the American Air Staff. The Report was to be rendered to the Combined Chiefs of Staff at Washington, to show just how much had been achieved and how very much more could be done, if only adequate forces were made available. The Report was a masterpiece of Staff work, most of it being undertaken by my boss, Syd Bufton. It was fully illustrated and generally most impressive. London had been searched to find suitable spring folders, quite a difficult problem, as about twenty copies had to be produced.

The Report was put to the Combined Chiefs of Staff with the recommendation that 'All evidence indicates that the Combined Bomber Offensive is achieving a profound effect on Germany's war economy, and the morale of its people. The offensive should be pressed on in accordance with existing Directives with all vigour, and its intensity increased'. The reaction to the Report must have been excellent for streams of bombers, and what was even more needed, long range fighters, came across the Atlantic. The long range fighters [P-51 Mustang] soon proved more than a match for the enemy, losses of bombers was greatly reduced, morale was on the uplift, and it certainly appeared that the Combined Bomber Offensive now had every chance of success!

If the attacks on Schweinfurt had been maintained, the German war effort would have been seriously impaired, but the Americans (and the RAF) would only return intermittently. One of the then unknown effects of the bombing raids was the chance destruction of a secret factory at Regensburg that had been producing the first Messerschmitt jet fighters.

It was not just the USAAF that was rapidly evolving. RAF Bomber Command's potency had been vastly increased by the widespread introduction through 1942 and 1943 of the Lancaster, which could carry up to five times the load of the old twin-engined Hampdens that John Collier had mostly flown. Aerial photographs gave proof of the efficacy of the heavier RAF raids, such as at Hamburg, which had been destroyed in July 1943 by a force of 791 aircraft deploying Window, strips of aluminium foil thrown from planes in bundles to confuse radar.

However, Bomber Command had not had it all its own way. The Ruhr had been subjected to consistent attack between March and July 1943 (the so-called 'Battle of the Ruhr') but although the first raid on 5 March had wrecked 160 acres of the city of Essen for the loss of fourteen aircraft, about 1,000 planes had been lost over the whole four months. Essen was now protected by a lethally-efficient system of searchlights, flak batteries and night-fighters (not to mention industrial smog). This gruelling campaign brought back stark memories for John Collier:

During the shorter summer nights Bomber Command paid special attention to the destruction of the industries of the Ruhr, which was then the centre of the enemy's heavy industries. Cologne, Dortmund, Duisburg, Essen and others became household names as the attacks were pressed home night after night. These attacks were not carried off without loss, and the hearts of all aircrew would sink slightly when the 'target for tonight' was given as 'The Happy Valley' as the aircrew nicknamed the Ruhr. Losses were not crippling, but certainly the aircrew had a really tough commitment – I know how scared of the Ruhr I was in the days that I operated, and then the defences were comparatively 'childs play'.

I found it irritating to notice that at this time the general public appeared completely apathetic about the attacks – I longed to shake people and shout, but don't you realize the hell our boys are going through night after night, how many are 'failing to return' and how

Germany is being devastated. The repetition of the attacks had killed appreciation – a terrific fuss would be made about some small naval engagement in the Channel – but fortunately later John Strachey's talks over the wireless did a lot to arouse interest and enthusiasm for the Bomber Offensive.

The development of the incendiary technique was one of our most successful weapons... Once more Arthur [Morley] had been the instigator. Standing on the roof of the Air Ministry [during the Blitz] he had watched the burning of the City around St Paul's. Here he thought is the real way to attack Germany – burn them out – saturate them with fire bombs – beat them at their own game! Up to that time we had used incendiary bombs more as an afterthought and make-weight than as a serious fire-raising weapon – saturation technique had not entered into it. Arthur consulted fire services, made transparencies illustrating the density of fire bombs that could be achieved. These transparencies covered with black dots, each dot representing a fire bomb, could be placed over scaled plans of towns, and clearly illustrated how impossible it was for any fire service to fight so many points of fire at once. Arthur 'sold' his idea – the 'incendiary technique' developed rapidly. Some idea of the extent of development can be gained when it is realised that nearly two persons in every hundred in Britain were engaged on making incendiary bombs at the peak of the Bomber Offensive.

After a year or so in his new job at the Air Ministry, John Collier could look back with some satisfaction on the Anglo-American effort:

By the Spring of 1944 the Combined Bomber Offensive had proved itself. The two great teams of day and night bombers had achieved the Primary Objective – the virtual destruction of the German fighter force. The Americans had destroyed the vital factories – a week of fine weather in February had provided the opportunity for the 'knock-out'; Bomber Command had levelled the cities associated with the enemy aircraft industry and many others.

There was no doubt that Germany would make supreme efforts to reorganise and disperse her fighter industry and 'policing attacks' would still be necessary – but the chief pre-requisite for the Invasion of Europe had been accomplished, and attention could now be turned to the destruction of the two other major factors of the German war machine – oil supplies and transportation.

High-level Mining

In June 1943 John Collier had presented his imaginative proposal for high-level dropping of sea mines as an alternative to the increasingly dangerous low-level mine-laying in areas of intense anti-aircraft defences [see 'Combined Bomber Offensive' above]. He had been rebuffed rather brutally by the Admiralty representative at the Air Ministry and this undoubtedly rankled. His memoir now turns to a complete change of mind by the authorities later that year. He had routinely taken part in these secret missions to mine continental waters from 1940, as part of what he called one of the war's 'silent services'. 'Gardening' operations were usually carried out when poor weather did not permit bombing missions:

The trips were often hazardous, for the enemy improved daily his defences against these low-flying mine-laying aircraft. It was not unusual to be met with a hail of light anti-aircraft fire from a 'flak' ship, just as one was about to lay mines. These ships could not be seen, and I had always found it quite a 'strain' flying low over enemy waters. I was always lucky, but every so often came back well holed. The need for dropping at such low levels had been stated as necessary to ensure accuracy and because the mines were unsuitable for dropping at high levels. One day, one of my old pilots [from 420 (RCAF) Squadron], now a Squadron Command, came to see me. He was operating on Halifaxes, and they were doing a lot of mining. Their losses were quite serious, and when I said that I could not see the need for mines to be dropped at a low level anyway he begged me to do something about it! Winston Churchill at this time had also sent a curt note enquiring why the losses during mining operations had been so heavy. I dug up my old folder [see Appendix] with proposals for mining the French ports from high levels. This time I took my ideas to my friends in Bomber Command,

Wing Commanders Ken Smales and Peter Cribb [CO of the Bomber Development Unit], who were both in positions to get the idea tried out, and they did! Trials were completely satisfactory, and showed that the mines could be dropped with considerable accuracy from any height, while with simple modification the mine would operate satisfactorily. How well I recalled the early obstructions put up by the Admiralty. In time large scale high level mining operations were undertaken by Bomber Command, losses were reduced to a negligible scale, and enemy sinkings were reported as being increasingly satisfactory.

The first operation using the new technique (which exploited the latest navigation aid, H2S on-board radar, which was at its most legible when overflying coastal areas) took place on 4 January 1944 when six Halifaxes laid mines off Brest, without losses.

As Collier declared in the first draft of his memoir, with a pardonable note of triumph:

The day was won, and Bomber Command took up this technique in a big way, with really excellent results… Mines could now be laid in heavily defended areas and the enemy were completely defeated as to where the mines were likely to be as they could no longer plot the aircraft and fall of the mines accurately.

Even if he had achieved nothing else in the war, this innovation, which was entirely his own, was a major contribution to lessening air crew casualties and perhaps should have been rewarded in some way beyond the private satisfaction of a personal vindication. It seems that others in B Ops 1 thought so, too [see 'An Honourable Mention' in Chapter Ten].

Some mine-laying operations, however, had to remain at a very low level:

Apart from sea mining, we were particularly interested in finding some means of interrupting the enemy's inland water transport facilities. Germany had built up a magnificent network of canals, linking up navigable rivers. Her barges were each capable of carrying a trainload of freight, and photographs had shown stretches of her more important canals, with barges almost in continuous stream! How marvellous if these lifelines could be blocked, but how was this to be done? The attacks with mines early in the war at the vulnerable Dortmund-Ems crossing, in which Squadron Leader Learoyd won his VC [and John Collier had been Mentioned in Despatches], had been spectacular and gallant in the extreme, but had achieved little. Opinion was generally against further attacks, and a suitable mine was not available. The Admiralty were entirely responsible for the production of mines, and although an order had been placed and the design approved for a suitable mine ['A' Mark VIII magnetic river mine], so little interest was displayed that the production of this mine was delayed and delayed, until all its usefulness was past. It must have been too much to ask the Admiralty to get interested in anything that had not the taste of salt water!

Although our aerial mines were generally unsuitable for laying in canals or shallow rivers, they were quite suitable for mining the larger rivers, such as the Danube and Rhine. The Danube at this time was of particular interest to us, for along it was carried in great barges, vital oil supplies from the Ploestie oilfields and Austrian oilfields. Closing the Danube to traffic was by no means an easy matter, and apart from the possibility of mining we had made a detailed study of all the 'vulnerable' points along the river. These points were few – hydro-electric barriers across the river and the famous Iron Gates appeared the most hopeful spots as far as we were concerned. We were greatly helped in this study because Army intelligence had made available to us dossiers, complete with excellent photographs and details, of both the Danube and the Rhine. The photographs of the two most beautiful rivers in Europe, and their cities and towns, would take my mind far away from the war, and I used to daydream, thinking how marvellous it would be to be holidaying in these lovely spots, instead of planning in a hot and stuffy office, how best to destroy them. Will the world ever be sane enough to let all men enjoy her bounty without fear or restriction?

The Iron Gates is a misnomer – the 'gates' are rapids, extremely difficult to negotiate. A special railway line with donkey engines provided the means of mounting the rapids. Should we try and destroy the engines? All sorts of plans were suggested and abandoned – in the end mining won the day, and very effective it proved.

Wellington aircraft, operating from the Italian base of Foggia, could just reach some of the more important stretches of the Danube, and they mined with great effect. Howls of rage were heard from [regimes in] Eastern Europe, who published stories of dastardly mining of peaceful passenger vessels. Traffic was brought to a standstill. Little publicity was given in England to this mining campaign, and it was not until later that the heavy loss in enemy traffic was confirmed – but this 'small' campaign had played a vital role in support of the Combined Bomber Offensive [and for D-Day; the Danube was 'frozen' between April and September 1944, greatly reducing fuel supplies to France].

'Gardening' in the Danube could be hazardous. Pilots were required to lay the mines from a height of 50 feet on moonlit nights, and often through searchlight and flak defences. As in John Collier's days in 83 Squadron, magnetic mines were on the 'secret list' and had to be brought back to base if not sown.

Duty Stooge

In Collier's second year in Whitehall he and his colleagues seemed exhausted by the strain of overwork, made worse by conditions of artificial light and wartime privation, but perhaps also by the great responsibility they shouldered:

Life in the Air Ministry was daily becoming more and more hectic, as the tempo of the war increased. The telephone in our office rang incessantly. We were all a bit run down after the winter – I had had incessant colds and seemed to have developed a permanent headache. Arthur [Morley] said the lights in the office were the trouble and I think he was right. Arthur himself was not in too good shape... he seemed to be developing a habit of deafness, his thoughts being miles and miles away from our conversation, he would give you a smile and a vague reply – 'Yes, old boy?' John [Strachey] seemed to be weathering well… Syd continued to work like an automaton.

God, how tired we got! We seldom packed up work before seven to eight o'clock at night, often we would work over a knotty problem to midnight. I used to arrive home in a kind of daze, hardly speak a word to my wife who was equally tired after a day of struggling with two children [after the birth of Richard in April 1944] and a house, with no help. We would finish our supper any time between nine and ten, sit in front of the fire and both fall asleep! Arthur lived at Gerrards Cross, about forty minutes run out of London. He was always missing his train, because he would not leave the office on time, so he would put up at his club for the night or park in the office on a camp bed. Time and time again he would go asleep in the train, and be carried past his station, only to spend half the night trying to get back again. Life was not being made any easier by the enemy's bombing attacks [the 'Little Blitz', from 20 January to 19 April 1944; Whitehall was hit several times, with damage done to the War Office] and later by his buzz-bomb and rockets. We had to take it in turns to sleep in the office – 'duty stooge'; I only once was called on to do anything useful, but it caused me no end of worry to be separated from my family at night, while those damn bombs and rockets fell around!

Our lives had settled down to a fairly stolid and monotonous routine: arrive in the Office just after nine, clean our buttons and discuss the news generally – what had happened the previous night – and what work lay ahead of us for the day. We all gathered round as in a family circle, for a family we were, amongst which all secrets were shared. We had an hour and a half for lunch. This sounds quite a lot, but by the time one had walked to the eating house and had queued up, one just got back to the Office in time. We used to lunch at those excellent charitable organisations 'The King George V Club' or the 'Queen Elizabeth Club'. Here the lunch was adequate, if not over-large. All the problems of the day would be thrashed out over lunch, if we had a table to ourselves – a very bad habit to talk 'shop' out of hours, but our interests were so keyed up that we found it hard to leave the subjects alone. The walk across St James's Park and Green Park was a life-saver, for it was the only fresh air we got for the day…

We used to have periodical visits from officers from [Bomber] Command. Like all keen officers they were of the opinion that only they were winning the war, but we used to get a bit peeved when they went to the lengths of remarking – 'Can't think what you chaps find to do all day!' Our offers suggesting they stayed to see were not accepted.

The Railway Row

What was keeping B Ops 1 so busy from March 1944 onwards was planning for Operation OVERLORD, the imminent invasion of Europe. The Luftwaffe was a beaten force, more or less, so the vital prerequisite of success was now the immobilization of the German army just before and after the landings. This would give the Allied forces time to build up sufficient numbers at the bridgehead to resist the inevitable counter-attack.

Weighing the strategic options for achieving this led to a furious debate in Whitehall:

The German air force had been accounted for – road and rail movement by the enemy were the next problems to be settled. Road and rail transport were complementary. The denial of the railways would throw German reinforcements onto the roads, while denial of the roads, which could be achieved by denying the enemy his oil supplies, would throw the load back onto the railways. It was necessary, therefore, that both transportation and oil should be attacked.

The attack of German oil supplies and the attack of rail transportation did not interfere seriously with each other, as the oil targets lay in Germany, Austria and Roumania, while the rail targets that we were chiefly interested in lay in France and Belgium. There were, therefore, two 'weather areas', and it would seldom occur that weather was clear over both oil and rail targets.

There were other very sound reasons for attacking oil, for its denial would not only immobilise road transport, but enemy tanks and aircraft would also not be able to operate.

The plan for the simultaneous attack of oil and transportation [backed by Spaatz] sounds a very simple and obvious thing, but there were many [principally SHAEF, who backed the Scientific Director of the British Bombing Survey Unit, Solly Zuckerman, advisor to Tedder] who wanted to place all the bomber effort on the attack on the railways, and they laid out the most elaborate and expensive plans to cause 'rail deserts'. Such elaborate plans were not justified, and in any case the [argument] for the attack of oil was extremely strong. The real answer to attack both was arrived at only after long and protracted argument between Staffs – tempers were at times ragged and it looked as if a settlement would never be reached. However, common sense won the day, and a really excellent Plan was drawn up for the immobilisation of the rail centres and also the destruction of oil. All parties were satisfied, except one [Harris] which had advocated that no direct help to the Invasion could be given by heavy bombers and that the best thing would be to continue with all effort on the destruction of German cities, Berlin in particular. Fortunately that party did not get much of a hearing!

In the first draft of his memoir John Collier made more of this long-running row, that dragged on until just a few weeks before D-Day, and perhaps edited it down for the final typescript for fear of causing offence to persons involved:

There was a very serious divergence of opinion between SHAEF and the Air Ministry, as SHAEF were very keen on the first priority being given to transportation, and not to oil, and the views of strong personalities clashed severely over this important factor. At one time the SHAEF plan was to cause a rail desert over the whole of France and Belgium, and parts of N.W.Germany. This involved the attack of well over one hundred major rail centres and would absorb every ounce of the bomber effort from the UK and allow nothing for the attack of oil. The Deputy Supreme Allied Commander, Air Chief Marshal Tedder, was naturally extremely anxious that all railway facilities should be denied to the Germans before D-Day, and he found it difficult to appreciate that the oil programme could be completed before the invasion took place, and that it could play such an important part.

There was one major factor which held the hand of SHAEF to some extent, and that was that both the Air Ministry Bomber Command and the American 8th Air Force were all dead against putting the whole of their effort on to the bombing of marshalling yards, which was the plan as advised by SHAEF. Further, the control of the Strategic Air Force [in essence the RAF and USAAF] still lay with the Chief of the Air Staff [Portal] and General Spaatz, and it was therefore not possible for SHAEF to thrust the plan down our throats, as until the control of the bomber forces passed to the Allied Supreme Commander, the final decision did not lay with him…

Every target was most carefully examined and separate estimates were made by SHAEF and by ourselves in consultation with our scientific advisors, as to the likely casualties that would occur to the civilian population. SHAEF were extremely anxious that their plan should be accepted, and were well aware how concerned the PM was [about] French casualties, and the result was that there was a very great divergence of opinion between the two parties, which were not in the slightest bit compatible. We were accused of bolstering our own estimate to destroy their plan, and we considered that they put their estimates at a ridiculous figure to ensure that their plan was accepted…

The arguments waxed hot and strong, and the position became very difficult. We were concerned that such an 'expensive' (both in bomb tonnage & human life) transportation plan was not necessary, and the same result could be achieved by the selection of certain key railway centres and the destruction of the rail bridges over the Seine and the Loire, and later over the Rhine.

This suggestion was put up by the AM, but largely ignored by SHAEF, who stated that in any case bridges could not be destroyed, except with a maximum of effort [assuming imprecise bomb-aiming], and that they were obviously not economical, as if you attacked a marshalling yard every bomb had some effect. In vain we argued that the marshalling yards were designed originally to accept the vast civilian and industrial traffic at these centres, and that the requirements of the Germans for military needs could not be one-tenth of that of the French civilians, and therefore, as it was known that the Germans intended to prevent all civilian traffic during the invasion, we would have to deny some 90% of the rail facilities before the German military needs were vitally affected. The achievement of a rail desert in France, Belgium and N.W.Germany we considered an impossible feat.

A big factor in the discussions and arguments which took place was Professor Zuckerman, who was Scientific Advisor to ACM Tedder. Z was a most unusual man. He had immense drive, was completely ruthless, and was extremely quick and ready to turn one's own arguments to his favour. I used to clash with him weekly at the Joint Technical Warfare Sub-Committees, which had met to study the transportation problem, and to advise. This Committee was unanimous in its views that the destruction of the bridges would be as big a factor in any transportation plan in France as the attempted destruction of every railway centre. The Committee, with the exception of Z, agreed with the view that the maintenance of through lines in marshalling yards was a simple problem, as one had all the facilities and men available, and that without the destruction of the bridges, any transportation plan would be extremely expensive. Zuckerman was furious at the Committee's decision, and refused to agree to the views. Asked to produce a minority report, he stalled the problem indefinitely, and in view of the fact that Z was working for ACM Tedder, and was one of his advisors, the Committee appeared to be unwilling to render its report without Z's minority report. This, I considered, was a disgusting sign of weakness, and I refused to take part in any further discussions of the Committee...

All these problems and arguments did not help relations between Tedder's Staff and that of Bomber Ops, and we were given a pretty rough ride at times, in fact, we all expected to be thrown out, as our views were not compatible with those of the Deputy SAC. Arthur Morley and Syd Bufton were, however, not easily frightened and stuck to their views.

The problem got to the point where it had to be dealt with by the Cabinet, and both ACM Tedder and Syd Bufton attended to express

Pilot Officer John Collier in late 1937, a flight commander with 83 Squadron at RAF Turnhouse.

'The Old Crowd': 83 Squadron in peacetime, 1938 or 1939; John Collier with Guy Gibson ('Gibbo'), Mulligan and others.

John Collier with his Handley Page Hampden, named 'Bet' after his wife-to-be, at RAF Scampton.

83 Squadron at Scampton as the 'Phoney War' sets in, 3 October 1939, after return from Ringway. John Collier, left; Guy Gibson, centre.

Flight Lieutenant John Collier briefing air crew, 83 Squadron, early summer 1940.

Squadron Leader John Collier DFC's Hampden after crash-landing at Scampton, 30 August 1940, on return from a mission to Magdeburg.

Flight Lieutenant James Pitcairn-Hill DSO DFC of 83 Squadron, John Collier's best man at his wedding in 1939, shot down and killed over Antwerp, 18 September 1940. (Portrait drawing by William Rothenstein.)

'RAF Hero and his baby son'. Press photograph of Squadron Leader John Collier with Mark at Buckingham Palace, 25 November 1941, to receive the Bar to his DFC for the attack on the *Scharnhorst* and *Gneisenau* at Brest, 24 July 1941.

Elizabeth 'Beth' Collier, nee Bishop.

Hampdens of 44 (Rhodesia) Squadron, 1941.

Avro Lancaster 'A for Queenie' of 97 (Straits Settlements) Squadron, 1942, signed by HM Queen Elizabeth.

Wristwatch presented to Wing Commander John Collier (against regulations) on leaving 97 Squadron in September 1942.

Wing Commander John Collier DFC and Bar with 97 Squadron at Woodhall Spa, 1942; 'the best squadron in the Command' according to Guy Gibson.

The staff of B Ops 1, Directorate of Bomber Operations, on the roof of the Air Ministry, c.1944: Wing Commander John Collier DSO DFC and Bar, seated left; Air Commodore Sydney Bufton CB DFC, seated centre; to his right Group Captain Arthur Morley OBE; standing at the back, on the left, Squadron Leader John Strachey.

Tallboy: Barnes Wallis's 12,000lb 'earthquake' bomb.

Group Captain John Collier DSO DFC and Bar and General Robinson, RAF Iwakuni, Japan, September 1946.

Joey the pet mongoose at RAF Kankesanturai, Ceylon in 1945.

John Collier as Assistant Chief of Staff, Allied Air Forces Northern Europe, at NATO headquarters, Kolsas, Norway in 1957.

John Collier's medals, from left to right: Distinguished Service Order, Distinguished Flying Cross and Bar, 1939–1945 Star with Bomber Command clasp, Aircrew Europe Star, Burma Star, Defence Medal, War Medal 1939–1945 with single oak leaf for three Mentioned in Despatches. Ribbons with rosette for Bar to DFC and oak leaf.

their views on the transportation plan before it could be finally passed by the Cabinet.

...Tedder stated that our proposal for the destruction of bridges was not practical. However, instructions were issued by the Cabinet that a trial attack on bridges was to be carried out. I think this came as a surprise, but was largely because we were able to pass our views to the Cabinet via an influential friend of Arthur's, and they were aware of the fact that the destruction of bridges had been carried out most successfully in the Italian Campaign over the last 7 months... Lord Cherwell, who was then the PMG [Postmaster General], and acknowledged as Scientific advisor to the PM, was a great supporter of our cause, and he was fully aware of all the problems involved, and I think he ensured that the PM was also.

We were on tenterhooks before the Cabinet meeting, and all felt that we would be removed as one body from Bomber Ops, to remove any further obstacles, and were relieved at the second Cabinet meeting, when my boss was not asked [to attend], that the PM enquired what had happened to 'the little Air Commodore'. 'Not banished,' he hoped.

In B Ops 1, according to John Collier, the Transportation Plan was known as 'Zuckerman's Folly'. Despite the openmindedness of the Cabinet, it was Tedder and Zuckerman whose rail desert idea prevailed at SHAEF for the vital months prior to D-Day:

Attacks on the French and Belgian railway systems with the vast forces available now at the command of the Combined Bomber Offensive... progressed rapidly, and soon chaos was rampant in all the major rail yards of Northern France and Belgium. The attack of the bridges was not commenced, as it was felt that it might give an indication of the invasion area, but the trial attack on the Seine [7 May 1944] had achieved the astounding results of destroying two major bridges by some eight Thunderbolts [each armed with two 1,000lb bombs]. This had proved our contention of the vulnerability of the bridge system to attack, and this theory was now accepted, and plans were made for the destruction of all the bridges on the Seine and the Loire, to be timed carefully just before the invasion took place so that the whole of the beach-head area could be isolated.

The vast scale of the attacks... can be judged by the fact that the 8th, 9th [both USAAF] and RAF dropped some 400,000 tons on the railway systems in the year March 44-45...

A very careful watch was kept on the French reaction to these attacks, as it was too much to expect that they would exactly welcome them. I consider that the French attitude was gallant to the extreme, and they suffered these raids, which must have appeared to them terrifying, with the greatest fortitude. French casualties were not heavy, except when a raid 'went wrong', which could happen occasionally, as in the case of Rouen, when some markers fell too close to the town, and the town suffered heavily, including severe damage to the famous Cathedral. These 'mistakes' were greatly regretted by the RAF, who tried to keep the casualties to a minimum, and BC certainly did their best about this, and the Prime Minister's own instructions were repeatedly stressed, that any negligence in bombing would be dealt with as a very serious offence. The result of this was an incredible concentration of bombing on the rail-yards, and literally the whole of the yards would be pot-marked with bomb craters that were lip to lip.

The bombing of the French railway yards required, as was expected, a vast effort, and terrible destruction to affect the German military machine, as they required only a very small proportion of the facilities available in order to maintain their military supplies. The Germans had prepared plans for the maintenance of the larger rail routes, but, of course, they were faced with a problem very much more difficult than bombing – that was sabotage, and the go-slow of the French railway employees. These employees were some of the stoutest supporters of de Gaulle and the Allied efforts, and the Germans finally decided that they were altogether too unreliable, and early in 1944 they drafted some 50,000 German railwaymen to France to keep the railways going, and to deal with bombing, strikes and sabotage.

As planned, to coincide with D-Day the Seine and Loire bridges were destroyed, and German reinforcements were unable to get directly to Normandy by rail.

Collier quoted an official report:

> The journey of two Panzer divisions from the East front to the West illustrates the difficulties which the enemy had to face. The two divisions raced across Germany in seventy-two trains, each division using three lines with twelve trains on each, but when they got to Nancy in eastern France it was found that they could only proceed from there to Paris with eight trains each day instead of seventy-two. There was, of course, no guarantee that the eight trains would not be destroyed or meet long delays on the way. Some of the two divisions pushed on to Paris in their eight trains that day, but the greater part of the force de-trained and went the rest of the way to Normandy by road... The German counter-invasion plan was to bring their reserve divisions to the battlefield at the rate of 48 trains a day. This was cut by bombing to six trains a day.

He concluded: 'The essential factor that the German build-up must not be able to out-race the build-up of our invasion force had been achieved!'

The Oily Boys

Having failed to reach the Caucasus and Baku, Germany's oil supplies depended on the vulnerable Romanian oilfields and an extensive system of well-defended refineries and synthetic oil plants in Germany, Poland and Austria. Vital motor and aviation fuel was produced there from brown coal in a hydrogenation process that also gave them synthetic rubber and materials for explosives.

In the first draft of his memoir John Collier had some key statistics at his fingertips:

> At the commencement of the bomber offensive on her oil in March 44 she [Germany] had approx a monthly oil production of some 1,344,000 tons of all oil. The vital fuel consisted of some 530,000 tons of motor and aviation fuel, and it was against this that the bomber offensive was concentrated. Germany's motor and aviation fuel was mainly treated at her 24 synthetic plants and 80 refineries. The great

majority of these were in six districts, with a concentration of refineries in the neighbourhood of Vienna and another concentration at Ploestie. With careful planning, each area was assigned to a definite bomber force. The RAF …were allotted the oil refineries of the Ruhr; the 8th AF undertook the refineries in Central Germany and the 15th AF undertook the destruction of those in the Vienna and P areas…

Harris had been very reluctant to divert forces to oil targets, as advocated by the Air Staff men (who he derided as the 'Oily Boys'), but in the summer of 1944 with Bomber Command subordinate to Eisenhower and Tedder at SHAEF for the period of the Normandy Campaign, he finally complied with the directive to attack oil.

Though it was late in the day, John Collier was impressed by a smooth-running campaign:

The attack on oil was launched with a bang, and the punches were not pulled until all German refineries were destroyed. In June alone some forty-three attacks were made against oil targets. The forces were operating with maximum efficiency. Radar aids had been perfected and it was possible to destroy the target without ever seeing it. The bombing was incredibly accurate by all the forces concerned. RAF Bomber Command were achieving concentrations of bombing never before achieved against industrial targets, and they were now making large scale sorties by day. Ploestie ceased to exist as a serious contributor to German oil supplies.

By April 1945 the production of enemy oil was down to approximately 7% of the original, while the output of the vital motor and aviation fuels were down to 2%. German reserves were used up, and nowhere could the enemy turn to save the situation. The results were catastrophic – in the air no training could be carried out, operational airfields would run out of fuel at the critical moments, standing patrols were cancelled, and only front line operational squadrons could be supplied even then.

General Galland, air chief of enemy fighters, stated that it was the Allied bombing of the oil industry that had had the greatest effect on the German war potential: 'We had plenty of planes in the Autumn of '44 and a considerable number of pilots, but lack of petrol did not permit expansion and training.'

The German Army was also in an extremely difficult position. Their motor transport was being drawn by horses, and tanks were allowed a minimum of fuel. Tanks were transported by rail to the fighting area, if that were possible, so as to conserve every ounce of fuel. By the time of the Runstedt Offensive ['The Battle of the Bulge', December 1944 to January 1945], the German Army had mainly to rely on horse-drawn vehicles, and motorized units were used only for attack...

It is likely that every German general will credit the reason for Germany's defeat to the cause most directly affecting him, but even so the denial of Germany's oil supplies was achieved with perfect timing, and undoubtedly led to the rapid defeat of the German Army. Again the Combined Bomber Offensive had achieved its aim, and again the policy recommended by Bomber Operations and our American colleagues was vindicated.

In his memoir Collier glosses over the bitter rows over prioritizing attacks on oil that rumbled on through an autumn and winter lull into early 1945 when Harris was still dismissing the policy as 'a chimera'. More deep-seated than the temporary row with Zuckerman, this was really a continuation of the heated debate that raged between advocates of precision bombing (the Air Ministry, inspired by the USAAF's example) and area bombing (Bomber Command under Harris). Heavy losses in the big raids on Berlin in the winter of 1943/44 had threatened Harris's position but, backed by Churchill and indulged by Portal, he had lived to fight another day and area bombing remained his strategy of choice until the end of the war.

Much later, in 1984 [see 'Forty Years On' in Chapter Twelve], Syd Bufton and John Collier corresponded about this battle of priorities and Bufton wrote: 'Re the oil offensive, they were down to 5% of aviation fuel by September 44, then the weather folded October–December; if we had started on oil in March instead of July [1944] (thanks to Zucherman [*sic*]) the war would have been over in 1944 or Jan 45.'

A Luftwaffe document dated 19 January 1945 and marked 'Top Secret' [translated and preserved in the papers of Sydney Bufton at the Churchill

Archive, Cambridge] shows graphically how restricted the German Air Force was by then, with flights only authorized in exceptional circumstances.

So were the 'Oily Boys' right? Zuckerman's Transportation Plan had sidelined the more wholesale targeting of oil which, if pursued in parallel with attacks on rail, would have had a truly devastating effect on the German war machine on all fronts. This very possibly would have shortened the war, as Bufton surmised. The screw was suddenly tightened on the Germans by the Red Army's advance into Romania, which signed an armistice on 12 September 1944, thus ending the Ploestie oil supply for good. From then on there was really only synthetic oil available, a very clear Achilles heel. Instead, thanks to both (initially) Zuckerman's 'Folly' and (latterly) Harris's intransigence, the impetus faltered.

John Collier himself had been deeply involved in lobbying for more attacks on oil in the summer of 1944. In the Bufton Papers is a memo from D.D.B.Ops 1 [Morley] to D.B.Ops [Bufton] dated 15 July 1944 and marked 'SECRET':

> I think you will agree that Collier put in some good work during his recent visit to 2 and 5 Groups. You will note the reaction of SASO [Senior Air Staff Officer] 5 Group to further attacks on the Ruhr oil plants. Unless considerable pressure is exerted by Bomber Command I fear that this primary task will be avoided or spread over many months…

Sir Arthur Harris had become autonomous once more, after Eisenhower relinquished overall control of Bomber Command in September 1944, and virtually ignored an Air Ministry Directive of 25 September making oil the number one priority. A new Directive in November forced him to do more, but in December 1944 Bufton was concerned that attacks on synthetic oil were dropping again. Among his papers in Cambridge is a graph, presumably the handiwork of B Ops 1, showing the averted crisis for the Germans of oil output in 1944: it declines rapidly from April to September, but recovers steadily between October and December; a period tellingly marked 'No Further Attacks'. This timetable slippage remains another of the great 'what ifs' of the war.

Reichsminister of Armaments and War Production Albert Speer could cope with most of the setbacks caused by the Allied bomber offensive, improvising brilliantly to recover aircraft or ball-bearing production after seemingly crippling attacks. However, even he had been worried by the disruption of oil supplies in the late spring of 1944, though he was confident that inconsistencies of policy would help, at least for a while. 'We have a powerful ally in this matter,' he declared. 'That is to say, the enemy has an air force general staff as well.'

When the attacks on oil resumed in earnest in 1945, the writing was on the wall for the Third Reich, but as a baffled Luftwaffe General Adolf Galland asked after the war, why had they waited so long?

OBOE Box

When Operation OVERLORD was being planned by Eisenhower and Tedder's SHAEF in the spring of 1944, B Ops 1 lobbied hard to promote the use of heavy bombers in close support of the invasion itself and the ground campaign in Normandy. Luckily, relations with the army – via the War Office – were much easier than with Bomber Command. In the first draft of his memoir, John Collier was full of praise for his opposite number there:

In Bomber Ops, for some time we had been keeping in close liaison with the War Office, whose... representative on our level was Colonel Patrick Browne. PB was an extremely intelligent man and a successful barrister in peace-time, and he now held the post of 'Air 1' at the War Office. Apart from his ability Patrick had a charming personality, and was a great friend of all in our Department. It was not surprising, therefore, that all matters between the War Office and the Air Ministry, concerning bombing, ran very smoothly. In particular, we had an excellent working agreement that all papers being presented to the Chiefs of Staff which concerned both our Departments would be prepared in draft together first of all, so that our views could be co-ordinated, and we could thrash out any problems beforehand. The result was that when these papers were presented to the Chiefs of Staff, the Air Force and the Army views always agreed and well-oiled the wheels. I had tried to start up a similar liaison with the Admiralty, but I was not able to find the same co-operative spirit, although the officers themselves were pleasant enough, but they always appeared to be too frightened of what their superiors might think, and so would not commit themselves at all.

As far as the Air Force was concerned, the plan for the Invasion was all carried out by SHAEF, and we had little to do except examine the requests put to us. We had, for some time, felt that in the Combined Bomber Offensive lay the strongest weapon of attack in support of the Invasion that had ever been conceived, but it was apparent that apart from bombing of beach defences and gun positions there was no plan to make use of heavy bomber forces in support of the Army. We realised that BC and the 8th Air Force could drop in a few minutes the same tonnage of explosives as it would take weeks of firing by artillery. The 'old school' were very much against using heavy bombers in close support of the Army. It had never been done before, and every difficulty was expressed instead of seeing what could be achieved and working out how this could be done. BC produced a folder expressing their views on how they could support the Invasion, and this consisted chiefly of the statement that they could do nothing but bomb Berlin. We objected violently to this view, and for once were in agreement with SHAEF...

In order to get across our idea of close co-operation for the Army we prepared a folder illustrating the devastation achieved in the attacks on the French marshalling yards, and pointing out the results that concentration and accuracy achieved during these raids, and what the result would be if this concentration were placed on the enemy lines... The book was well-prepared and illustrated, and quite well received by BC as it 'laid on with a shovel' the high standard that Command achieved with its bombing. It was a more difficult proposal to overcome the objections raised on tactical grounds by the other Commanders, and it was obvious that we were getting nowhere with this idea, although it had been placed to the War Office and all responsible parties, no plan had been put forward for including BC and the 8th Air Force as heavy bomber support for the Army. Exasperated, we tried every avenue of approach and at last Arthur Morley struck on the bright idea of going down [to Portsmouth] and seeing General [de Guingand], who was Montgomery's Chief of Staff. Arthur immediately ordered a car and set forth to see this officer [with Bufton? – see 'Forty Years On' in Chapter Twelve], who was in such a vital position for affecting decisions concerning the Invasion.

Arthur came back delighted. [De Guingand] had immediately appreciated the immense value of the support that could be given by the heavy bombers, and was amazed that all this had not been done by anybody else much earlier. I do not know how [de Guingand] set about it, but we soon found out that plans were being laid on for close support of the Army, when required, and our point had been won, although it was yet to be proved, and we had to suffer complaints from various high quarters about 'unofficial methods of approach'.

Collier further stressed the potential of close support in his memoir: 'How could an army survive under such concentration of high explosive? …why not make use of the colossus?' In practice, though, in the confusion of the battlefield, the use of heavy bombers, though spectacular to observe and devastating for the enemy, had limits:

The 'heavies' were able to carry out some very useful bombing of coastal targets before and on D-Day, and afforded some measure of support for the landing, but poor weather prevented their full benefit. It was not until later and with the bridgehead stabilised that the heavies could carry out saturation raids on the German army. A trial raid was carried out on 30th June against the village of Villers Bocage. The village was some way behind the lines, but was a focal point for important military roads, and it was expected that two Panzer divisions would pass through… The attack was accurate and extremely concentrated, and although only one or two tanks were afterwards found in the rubble, it proved that the concentration promised could be achieved, and that the heavies could be called on at reasonably short notice for support.

The first large scale attack in support of the Allied armies was carried out on 18th July [Operation GOODWOOD], when approximately 1000 Lancasters, 600 Liberators and 300 medium bombers attacked enemy positions east of Caen. Whole tracts of country were saturated with fragmentation bombs and bombs of heavier calibre. Never had armies seen such a display of air power: the plan was well-conceived, the high ground on either side of the proposed line of advance of our Army was 'neutralised', whilst an enemy strongpoint – a steel mill – was obliterated. Our Army advanced almost without loss, and if it had been able to exploit the advantage there might well have been a complete rout of the [German] Army. What exactly went wrong I have never been told, except that it appears that the enemy were able to rush a line of anti-tank guns across the line of advance of our tanks, and such heavy casualties of tanks resulted that the whole advance was halted.

The technique of close-support saturation bombing was christened the 'OBOE Box' method, whereby Mosquito craft using the OBOE guidance system would precision-mark an aiming point, guiding in wave after wave of Lancasters – each loaded with fourteen 1,000lb bombs – to obliterate a military target.

The all-weather OBOE system had already proved itself in bombing raids on Germany, although its intersecting radio beams had a limited range. German defences could do nothing to intercept the fast Mosquitos flying at high altitudes who were free to drop their marker bombs.

Sydney Bufton was on the ground in Normandy to witness the apocalyptic debut of the OBOE Box that launched Operation GOODWOOD, which he recalled in an interview in 1990:

...the four of us landed on the beach head and went with the DGS Ops in a jeep and we were taken to a slit trench where the Huns had been evicted from earlier in the evening, 2000 yards from the aiming point... and at 6AM precisely... a marker bomb came down at the aiming point... exactly spot on time and three Lancs appeared against the dawn sky and they dropped their bombs and then five Lancs and then ten Lancs and the sky was filled with Lancs and every time they dropped fourteen 1000lb bombs our trousers went fourteen times like that and in five minutes you couldn't see twenty yards for dust, but the markers could be seen from above and they dropped I think 5,000 tons... Anyhow that was the Oboe Box...

This mixed success was followed by 1,000 USAAF planes 'and practically every fragmentation bomb they had left in this country' (reckoned Bufton), being dropped, triggering General Patton's sweeping advance from St Lo to cut off the Cherbourg Peninsula. Subsequently heavy bombers were used to pulverize the German garrisons holding out in French ports stranded by the Allied advance and, claimed Bufton: 'After one saturation bombing raid these garrisons would surrender without casualty to our troops.'

For John Collier these 'immense displays of air power' gave 'great moral uplift... to our armies' and 'despair... to the enemy troops'. The awesome power of OBOE Box bombing achieved, in a confined area, what Harris had grandly foretold for Germany as a whole: a vengeful scourging from the skies. Also, rather disturbingly, it seems like a foretaste of modern warfare's 'shock and awe'.

The Warsaw Uprising

While the RAF and USAAF were 'causing hell' in Germany and enabling the Allied armies to break out from Normandy, on the Eastern Front the rapid advance of the Red Army brought them to within sight of Warsaw. On 1 August 1944 the Polish Home Army rose up against the German occupiers, but the Russians, who had been checked by fresh German divisions, were content to sit on the east bank of the Vistula and regroup. They did not want to get involved in street fighting, Stalingrad-style, and had problems of supply after their 450-mile dash. During the two months of the Warsaw Uprising they did not make even a token move to assist this non-Communist revolt, which can be ascribed to some extent to these practical difficulties, but more plausibly to Stalin's cynical calculation, especially as Radio Moscow had initially called on the citizens of Warsaw to rise up. For their part, since the discovery in April 1943 of the 4,000 murdered Polish officers in Katyn Forest, the Polish government-in-exile in London had had nothing to do with the Soviets, so co-operation at the highest level was non-existent.

John Collier and his colleagues followed events, and what he described as 'one of the most tragic, but heroic and hopeless incidents in the war', and agonized over how they could assist the patriotic Poles. He revisited the fraught discussions in B Ops 1 in his memoir:

It was not long before we received the first requests for aid. Air supply of arms was the main call, and desperate the call. The texts of the [radio] messages were passed on to us, with instructions to study the problem and advise as to what help could be given. Specific dropping areas were described in the messages passed from Warsaw, and we hastened to try to identify them. This proved no easy matter for the directions were not clear, but the mention of a large wood adjoining the city was the chief guide. Warsaw lay some nine hundred miles in direct flight from England and was well out of the range of all but our latest heavy bombers. The C-in-C Bomber Command said that even so it would be necessary for the aircraft to land in Russia, for some time would have to be spent searching for the target area. Plans went ahead for a force of heavy to provide supplies, and permission was asked to use Russian bases. It was refused by the Russians! We were virtually stumped, but there was one other possibility – Warsaw lay just in range of Wellington aircraft operating from the Mediterranean. The cries for help daily grew more desperate, and one felt terrible in the office putting pen to paper stating that if aircraft could not land in Russia then little help could be given, and that anyway dropping under conditions of heavy 'flak' after a long flight, with scanty information, would hardly justify the losses… It was a shocking experience to know that that gallant band of Poles were doomed to annihilation, but the help we could give would be so limited that it would only prolong the agony rather than materially help.

It had been decided that Polish Wellington squadrons should be sent to the Mediterranean to operate from there, and additional aircrew were flown out by special Sunderland aircraft. A WAAF I knew, who had been responsible for making out their tickets and papers for the journey, told me that the Poles were viewing the trip with very mixed feelings. Many were now married to English girls, and much of the original Polish airmen's zest for throwing away their lives 'in a blaze of glory' had died. They realised that for many it was a one way journey.

I have always had great admiration for the Polish airmen. They fought their way out of Poland to find their way into the Royal Air Force, after incredible hardships and difficulties. They had fought magnificently in the Battle of Britain and earned undying fame. I had met their bomber crews in the early days, when they had found their way onto our airfield to watch us operate, as their squadrons were not yet formed. They came up regularly and begged me to allow them to fly with me – 'just to drop a bomb on those damn Germans!' I had met them again at the Nottingham Palais de Danse. Noticing that they did not dance, I asked them why – 'We do not dance while our country is in danger' was the reply. It was genuine – I know later the Pole had a reputation as a ladykiller, but those early boys were tough and filled with intense feeling and hatred that we would find hard to understand.

The dropping operation over Warsaw was carried out. Conditions were very difficult – a very long flight and serious 'light flak' over the target area, apparently from both the German and Russian areas. The dropping area held by the defenders by now was seriously reduced and even doubtful – but in spite of all these difficulties many of the aircraft must have been successful for a grateful message was received by the beleaguered garrison. Losses in aircraft had been serious and further operations were not possible.

The gallant and hopeless resistance went on to the last – until the last shot had been fired… A glorious example to the world of real fortitude and courage, that pray God we never forget.

Chapter Seven

The Blackmail Committee

A Spanner in the Works

The Warsaw Uprising may have been doomed by geography as much as ideology and military realities but France, a short hop across the Channel, was another matter when it came to stirring up trouble... When John Collier first arrived at the Air Ministry in early 1943 the Special Operations Executive (SOE) was at a formative stage of its existence, assisting the small-scale sabotage operations of the French Resistance, and had yet to establish a co-ordination with the Combined Bomber Offensive. By chance Wing Commander Collier would be the key person from the Royal Air Force side to set up and maintain a creative partnership between Bomber Command and the activities of the SOE's agents. His brief account of the organization, written in 1946, is a very early one:

> My first introduction to SOE came as a result of a request from them that they should be given guidance as to the Bombing Policy so that they could assist in a small way. I went over to their headquarters to let them know what we wanted, and to find out what if any assistance there really could be [from them], for we were inclined to be sceptical about all this 'cloak and dagger' work, as we termed it. There I met a Flight Lieutenant Spinks, who appeared to be the 'live wire' of the party, and to have an amazing knowledge of factories in France. He had acted as an insurance agent in the country, and it seemed that he had visited a large number of the factories that we were interested in.

The first draft of his memoir makes more of his first encounter with this mysterious entity:

...I had not heard of this body of men [many of the SOE's most celebrated agents were, of course, women] known as the Executive... This was a new one on me, as we were all rather sceptical as to the effectiveness of such an organisation and thought that they [would be] better concerned just 'playing at spies'. Our amusement was increased because when we arranged to go to their Headquarters we had strict instructions that we were to meet certain persons at certain street corners who would then guide us to [HQ].

Having proceeded by Underground to Baker Street I met my 'contact' and was ushered into an odd-looking building, the [location] of which is still secret [later revealed as 64 Baker Street, hence the SOE's Sherlock Holmes-derived nickname 'The Baker Street Irregulars']... There were a lot of odd Army and Air Force personnel rushing about this building and somehow an Army officer dressed in a kilt struck a contrast to the black cloaks that I was mentally prepared for. However, I was most impressed with Spinks... my respect grew daily as I discovered that there was hardly a factory in France that you could mention that Spinks had not visited, or an underground storage that he had not somehow found a way into before the War...

It was the increasing activity of Bomber Command in France that made co-operation between B Ops 1 and the SOE an urgent priority and a practical prospect:

It was our job in Bomber Ops to select all industrial targets of importance in occupied territories, examine their relative importance against the possible implications of bombing friendly nationals, and decide whether this should be done. Bomber Command, due to the increasing effectiveness of the enemy night fighters, was finding it increasingly difficult and dangerous to carry out bombing missions of deep penetration into Europe by night, except during the dark periods. This meant that for half of every month Bomber Command's bombing was restricted to occupied territories...

Together the SOE and Bomber Command could help the Resistance achieve more ambitious aims, as Collier made clear in his memoir:

It was apparent that the sabotage then being carried out was not of a very useful nature. It consisted largely of pulling down high tension cables. SOE of course had many other duties, the chief of which was the organisation of the French Underground movement, a difficult and dangerous task. Although SOE had operatives in all occupied countries, France was by far the most lucrative, and contact with agents was reasonably [straightforward], as our light aircraft could easily maintain a shuttle service, although such trips were often fraught with danger.

Our first 'big business' with SOE came unexpectedly. Bomber Command had carried out a bombing attack [15/16 July 1943] against the Peugeot motor works at Montbelliard [which made tank turrets and aero engine parts]. Although the bombing had been very concentrated, it had just 'missed the mark' and little serious damage had resulted. However, it appeared that the workers and the management were thoroughly alarmed, and had hastened to make contact with England with a view to preventing further attacks. In view of the proximity of Switzerland, contact had not been difficult. The management begged that further attacks should not take place, and they offered to so reduce output by sabotage and a 'go slow' campaign that bombing would be unnecessary and unjustified. SOE pressed strongly that further attacks be withheld and that the management be given a chance of proving their word. They explained that the Montbelliard district was one of the strongest centres of the French Resistance Movement, and our 'co-operation' would have a most favourable impression, while the deaths of a lot of Frenchmen as a result of bombing might have a disastrous effect on 'relations'.

The implications of the request by the Montbelliard factory were tremendous. Would it not be possible by threat of bombing alone to induce many factories in France to 'go slow' and to sabotage? I put the proposals to my Director, who agreed that a trial case should be made of Montbelliard and that we should form a small committee with myself as Chairman to study with SOE and the Ministry of Economic Warfare factories in France suitable for our 'blackmail technique'.

The Peugeot factory was first hit by saboteurs on 5 November 1943, apparently with the connivance of the owner Rodolphe Peugeot. Although Collier states that it was the staff of the factory who proposed self-sabotage, according to M.R.D. Foot's history of the SOE it was their own man in the rebellious Jura, Harry Rée – code-name 'César' – who had thought up the 'blackmail' plan after witnessing the ineffective bombing raid of 15 July 1943. (Or perhaps Rée and the staff had come up with the plan in concert.) According to Foot, Rée had visited the manager and made him an offer he couldn't refuse, and arranged for a special codeword to be used in a BBC broadcast to prove his bona fides. It was Rée himself who nonchalantly left a rucksack full of plastic explosive and a timer next to a key piece of plant during a lunch break. It took six months for a replacement machine to arrive from Germany, and that was blown up even before it was unloaded in the goods yard.

A series of rather frantic 'Immediate Most Secret' cypher messages from the Air Ministry was sent to Bomber Command and the Eighth Air Force. On 5 October 1943: 'Request no further attacks be made upon Peugeot factory at Montbelliard (Sochaux) until further notice'; on 12 November 1943: 'Information received factory concerned successfully put out of action. There is now no need for this target to be attacked'; and on 4 December 1943: 'We have given an undertaking that as a test case Montbelliard would not be attacked till opportunity had been given for factory to be put out of action by other means.'

John Collier's committee, which met fortnightly in his office, began applying the blackmail principle methodically 'under the guidance of the Ministry of Economic Warfare':

One of the chief considerations [for planning bombing raids] was the possibility of civilian casualties. It was of the utmost importance that civilian casualties should be avoided whenever possible, and if a target was in a heavily built-up area, then we usually ruled it out as unsuitable for attack.

Targets not suitable for attack by Bomber Command were given first consideration for attention by the SOE organisation, who would either 'blackmail' the factory, or if necessary take direct action to sabotage the works. Two lists of targets were therefore prepared, those for attack by Bomber Command and those 'reserved' for SOE. The list was amended at each meeting and presented to my Boss for approval.

SOE got busy and sent their agents to contact the factories to inform them of 'the excellent opportunity to avoid bombing'. If the management would not 'play', then word to that effect was sent back. A case in point was the large [Michelin] rubber works at Clermont-Ferrand. The son of the owner of the factory, who had escaped to England, volunteered to be dropped by air to see the new management and try to induce them to 'go slow'. Rubber at that time was of extreme importance to the enemy, and we had it down as 3rd Priority on the Bombing Priorities. The management were duly informed that if they did not cut down production considerably they must expect to be bombed. The offer was refused, and its originator was lucky to arrive back safely in England. Here was an opportunity for the 'Blackmail Committee' to back its threats with action – for it would have a profound effect all over France when the news had been suitably published.

Examination of the target showed that the works, which consisted of two main blocks, lay a good distance from the worker dwellings, and with careful bombing few casualties should result. A special request was made to Bomber Command to attack the works at the earliest opportunity, and they laid on their Specialist Squadron [see Chapter Eight], led by Wing Commander [Leonard] Cheshire, to carry out the attack. No.617 Squadron took off on a clear moonlit night [29 April 1944], each aircraft carrying one 12,000lb bomb, with strict instructions to place it on the target only! Over the target Cheshire controlled the attack with his usual excellence and full use of the Squadron was not required for the early bombs were placed fairly on the target, and had caused all the havoc necessary. Photographic evidence showed little civilian damage.

This was a lesson that we did not intend should be forgotten by possible 'delinquents', and suitable messages were passed over our radio transmissions to France. Such was the fate to be expected for all those who would not obey the instructions of the 'Blackmail Committee'!

The most ingenious methods and instruments for sabotage were employed by SOE and distributed to 'loyal' workers. One of the favourite and most effective methods of destroying machinery was with the use of plastic explosive. This material could be moulded into any shape and stuck onto machinery, and by a simple fusing device could be exploded in that position. The charge was not great, but all that was necessary was to crack the machine to render it completely unserviceable. Other methods of sabotage were to use strong acids, sand and cruder methods such as literally putting a spanner in the works were often most effective.

It was not long before the Germans noticed the increase in sabotage in certain factories and they immediately took counter-measures. In the case of Montbelliard the colonel in charge of the district called all the workers together and threatened them with the most dire punishments and deportation if production was not maintained. We received regular reports on the position and the action being taken for sabotage and counter-action by the Germans. Reports on production would be studied by the Ministry of Economic Warfare who would say whether they considered this to be too great after making allowances for the fact that if production fell to too low a level the Germans would deport all the workers in the factory. One felt a certain amount of sympathy for the workers who were threatened with deportation if they did not produce the goods, and threatened with bombing if they did!

Hardened Steel and Heavy Water

The targets selected for the Special Operations Executive and Bomber Command's joint attention spread further afield and into some strategically vital scientific areas:

There were many occasions when SOE were particularly helpful. An example was when we were planning an attack on the Knaben molybdenum mine [referred to as simply the 'K-M mine' in Collier's first draft]. This target was of considerable economic importance, but was a difficult problem for attack as it was situated well inland in the high mountains of Southern Norway.

Molybdenum was a metal of vital use to the enemy. It was used as a hardening agent for all steels, where particular toughness was needed, such as with aircraft crankshafts. The Germans were desperately short of all hardening agents for we had bought up the supplies from Spain, and had brought pressure to bear to cease supplies from Turkey. They had little reserves and their main source of supply, the Petsamo mine, which lay in the very north of Finland, was liable to be captured by the Russians at any time. At this time we were attacking the German aircraft industry, and the denial of Knaben supplies alone might well necessitate the enemy reducing his grading for steel, a step which would hold up production.

A request was made to [Bomber] Command to carry out an attack on the mine. However, certain officers there considered the target tactically unsuitable for attack, and anyway they said it was just another Air Ministry 'panacea' ['I was met with a jeer of "I suppose you have brought another of your panaceas?"' wrote Collier in his first draft]. Defeated for the moment, I returned later to the attack with a written report by a Norwegian Mosquito pilot, to whom we had given details of the target, that he considered it could be destroyed with twelve Mosquito aircraft, and that [the mission] was not tactically impossible. Bomber Command were satisfied and the attack was on.

Undoubtedly the target was difficult to find under any conditions, but the position was further complicated by the fact that it was liable to be covered under a heavy snow fall. We had plenty of photographs of the target under normal conditions, but it was necessary that the pilots should be given some idea what it would look like under [current] conditions... SOE said that they could find out what the depth of snow was, and let us know in a few days. This sounded a bit of a tall order, but the information was forthcoming. Apparently some signal had been sent to agents in Sweden, who had gone over and had a look at the mine. With this information it was possible to produce for the pilots a good 'artist's impression' of the target, as it should appear when attacked.

The attack by twelve Mosquitos of 139 Squadron succeeded brilliantly and the Germans were denied use of this vital mine for at least six months, when it was bombed again by the USAAF. With further sabotage it was never much use again to the enemy. John Collier considered the initial raid 'one of the finest bombing exploits of its kind in the War'. He also took a sideswipe at the doubters in Bomber Command, especially Harris with his dismissive talk of 'panacea mongers':

> Whether the target was a panacea or not can be argued by others. It had been strongly recommended for attack by those whose job it was to study the enemy's weak points, and at later dates we received ample evidence that the enemy aircraft industry was held up because of hardening agents. A large dividend for a small outlay? [Or, as he put it sardonically in his first draft: 'Maybe it was a coincidence.']

Of even greater significance were the various attacks on the heavy-water Norsk Hydro plant at Vemork in the remote region of Telemark in Norway (but which Collier wrongly identifies in his memoir as at Haroya, which was in fact another Norsk Hydro plant producing aluminium). Heavy water – 'spoken of with hushed breath and complete vagueness' as he put it in his first draft – or deuterium oxide was a key element for obtaining plutonium from a nuclear reactor, and thus for the development of an atomic bomb; it was therefore a vital objective for the Allies to deny it to the Germans who had increased production at Vemork during the occupation. An attempt at sabotage by commandos, brought in by glider in November 1942, failed and the captured men had been interrogated by the Gestapo and shot. At the time he was writing – in 1946 – a German general was being tried for this war crime and John Collier was keen that 'all those responsible for the dastardly action pay the penalty'.

B Ops 1 looked at the feasibility of bombing the heavy-water plant:

> A careful study of the target showed that it was not very suitable for bombing attack, except with very heavy bombs. The building was extremely solidly built, and we were informed that it was necessary to destroy the plant which was situated in the 'basement'. However,

the importance of 'heavy water' was daily becoming greater, and the rumours of enemy preparation for attack on England by secret weapons was an added incentive for attack. Personally I found it extremely difficult to understand exactly what heavy water was, but it had been made fairly obvious that the enemy were developing it along with some secret weapon.

A bombing attack was carried out by the American Eighth Air Force. The attack was accurate, but it was considered that no guarantee could be given that the heavy water plant had been put out of commission.

This bombing raid was in fact preceded by the successful sabotage by Norwegian agents (on 27 February 1943) that was later immortalized in the film *The Heroes of Telemark* but was not made public at the time. When John Collier was writing his memoir the full story had not been revealed, and as his involvement in it had been limited to planning the single air-raid, he was reporting hearsay about other aspects of the SOE's operations there. He knew, however, that the final sabotage attack on the plant had been a 'one hundred per cent success', the German guards having been caught by surprise.

It was the USAAF raid on 16 November 1943 (nine months after the successful sabotage and on the same night as the second raid on the Knaben molybdenum mine) that prompted the Germans to abandon the Vemork plant altogether in February '44 and transport the remaining heavy-water stocks to Germany. This plan was then foiled by more Norwegian SOE men blowing up the ferry that was carrying the single consignment across Lake Tinn.

Collier concluded: '...the enemy "Atom" potential had been seriously disrupted, and another illustration had been given of how sabotage could assist and achieve results with a great saving in bomber effort.' In fact, the German atomic programme, so worrying in combination with the massive investment in rocket and flying-bomb development [see Chapter Nine, 'Buzz-bombs and Rockets'] was completely abandoned.

Resistance Heroes

John Collier was also working with the SOE in The Netherlands, as well as the Dutch government-in-exile and their air liaison officer Commander

Cornelis Moolenburgh, a former naval attaché (and 'a very fine officer' in Collier's opinion), who became a regular visitor to the B Ops 1 office and a personal friend. The usual targets in Holland were industrial, but there were some sinister developments afoot as the occupation entered its fourth year:

The Dutch Government in England were particularly worried about the wholesale transportation of population to Germany that was taking place. With usual German thoroughness an efficient record of 'suspected' persons had been prepared... and such persons were rapidly being rounded up and deported. The records [of the Dutch Central Population Registry] were kept in one building in the Hague.

One day the Commander came around to say that his Government were most anxious that the German records kept in the Hague should be destroyed. We examined the target [the Kleizkamp art gallery] and pointed out that it must mean risking civilian casualties, possibly quite heavy, and that he should make sure first that such casualties were acceptable. He returned later and said that the position had been discussed and that they wished the attack to go ahead, as it was of vital importance to destroy those records.

The building in the Hague was quite unsuitable for attack by heavy bombers, so we passed the problem over to the Directorate for Tactical Operations, with the recommendation that fire bombs should be used with high explosive. A most excellent low-level attack with light bombers was carried out [on 11 April 1944, by Mosquitos of 613 Squadron], and the building housing the documents was destroyed. We heard, subsequently, that all the records were not destroyed as some had been kept in steel cabinets, nevertheless the Commander was well pleased with the raid, which achieved very useful results with light casualties.

A few weeks later 613 Squadron carried out an equally daring low-level attack on the Gestapo headquarters in Copenhagen, which was completely destroyed with all its documents.

* * *

Not every meeting took place in cramped offices, mysterious SOE headquarters or the underground Whitehall War Room:

> I attended a dinner at Claridge's, given by the SOE organisation. The dinner was really excellent, and a very nice change from the austerity meals that I had been used to. As my boss had been unable to attend, I was given a seat of honour next to General Koenig [CO of the Free French Forces in the Normandy campaign, and in charge of the French Forces of the Interior, the Resistance fighters loyal to de Gaulle]. My French being of the 'la plume de ma tante' variety I was a bit nonplussed at the fluent conversation everybody was carrying on with the many French guests. However, General Koenig kindly came to my rescue for he could speak English perfectly.
>
> After dinner three Frenchmen of the Underground movement were decorated, two were awarded the Military Cross and one the Distinguished Service Order... Colonel 'Passy', who was head of General de Gaulle's intelligence service, came up and said to me that he had been told that I had been most helpful over operations with SOE and he thanked me most pleasantly [and as Collier had it in his first draft, 'said I was a good friend of France']. Colonel Passy's real name was Dewavrin. He appeared to be a very strong character, and I was told he had many enemies. I was not, therefore, very surprised to read recently that he had been cashiered and stripped of his decorations and thrown into prison. The French seem to have a different form of justice to the British, but even so this ruthless treatment could hardly be justified even if the charge of 'very serious administrative faults' were true. I wonder what the French authorities did about the DSO that Dewavrin had been awarded? [André Dewavrin was jailed for four months in 1946 on a charge of embezzling Free French money, then aquitted.]

Collier's regular link to the SOE meant that he heard of and was occasionally concerned with some of its other activities. For instance, his committee monitored SOE agents in France who 'did a truly magnificent job' in trailing a convoy of undamaged ball-bearing machinery that was being moved from a bombed-out factory at Annecy to a new underground installation near Paris:

> The Directive went out 'Destroy these machines or prevent their passage', and well and truly this was done. We got almost daily reports given to us about the movement of each of these machines and how they were being sabotaged. I can only remember one machine which reached its destination, and that arrived so late it never operated.

Agents on the ground would supply the SOE and John Collier's committee with photographs of the effects of bombing attacks:

> ...many very fine ground photographs were taken at great risk to the photographer... They served as a great encouragement to all concerned as aerial photographs tend to minimise the fantastic confusion caused as a result of the raids, and this can only be appreciated when one sees photographs taken from the ground. I was told that the cameras... were often of minute size and that the button of the coat would disguise the actual lens.

In return for all this voluntary effort, in the build-up to D-Day Bomber Command was extremely busy supplying the Resistance, usually via capacious Stirling bombers that could carry a large number of containers. Night drops were made at prearranged sites identified by Eureka beacons: 'a device whereby the aircraft could transmit a signal [Rebecca] which would be reflected by the beacon. This was particularly useful as the beacon could not be discovered by the enemy.'

The heavy bombing of French railways prior to the invasion was much assisted by sabotage, as Collier stressed in his first draft:

> There is no doubt that the French railway workers as a whole were ardent patriots and during the Invasion this was proved as they withstood the most terrific bombing attacks, which often destroyed their homes and livelihood, but nevertheless did all in their power to assist the Allies... Their favourite trick was to set the turntable outside the engine sheds

so that the engines, when started, would fall into the pit and take several days to remove them. This used to particularly irritate the Germans…

ULTRA decrypts seem to have helped finesse the targeting of French railways, by revealing the enemy's contingency plans:

The Germans were more or less prepared for large scale sabotage and stoppage of work by the French railwaymen in the event of an invasion and we had a copy of their plans which showed that they intended to keep open the five main railway arteries. It was not difficult, therefore, to counter this plan. The main operatives of the underground movement had to lie quiet until the moment to strike arrived, and it was one of the most difficult things for SOE to keep this organisation alive and in working order month after month, and yet not be allowed to give them any work.

Close monitoring of activities across the Channel gave John Collier a strong appreciation of the sacrifices of the French people:

Before the Invasion took place there were many sceptics about what part the French would play, and whether they would really rise. I always had considerable sympathy for the French because they were subjected to the most appalling bombing at the hands of the Allies and they had endured this with hardly a murmur. I always felt that when the time came they would prove their mettle, and I feel that this view has been fully confirmed.

He ended his record of his collaboration with the SOE with a heartfelt tribute:

…all this was not achieved without loss of many brave operatives of SOE and large numbers of patriots, but the spirit of resistance was kept alive and the honour of France was saved.

When I was shown maps of dispositions of agents in occupied countries, with special coloured pins indicating agents and areas that had been 'cleaned up' by the enemy, I was able to appreciate a bit just what the maintenance of this resistance must have cost.

Chapter Eight

Specialist Squadrons

Wallis, Gibson and Upkeep

John Collier had only been in his new job at the Air Ministry a few days in January 1943 when Sydney Bufton, then Deputy Director of Bomber Operations, took him to visit an experimental research centre run by Vickers Armstrong. They were conducting preliminary trials of a new weapon that had the potential to destroy German dams and was the invention of their chief designer, Barnes Wallis:

Wallis had made a really thorough examination of the problems involved in destroying dams, and had... carried out secret experiments in South Wales with large scale models of the dams he wished to destroy. These models had been destroyed many times with explosive charges so as to determine exactly the strength of charge needed and the exact spot of detonation. Wallis explained to us the many problems involved, and how invulnerable dams were to attack by normal weapons. We were aware of the difficulties to some extent, and had not contemplated attack to date for from the normal bombing point of view a dam presents a knife-edge target, while attack from low level on the outer surface had no hope of success with existing weapons. The enemy had taken precautions to place booms and nets on the water side, so again attack with torpedo was out of the question.

Wallis was proposing a new form of attack with a new weapon, one that would skip over the water, pass over the booms and nets, and finally strike the inner face of the dam and sink to a correct level to ensure maximum tamping effect [using water pressure to concentrate the blast] before exploding. Only thus could the dams be destroyed.

We watched the demonstrations which took place in a large tank. To see the model weapons skimming along the surface of the water was sufficient to make one realise the potentialities of this new form of attack, and after listening to Wallis – who was burning with enthusiasm – and seeing films of trial 'drops' carried out from Wellington aircraft, one was convinced. Like all good ideas, the principle was extremely simple, and therefore likely to be successful.

Wallis had in mind particularly the destruction of the Mohne Dam, in the Ruhr... but the weapon could be applied against all concrete or stone built dams, provided there was sufficient depth of water. The weapon was, however, unlikely to be effective against 'earth filled' dams which relied on their great depth of material for their strength. One of the chief problems was the 'tactical angle' – the attack would have to be made from a very low level, and because of the great weight of the weapon only four-engined aircraft could be employed. It was obvious that the attacking aircraft would be very vulnerable to anti-aircraft fire, but if surprise could be achieved, I said I thought the attack could be carried out successfully and the dam destroyed.

In the first draft of his memoir John Collier described the demonstration model:

It consisted of a long tank, with a board at one end, and a form of elastic catapult at the other, with a spinning [rotor mechanism]. A small metal sphere, little larger than a golf ball, was employed. Whilst we were waiting, Wallis explained to me the system by which it would work, and he was incredibly enthusiastic about it. I was immediately most impressed by this man whose name is now so well known. His piercing eye and resolute appearance defied argument, and I found later that if you did his amazingly quick brain always ensured that you got the worst of it. The tension on the elastic would enable the sphere to be catapulted at an equivalent speed of release as from an aircraft. The sphere itself was modelled to represent approximately a 9000lb projectile. Before release it was rotated anti-clockwise at various speeds. According to the speed of release and rotation so the distance the sphere would travel over the surface of the water could be varied. The ball, on striking the board at the far end of the tank, which represented the internal surface of the dam, due to its backward rotation, would adhere to the inner surface… and climb down it. A real weapon could be detonated at any suitable depth to ensure the most effective tamping and explosion opposite the more vulnerable area of the dam itself. Simply, it might be described as a form of 'Ducks and Drakes'.

Bufton had been sceptical about the chances of success of a low-level attack at an Air Ministry meeting on 15 February 1943, which had nevertheless approved production of the Wallis bombs – not popularized as 'bouncing' bombs until after the war, due to continuing secrecy – and the adaptation of thirty Lancaster bombers to carry them. Bufton had been asked to prepare a report on all operational aspects of the project and Collier's clearly expressed confidence in the plan reassured him about the practicalities.

Bufton subsequently reported favourably to his superior Bottomley, but Arthur Harris at this time still considered the idea 'tripe of the wildest description' championed by 'panacea mongers' who disdained the serious business of demolishing German cities night by night. It would not have helped in this context (as in others) that Sydney Bufton was the junior officer who had outmanoeuvred him over the Pathfinder Force.

John Collier did, however, understand Bomber Command's doubts:

[The Mohne Dam] lay in a hilly, wooded district, and the tactical difficulties of attack were undoubtedly considerable… A special form of low level attack was necessary, and the approach could only be done from one direction. Flying four-engined aircraft at low level around the Ruhr area was in itself a very considerable hazard, and it only needed searchlights and light anti-aircraft defences to make any such low level attack an almost impossible proposition.

The key moment for the project came when Portal overruled Harris and gave the go-ahead for more trials. A meeting at the Ministry of Aircraft Production on 26 February 1943 established a deadline of just eight weeks for delivery of bombs and adapted planes. The weapons would have to be used by 26 May at the latest to take advantage of the high spring water level in the reservoirs. For a bomb that was still at the experimental phase, this was an extraordinary commitment – and an extraordinary gamble – by Portal.

John Collier and B Ops 1 were aware that, if the gamble came off, the raid had tremendous potential to disrupt the German war effort:

> The Mohne Dam, which was one of Germany's latest and largest constructions, was the chief source of water supply for the Ruhr. It also supplied considerable electrical power to the Ruhr industries. It contained some three hundred million cubic metres of water, and this, if released suddenly, was likely to flood a large area of the Ruhr valley and sweep away bridges and many important lines of communication.
>
> Photographic reconnaissance of the Mohne Dam, taken with great care to ensure security, showed that the defences were comparatively light, and that no balloons were operating.

Analysis by the RAF Photographic Interpretation Unit at Medmenham revealed belts of fake fir trees around the Mohne, an attempt to camouflage its vast concrete structure. The Eder Dam, set in a twisting valley, had no defences at all. The easier conditions reinforced Collier's confidence in the operation, and he made it clear in the first draft of his memoir that his approval carried some weight with the planners: 'It appeared... that the aircraft, if they could achieve surprise, would have a reasonable chance of success and survival, and my views that the operation was feasible were listened to as I had so recently commanded a Lancaster squadron and should have a good idea of the problems involved.' Accordingly the Air Ministry issued instructions for the manufacture by Vickers of these special weapons, which were given the code-name of 'Upkeep', and a Directive was sent to Bomber Command for the formation of a special squadron.

Meanwhile, John Collier was closely following the refinement of Upkeep from a sphere to a cylinder through regular contact with its creator:

> Wallis, once he had been given the order to go ahead, worked with absolutely untiring energy. He had many difficulties to overcome and many initial disappointments, for the trial weapons would not operate satisfactorily. The outer cover would come off when the weapon was

'skipping'. However, by chance a trial showed that the outer cover was not necessary, and that the core could operate satisfactorily on its own. So one of the greatest difficulties solved itself.

The more I saw of Wallis, the more I was impressed. He had a piercing way of looking at you, and had such a 'rapier' brain that I used to feel somewhat stupid when conversing on any technical subject with him. However, he always went out of his way to be most helpful, and did not even mind when I used to invade his privacy at his home on a Sunday.

Wallis had his office at a country house well hidden away near Wadebridge [Burhill Golf Club, close to Brooklands]. With him were all his technical staff and other operatives of Vickers. It was always a great treat to get away from the Air Ministry for the day and motor down to see him, and listen to his many technical wonders, for he was the inventor of the famous 'geodetic principle' employed on airships and aircraft [the lattice space-frame, used first in Wallis's R100 airship and later for the sturdy Wellington bomber]; he also was busy planning new long-range aircraft with new principles of construction, and new weapons which he hoped to interest the Air Ministry in. There seemed few things he could not turn his hand to and solve in a 'flash of his slide rule'.

In parallel with the testing of Upkeep for the RAF, the navy were trying to get Vickers to work on a smaller weapon – code-named Highball – derived from Wallis's spherical prototype. They hoped to use it to attack capital ships (notably the *Tirpitz*) when they were thought to be safe behind anti-torpedo booms. The Admiralty was keen that Upkeep would not be used first and so give away the principle of the new weapon. The Air Ministry naturally wanted first use, but as it was the Admiralty who had sponsored the initial trials at Chesil Beach and were now busy with their own tests, this situation required John Collier to be the diplomat:

The use of Upkeep could not be delayed indefinitely, for its success was dependent on the level of water in the dam, and with the... summer the level would drop and drop. Admiral Reneouf [Edward de Faye Renouf, Director of Special Weapons] was looking after the interests of the Admiralty… over the use of the weapons, and I had long discussions with him with a view of impressing the importance of there being no hold-up with the planned attacks on the dams. The Admiral was most pleasant and gave me tea and buns in his office high up in the old Admiralty building. The office was more like an attic, and I could not help thinking how unsuitable it was for an admiral, but office accommodation was apparently terribly scarce, and like the Air Ministry little thought was given for the comfort of the Service members.

As well as these informal meetings an Ad Hoc Committee (of which Joe or a B Ops 1 colleague would have been a member) was set up in early March, at Admiral Renouf's suggestion, to co-ordinate the different activities of the RAF with Upkeep and the navy with Highball. It may have been significant that Air Vice Marshal Bottomley, and not an admiral, was in the chair. Before the inaugural meeting on 18 March, B Ops 1 produced a preliminary survey considering other targets such as dams in Italy, ship lifts and canal locks in Germany etc, but the Ad Hoc Committee agreed to focus Upkeep on the Mohne and Eder dams in the Ruhr, with *Tirpitz* the objective for Highball.

A specialist squadron was to be formed for the dams raid, but it was not initiated until mid-March 1943:

Wing Commander Guy Gibson was selected by the C-in-C Bomber Command to form and command the now famous 617 Squadron. I was particularly happy at the choice, as Guy was an old friend of mine, having served in the same squadron with me for some three years in peace and war. It was not until I crashed an aircraft on landing and was carted off to hospital, that Guy and I parted company for any time. He went on to continue his fine record with a night fighter squadron, while I was 'grounded'. Later, when I was flying again, we joined up again and both commanded Lancaster squadrons under the same Base Commander [at Coningsby/Woodhall Spa].

When Gibson wrote his book *Enemy Coast Ahead* in the year after the Dambusters Raid, he was obliged to keep many aspects of it obscure. The bouncing bomb was still a secret weapon, and he could not mention his friend Joe Collier's involvement, or anybody else's.

Gibson had been (unhappily) resting for a while at 5 Group HQ when he was asked whether he was up for 'one more trip' against an unspecified target. He jumped at the chance, and described the mad, breathless rush to form the new Squadron 'X', having been given only two days to select air crew from the creme de la creme of Bomber Command.

On 24 March he was taken by 'Mutt' – Mutt Summers, test pilot for Vickers – to an undisclosed destination in the south of England where he met 'Jeff' – aka Barnes Wallis – in his underground lab and where he was told he was only the seventh person to be 'in the know' about the new weapon, to which Gibson gave the code-name 'Downwood' rather than 'Upkeep'. He was shown film of the Chesil Beach tests, which revealed the skipping motion of the bomb, but was not told what the target would be.

The next day the Ad Hoc Committee met for the second time at King Charles Street and confirmed the code-names for the two rival operations as SERVANT (for Highball) and CHASTISE (for Upkeep), and on 27 March Portal presented a paper to the chiefs of staff devised by the Ministry of Production: 'The Economic and Moral Effects of the Destruction of the Mohne Dam and the Added Effects which will result from the Destruction at the same time of the Sorpe and Eder Dams.' The Air Ministry was spelling out its intentions and pressing harder for primacy over the Admiralty's plans for Highball. A complementary analysis by the Ministry of Economic Warfare concluded that only if both the Mohne and the Sorpe were destroyed would the economic effect on the Ruhr be really significant, but somehow this reservation was put to one side in the future planning of CHASTISE.

On 29 March Guy Gibson was finally shown three model dams (though not told their names), which brought the private response: 'Thank God it's not the *Tirpitz*.' He attended more trials of the weapon, the first of which at 'Parkstone' – Reculver, on the Kent coast – failed because of the difficulty of correctly judging the aeroplane's height above water: 'The problem was later solved by mounting spotlights on each wing that were set to converge at first 150 feet and then, at Jeff's request, a mere 60 feet.' The bomb's wooden outer casing, held together with metal bands like a barrel, shattered; however, the cylindrical steel core did bounce.

Gibson described a further trial (without the wooden casing):

Then one morning early in May, Mutt flew over and dropped one which worked. The man on the ground danced and waved his hands in the air and took out his handkerchief and waved it madly. I threw my hat in the air. I could see Mutt in his cockpit grinning as he banked around after his run, and I waved back at him and shouted into the noise of the engines. I believe, although I do not remember very well, that Jeff threw his hat into the air. This was a wonderful moment.

What Gibson could not reveal in his wartime account was that the marvel that set this select group of military men and scientists dancing like wild things was the sight of a bomb skipping across water to its target. John Collier was present at '…one of the final trials and it really was an amazing sight to see this "tar barrel" weighing some 9000 pounds leaping towards you across the water. If I had not seen it I would not have believed it possible.'

The Admiralty's trials for Highball were now lagging behind Upkeep; there were inadequate numbers of Mosquitos available to carry them and any low-level attack on the *Tirpitz* was generally viewed as 'suicidal'. It was officially 'off'. As an alternative, the Admiralty had been considering a Highball attack on the Italian fleet, but pressure was brought to bear to prevent this complication. Finally even Admiral Renouf, in many ways the godfather of the whole bouncing bomb project, came round to the RAF point of view that CHASTISE could go ahead without compromising SERVANT. Perhaps tea and buns with John Collier had done the trick:

Eventually the time came when a definite decision had to be taken, for the attack on the dams could not be delayed any longer. Appreciations were written by both the Admiralty and ourselves outlining the two different viewpoints, but Bomber Command and Wallis were ready for the operation, the time was ripe, and the Admiralty were not likely to have their special squadron ready for months. The decision was taken by 'higher authority' that the attack on the dams should proceed as soon as possible.

Bomber Command planned for the attack of the Mohne Dam as the primary target, and if this attack was successful then the Eder Dam, which lay above Kassel, should be destroyed. The Eder Dam, though not of the same importance as the Mohne Dam, was of almost equal capacity, and the flooding effect resulting from a breach in this dam could also have serious consequences. The successful attack of both would have a most profound morale effect on the whole of Germany. A third but much smaller dam, the Sorpe Dam, also supplying the Ruhr area, was the last alternative. It was an earth-filled dam, with a thin concrete core. It was appreciated that an immediate breach in the dam could not be caused, but it was considered possible that the dam could be rendered dangerous and might even collapse eventually if the concrete core could be cracked. The whole plan was very ambitious, and beyond our original hopes and expectations.

A progress report on the two competing operations was submitted to Churchill and the chiefs of staff when they were in Washington in the very week before the proposed date for CHASTISE. It was these 'higher authorities' who now made an unambiguous decision for 'immediate use of Upkeep without waiting for Highball'.

After intensive low-level training over lakes and reservoirs all around the UK, 617 Squadron was ready to go, flying its specially-adapted and stripped-down Lancasters. Ralph Cochrane, the new CO of 5 Group, sent a message to Gibson and his crews at Woodhall Spa on 16 May 1943, the evening of the attack: 'Bomber Command has been delivering the bludgeon blow to Hitler. You have been selected to give the rapier thrust which will shorten the war if it is successful.'

To read Guy Gibson's businesslike account of the Dambusters Raid – already too well-known when John Collier was writing his memoir in 1946 to need retelling then or now – is to be awed by his preternatural coolness in controlling the individual attacks by other planes, his own crew's courage in distracting the German anti-aircraft gunners and consistently taking the flak on themselves, and his single-mindedness in getting the job done.

Vast quantities of water were released, and much damage done, in what the Germans called the *Möhne-Katastrophe*. Tragically, over half the victims of the flood waters were foreign slave labourers of the Organisation Todt who were trapped in their barracks. Perhaps the most crippling effect of the raid was simply the massive diversion of resources needed to rebuild the Mohne and Eder dams over that summer, a propaganda imperative for the Germans as much as an economic one. The bulkier, more massive Sorpe dam was not destroyed.

Only one plane was shot down at the dams, but Gibson mourned that so many comrades and friends 'got the hammer' on the way out or on the trip home. Barnes Wallis, too, was deeply shocked at the high level of casualties. John Collier did not dwell on the raid's spectacular success in his memoir, but he also regretted the personal losses in a raid in which eight out of nineteen aircraft were destroyed and fifty-three crew died: 'Many of the aircrew operating with Guy were killed and I lost a number of old friends, almost the last of the original "crowd". In particular I mourned Squadron Leader Henry Maudslay, who had always set an example of perfection in my old Flight…'

Maudslay had served under John Collier in 44 Squadron in 1942. His bomb hit the parapet of the Eder Dam and the explosion seems to have fatally damaged his plane. He was just 21 years old. In the first draft of his memoir Collier wrote a eulogy for this beau ideal of the RAF:

> I felt a particular sorrow over the loss of Henry Maudslay. Henry came to me almost direct from Eton. He was very young, but he was perfect in his flying and in his behaviour as an officer. He never allowed himself to get flustered, nor did he ever allow himself to lower the standard of his behaviour or conversation below that of a perfect young gentleman…

That was the sober aftermath of the raid, but John Collier's first reaction on hearing of its success had been pure elation:

> On the night of Gibson's attack on the dams, I was sitting with my wife in a small 'artists' cafe in Chelsea. I had known that the attack was likely to take place any night and I had worked myself up to an intense state of excitement. My wife could not understand why, at just before the nine o'clock news, I insisted on disappearing into the rather dirty

kitchen of the cafe where they had a wireless. Ah! At last the attack had come off!! Far, far beyond my expectations – both the Eder and Mohne Dams were smashed and 'water was pouring as one vast flood over the German countryside'. I am afraid my enthusiasms ran away with me, and I dashed back to my wife saying that the destruction of the dams was 'a crippling blow' to Germany. My wife later reminded me of my claims, and asked me why – when I said the Ruhr would be flooded – it was still necessary to bomb it!

Shortly after the attack Guy was awarded the Victoria Cross, and this in addition to his many other awards made him the most highly-decorated pilot of the war. Guy was more or less 'retired' from flying, and we used to see quite a lot of him as he had a job in the Air Ministry for some time.

Gibson described his feelings when finally clear of the Dutch coast and heading home:

We did not know anything about the fuss, the Press, the publicity which would go round the world after this effort. Or of the honours to be given to the Squadron or of trips to America and Canada, or of visits by important people. We did not care about anything like that. We only wanted to go home. We knew that the boys had done a good job...

We did not know that we had started something new in the history of aviation, that our squadron was to become a by-word throughout the RAF as a precision-bombing unit – a unit which could pick off anything from viaducts to gun-emplacements, from low level or high level, by day or by night. A squadron consisting of crack crews using all the latest new equipment and the largest bombs, even earthquake bombs. A squadron flying new aeroplanes, and flying them as well as any in the world.

Cheshire and Tallboy

Another division of opinion arose over the future of 617 Squadron after the Dambusters Raid, while Guy Gibson was off on a morale-boosting tour of

Canada and the USA. Bomber Command now wanted every plane there was for the mass raids on German cities, so the pressure was on to justify the continued existence of a specialist squadron.

The other German dams were now heavily protected from attack, and as it turned out Upkeep would not be used again, and Highball was never used in anger against the *Tirpitz* or any other big ship. Also ironically, because the Germans had recovered a bouncing bomb intact from a crashed plane, precautions had to be taken against a copycat attack by the Luftwaffe on British dams. Luckily the principle of backspin was never understood by the non-cricket-playing Nazi scientists, who tried a spherical version of Upkeep, similar to Highball and code-named 'Kurt', that used a rocket booster to create a skip. This failed and the project was abandoned.

The Air Ministry were keen to retain the squadron as a force of highly-trained men who could use specially-designed weapons against vital enemy installations. John Collier suggested in his memoir that a major justification for this elite unit was the continuing inaccuracy of many of Bomber Command's saturation attacks, and the need for pinpoint targeting of aircraft factories and oil refineries, the items of most interest to B Ops 1. A squadron trained in precision bombing by night could also lead in the bomber stream and thereby ensure greater accuracy than that achieved by the Pathfinders.

Collier and his colleagues were also looking some way ahead to a worrying scenario:

> A final consideration was the fact that if the enemy developed his long threatened 'secret weapon', such weapons were likely to be buried under concrete and it would need a specialist squadron equipped with specially heavy bombs to 'winkle' them out. In fact it might be our only form of retaliation. Wallis at this time had put forward proposals for the production of his 12,000lb 'deep penetration bomb' [code-named Tallboy and known as the 'earthquake' bomb], and this weapon, in conjunction with the Specialist Squadron, was the obvious answer. I can remember John Strachey and myself putting up a long minute to our Director stressing the need for such a force and weapon for dealing with possible enemy secret weapon sites. Our guess was not far wrong!

It was finally decided to maintain 617 Squadron and to re-equip it to operate with the 12,000lb Wallis bomb.

The development of the Wallis bomb took longer than was expected, for the bomb employed new principles of travelling at supersonic speeds to ensure deep penetration. The bomb was not heavily cased, for again speed was the agent by which penetration was to be achieved without the bomb casing breaking up – Wallis explained that 'a candle could be fired through concrete without disintegration, provided that its velocity was sufficient'. Wallis claimed that his bomb would penetrate through anything up to about twelve feet of concrete – this was certainly a weapon with possibilities, for the enemy had taken to covering all his really important projects with heavy casings of concrete: the Todt Organisation were past masters at such constructions…

It was a big thrill to watch the early trials with the 12,000lb bomb, and to feel the earth tremors as the bombs exploded deep underground. The crater caused was impressive, but it was the underground disturbance that was the main feature of the weapon.

One of the first tests for the Tallboy was intended to be the extraordinary Rothensee boat lift, near Magdeburg, completed in 1938, that could lift a massive 1,000-ton barge. This lay on a key route from central Germany and Berlin to the Ruhr, and linked the River Elbe with the Mittelland Canal. The idea was for the bomb to penetrate deep underground to destroy the balance shafts and their concrete floats that, powered by compressed air, acted as counterweights to the lifting trough that held the barge. Luckily for engineering history, the boat lift was deep inside Germany and needed long dark nights to be safely reached from Britain. Correspondence between Collier, Bufton and Wallis also makes it clear that the latter, after making a scale model of the boat lift, decided that only the 'large' Tallboy – i.e. the 22,000lb Grand Slam – would work, but that was still in development in 1944. So an attack was put off, then superseded by more urgent targets. The boat lift is still working today.

Wing Commander Leonard Cheshire was appointed the new CO of 617 Squadron (thereafter christened the 'Cheshire Cats') in mid-September 1943, following the death of Guy Gibson's replacement Squadron Leader

George Holden in a failed raid on the Dortmund-Ems Canal. John Collier visited Cheshire shortly after he took up his new post and stayed at 617 Squadron's mess at the Petwood Hotel, Woodhall Spa, which brought back many memories of his time in Lincolnshire with 97 Squadron when the hotel had been a favourite spot for him and Beth: 'It seemed difficult to associate this quiet and beautiful house and gardens with the desperate deeds that its inmates might be called on to perform at any time.'

Collier found Cheshire

...to be the most unassuming of men. I have often been accused of looking much too young to command whatever job I held, but I must admit he looked to me even younger. He had already won the DSO and bar and the DFC... and he had now given up a rank and reverted to W/Cdr to take over the famous 617 Sqdn.

They discussed getting the squadron back into action:

For a number of months things were not very satisfactory for the squadron, for the development of the Wallis bomb was still delayed. The squadron were getting restless, although they were busy all day perfecting their bombing to a very high degree of skill. But they wanted action. It was decided that the squadron should operate with the normal 12,000lb HC [High Capacity] bomb, pending completion of the Wallis bomb. The former was a blast bomb of great effectiveness, but it had no penetrative powers as in design it resembled three large barrels tied together.

We selected a number of important targets in France which were suitable for an attack by 617 Squadron. These factories had not been attacked to date, for they were unsuitable for the main bomber force. The first attack took place [8/9 February 1944] against the [Gnome & Rhone] aircraft factory at Limoges, [which] was modern and of increasing importance.

On arriving over the target in bright moonlight, Cheshire found that the lights of the factory were full on, and apparently it was in full operation. Not wishing to cause unnecessary loss of French lives, Cheshire flew low over the factory several times to warn the workers and allow them time to vacate the factory, which they did. [He then marked it with flares and incendiaries.] The attack was brilliantly executed, and the target was completely destroyed. We heard later that the only casualty was one nightwatchman, in spite of the fact that hundreds of women were employed. The French were delighted with the consideration shown for their safety and word of the attack soon spread over France, and opinion of the RAF was very high.

A similar raid in March 1944 on the Michelin factory at Clermont-Ferrand by Cheshire and 617 has already been described [see 'A Spanner in the Works' in Chapter Seven]. The first use of a Tallboy bomb in anger came with an attack by 617 Squadron on a railway tunnel and bridge at Saumur on the Loire, two days after D-Day, preventing German reinforcements from reaching Normandy. Tallboy attacks on concrete E-boat pens at Le Havre and Boulogne followed, protecting the flank of the cross-Channel supply corridor to the invasion forces.

Though the weapon was a fearsome one, the risks facing the bombers on precision raids were perhaps greater than usual. Leonard Cheshire's low-level marking technique, whereby he would fly ahead of the main force in a fast Mosquito (and later a P-51 Mustang) meant that he often lingered over a target, as at Limoges. On 24 April 1944 he had proved his expertise to a sceptical Bomber Command by marking a target in central Munich 'right on the dot'. Not only that, there had not been time to fit extra fuel tanks to the Mosquito, so Cheshire had had to fly to Bavaria over defended areas rather than fly round them as the main bomber stream, consisting of 220 Lancasters, could.

The low-level method was subsequently taken up by 5 Group, under AVM Cochrane, but the rest of Bomber Command continued with the Pathfinders of 8 Group (flying much higher, in Lancasters), who were stimulated to improve their accuracy. The two rival marking techniques continued throughout the rest of the war 'and the tension between the two Bomber Groups at times was pretty strained'.

Although 617 Squadron was now set up with weapons and target-marking techniques to become Bomber Command's elite force, it was decided that Leonard Cheshire would not be the man to continue the task. John Collier approved of the fact that his two exceptional RAF friends – Leonard Cheshire and Guy Gibson – were following him into planning roles:

> When the low-level marking technique was well under way, Cheshire was 'retired' [in July 1944, after his 100th op, which destroyed the V3 launch site at Mimoyecques]. A splendid decision as so many gallant aircrew will continue to the last, if they are permitted to do so, while they are of far more value alive passing on their experience and knowledge to others. Cheshire was pretty glum about being taken off operations, and in the hopes of cheering him up a little I took him along to the RAF Club for lunch. I had heard that morning that he had been awarded the Victoria Cross for his outstanding leadership and daring, and I found it a bit of a strain to sit through lunch without dropping a hint! However, I was able to ring him up at the Ritz Hotel the next day and congratulate him, for the news had hit the headlines of all the daily papers.
>
> Guy Gibson VC did not find Staff work much to his liking, it was too irksome after the many years of freedom he had enjoyed in the squadrons, and nothing would do but that he get back near operations and flying again. He was given a ground job at a bomber base, but of course it was not long before he had talked his way into being allowed to lead a few attacks. He operated as 'Master Bomber', flying a Mosquito and employing the Cheshire low-level marking technique.
>
> The attack was made against Monchengladbach [on 19 September 1944], an important rail centre just inside Germany, the attack had gone well and Guy was heard controlling the operation almost to the end – what went wrong no one is quite clear, but Guy did not return, and it was not for some months that confirmation of his death and that of his navigator were received. Guy had operated almost continuously since the first day of the war, and he almost saw the finish – and so England lost one of its finest pilots and I an old friend...

Bowling Highballs

B Ops 1 also applied its imagination to new ways to use Highball, the spherical bouncing bomb that Barnes Wallis had devised for the navy but which had been laid aside by the Admiralty. The immediate problem, as John Collier stressed in the first draft of his memoir, was trying to delay German reinforcements reaching Italy to counter the imminent Allied invasion of Sicily in the summer of 1943:

> I was instructed to prepare a draft plan for the interruption of all communications into Northern Italy… There were only four or five [rail] routes. Two routes from France – one along the Riviera, and one through the Modane tunnel; the main Brenner… from Austria; and two less important routes through Trieste and Yugoslavia. This did not include the routes from Switzerland, through which the passage of military supplies was prohibited under the existing treaties.

A target list was drawn up that included the Avisio viaduct in the Riviera and the Bolzano viaduct on the Brenner route, marshalling yards at Modane and elsewhere (with possible involvement by the Resistance), and if feasible the destruction of the Modane tunnel. The specialist squadrons would take on the French targets, and the US Fifteenth Air Force the Italian.

Collier now had to convince the top brass:

> The plan was generally approved by the Air Staff and I was instructed to take it personally to Bomber Command with a view to 'selling' it to them. After I had been thoroughly discouraged by all the junior members of Harris's Air Staff, and rather laughed out of court, I was allowed to see the great man himself. He greeted me with 'I suppose this is another of those damn-fool Air Ministry ideas.' However, I was allowed to put forward the plan and he eventually agreed that it was possible, and would have his support.
>
> The closing of the Brenner route, of course, was the real plum, as this world-famous railway was the main …artery to Kesselring's armies in Italy. It was with this in mind that the idea was put forward [by Wallis] to destroy certain tunnels on the route with the use of 'highball' dropped from Mosquitoes.

Wallis wrote to Bufton from Weybridge:

It is my opinion that for this purpose the Mosquito aircraft, carrying two of the new steel case Highball stores [i.e. bombs] with forward spin [for propulsion, as opposed to the backspin of Upkeep] would be sufficient to bring about a heavy fall of roof, and certain experiments which we have been doing on model scale here leads me to believe that a pilot would have no difficulty in placing his store accurately some considerable distance up the tunnel.

The manoeuvrable Mosquito would need to travel at a much lower speed than when launching Highball over water, enabling it to make rapid turns or to climb out of an Alpine valley.

'Bowling' the spherical Barnes Wallis naval bomb on land would need to be rehearsed, as Collier explained:

This... needed to be pretty comprehensive for complete air cover of the route was necessary, and then a study of the tactical problems of low-level approach with Mosquito aircraft, a difficult problem in mountainous country, and finally a geological report was necessary from the experts... solid rock would be invulnerable, and a lined tunnel with 'loose' earth and rock would be necessary if a collapse of the tunnel was to occur.

Trial drops of the Wallis weapon into tunnels were necessary to ensure that the idea was practical, and trial detonation of explosives were necessary to ensure that the weapon would be effective. The Great Western Railway were most helpful and kindly arranged for a section of line in a remote part of Wales to be closed for the dropping trials. In addition they laid on special coaches of a most luxurious nature [one of them formerly part of George V's Royal Train], plus dining car and special attendants to look after us. Drink and food were 'ad lib' and it was a really marvellous treat for myself and the half dozen RAF officers that also came. Wallis, of course, was with us. After disembarking at a remote Welsh station, we re-embarked into a small 'mountain train' and puffed our way to where the trial was to take place.

The area around the single-track Maenclochog Tunnel in Pembrokeshire had been sealed off '…and cleared of all the prying public. Nevertheless, you could see, on distant hills, civilians being chased by the local police, which afforded us much amusement.' Then the real fun began:

It was a lovely day [in October 1943] and exactly on time 'Shorty' Longbottom, test pilot for Vickers, arrived overhead in his Mosquito. Wallis, who was very excited about the trial, would insist on standing practically at the tunnel entrance. He knew the expert touch of Shorty better than we did, and I personally stood well back, as I did not want to be bowled over by 2000lb of bomb, even if it had had its charge extracted. Shorty's aiming was excellent, and he bowled about three out of six of the weapons into the tunnel, having flown back and bombed up after each drop. It was a surprising sight to see these large spheres bouncing their way into the tunnel, and in one case rolling right out of the other end.

Film footage of this extraordinary sporting activity exists at the Brooklands Museum. John Collier reported on the trial in more sober terms at the time: 'As instructed I attended the trials of HIGHBALL weapons which took place under ideal weather conditions on 7th October 1943, against a tunnel on the single track line near Clynderwyn.' At the time it looked very promising:

We thought that we could now 'bowl' the 'Highball' down almost any tunnel on the Brenner route, and our imagination ran riot with pictures of German troop trains going in one end of the tunnel whilst pilots bowled Highballs down the other end.

Unfortunately, the scheme was eventually squashed, because we found that the explosive charge of the Highball was not sufficiently great to ensure the collapse of the inside of a tunnel [as shown in a subsequent test with Torpex explosive in an old tunnel near Wrexham, designated 'Grouse Shooting Part 2']. A collapse was only likely when certain geological formations existed, and a run of loose stone could be created by breaking the inner lining… Our geological experts informed us that in many cases on the Brenner route... the tunnels were hewn out of pure rock...

So it had all been something of a B Ops 1 pipe dream, maybe even a panacea... More conventional attacks were carried out on the Italian railways, but the bowling technique was not entirely forgotten: Upkeep was successfully bowled on land at a bombing range, although debris tended to fly up and damage the low-flying Lancaster. Highball was retained for possible use against the Japanese fleet, and thirty converted Mosquitos were kept in reserve.

Collier concluded:

The plan was never really successfully carried out, as the first and essential factor of timing and concentration, was not adhered to. Every route was closed at various times, but seldom, if ever, were all the routes closed at any one time, and so, although there was dislocation, it was never absolutely fatal to the enemy.

Sometimes Bomber Command seemed dilatory and tardy in the extreme. Collier much later recalled the marshalling yard at Modane being known to contain at one time forty troop trains which 'sat there for days' unbombed.

Tait and *Tirpitz*

Wing Commander 'Willie' Tait took over as the third and last wartime CO of 617 Squadron; a 'worthy successor' to Gibson and Cheshire, thought the admiring John Collier who found Tait

...a very quiet character... reputed to be extremely shy. I must say I got this impression when I went up again to Woodhall shortly after his appointment to discuss some of the future targets, and to keep myself in the picture as regards their problems. Willie, of course, would not have been chosen if he had not had a specially fine operational career, and he was already heavily decorated, with the DSO and bar and DFC.

Under Tait, 617 Squadron – and the second specialist bomber squadron, No.9, active from October 1944 – pressed attacks against enemy rocket-launching sites, forcing delays in the construction of the massive and mysterious bunkers in the Pas-de-Calais, and succeeded in collapsing the great reinforced concrete dome at Wizernes [see Chapter Nine, 'Buzz-bombs and Rockets'].

Collier was full of admiration for Tait and 617:

> The attacks on the rocket sites were no laughing matter, as they were carried out in daylight and these sites had become some of the most heavily defended targets in the world. At one time there was something like forty heavy anti-aircraft guns around the Watten site alone, and as accurate bombing necessitated accurate flying, 'steel nerves' were needed if the attack was to be successfully carried out.

However, despite being forced to abandon the most prominent sites, the Germans pressed on remorselessly with these sinister projects.

There had been some argument over the equipping of 9 Squadron and an internal B Ops 1 memo, from Morley to Bufton, dated 15 July 1944, is preserved in the Churchill Archive in Cambridge:

> 2. Collier also mentioned to me the question of bomber-sights. The new squadron (No.9 Squadron) recently formed is being fitted with MkXIV. Tate [sic] is of the opinion that their bombing accuracy will be affected, although apparently the SASO [Senior Air Staff Officer] is satisfied.

The very precise Stabilised Automatic Bomb Sight (SABS) was used by 617 Squadron for Tallboys, which could be dropped to within 20 to 30 yards of an aiming point from 20,000 feet. The older MkXIV sight was easier to use, especially at night, requiring much less data and computation, but was less accurate. The two alternative devices seem to physically embody the differences of approach, philosophy and technique between Bomber Command and B Ops, between the regular bomber squadrons and the specialists: SABS was known as the 'precision sight'; MkXIV was known as the 'area sight'.

More frustrating was shortage of supply of the complex new bombs. Production of Tallboys was limited to one a day in Britain, and although thirty per week were being made in America, the convoys bringing them over could be held up by bad weather and the continuing (if decreasing) threat from U–boats.

When conditions permitted, the specialist squadrons achieved yet more spectacular results. On 23 September 1944 Tait's 617 dropped Tallboys on the Dortmund-Ems Canal and drained a 10-mile section; then on 7 October they hit the Kembs Barrage, part of the Rhine river system, using Tallboys and attacking from a very hazardous low level. The Germans were thus prevented from using it to flood the area of the US army's advance; a defensive tactic that would be much on John Collier's mind over the next few months and feature as his final and most urgent collaboration with 617 Squadron [see Chapter Ten, 'The Siegfried Dams'].

Attention switched to that seemingly perennial maritime threat, especially to the convoys to Russia: the *Tirpitz*, lurking in a fjord in the far north of Norway. In the absence of a functioning Highball, it was to be attacked with Tallboys.

Lancasters of 617 and 9 Squadrons were sent off across occupied and neutral Scandinavia to a temporary base at Archangel, on the White Sea, in order to get within range of the battleship. Forced landings in abominable weather in Russia had, despite much initial suspicion in the Kremlin, allowed the Soviets to join in with a will. Collier reported:

Fortunately no lives were lost, but a number of the aircraft were rendered unusable. I heard that the Russians, having decided to permit the operation, did things in a big way, and parachuted mechanics to the aircraft that had force landed. ...they manhandled one of the Lancs loaded with a 12,000lb bomb about the airfield, whilst it had its brakes on; but nevertheless, in true Russian style, and weight of numbers, they managed even this.

Despite delays, and then a very effective smokescreen in the fjord, the Lancasters managed to damage *Tirpitz* with a single Tallboy on 15 September 1944, and the ship was towed south to an island near Tromsø. The Germans now considered her unseaworthy, but the Allies did not know that, so a second attack was carried out from Lossiemouth on 28 October.

Tirpitz survived this raid and so the specialist squadrons mounted a third, also from Lossiemouth, on 12 November 1944:

> The *Tirpitz* had been in its new anchorage for a brief time only, when in perfect weather, in daylight, both specialist squadrons – led by Willie Tait – arrived on the scene. The attack had been brilliantly planned, for it necessitated stripping the aircraft of armament and fitting of additional petrol tanks. By this means the Lancaster had been given a range and bomb load capacity never considered possible before. The enemy were unprepared, and our aircraft were not hampered in their attack by smokescreens or strong defences. Each aircraft delivered its deadly load of the Wallis 12,000lb penetration bomb and after being struck by at least two bombs, with other near misses, the *Tirpitz* slowly heeled right over until only her keel was to be seen. Thus ended the inglorious career of another of Germany's battleships, and Air Chief Marshal Harris had achieved one of his ambitions, and had released once more the bitter controversy between the Navy and the RAF of battleships versus bombers!

In total seventy-six Tallboys had been used against *Tirpitz* and only one plane was damaged. When he stepped down as CO of 617 Squadron in December 1944, Tait had completed 101 operations and was awarded an unprecedented third Bar to his DSO.

John Collier moved on from B Ops 1 and his close liaison with 617 Squadron in the winter of 1944/45, and so missed the finale of the specialist squadrons' role: the use of Barnes Wallis's ultimate bomb, the 22,000lb version of the Tallboy, known as the Grand Slam.

Collier and his fellow-planners had had their collective eye on one particular target:

There would be many uses for this very large bomb, in particular we wanted to destroy the Bielefeld Viaduct. This carried four rail lines, which formed the main trunk route for East and West rail traffic in Germany. The attack of transportation was well under way, and the destruction of this viaduct would seriously dislocate enemy military reinforcements. The viaduct was of ferro–concrete construction and was to date considered virtually indestructible.

Specially strengthened Lancasters were built to carry the bombs. All went well in the development of the weapon and aircraft, and the destruction of four bays of the viaduct was achieved [at the sixth attempt, on 14 March 1945]. A main artery had been severed at a critical time.

John Collier drew general conclusions from the deployment of 617 and 9 Squadrons as a vindication of a precision strategy for the Combined Bomber Offensive:

The Specialist Squadrons had been a revolutionary feature of the Air War. Britain's finest pilots and machines, with their latest weapons, had been pitted against Germany's most vital targets. Almost every attack had been a telling blow, and a very serious loss to Germany. One squadron alone produced two VCs and a quadruple DSO, which is worthy testimony of their courage and efficiency. Apart from the damage to the enemy that these squadrons effected, the development of their precision attacks had a resounding effect on the whole course of the bomber strategy. The value of precision attacks were proved and the argument of accuracy, with smaller numbers, as against saturation, made its point at the right time, and Bomber Command, in the later stages of the war, carried out some of the finest precision attacks ever seen with their main force, as a result of the lead given them by this courageous band of pioneers.

Chapter Nine

Buzz-bombs and Rockets

Retaliatory Weapons

Bomber Command's attacks on German cities were becoming increasingly accurate in 1943, as the OBOE system used to mark targets was proving pretty much infallible. After a notably precise attack on Wuppertal in May 1943, Goebbels had visited the devastated city and made a speech promising that Germany would retaliate soon. The British now knew that there was the possibility of something very unpleasant in store for them, but what would it be? John Collier and B Ops 1 were worried:

Discussing Goebbels's speech in our office we were all agreed that it really looked as if something pretty serious would be cooking soon, for Germany's leaders could not make statements of so definite a nature without backing them by action.

Receiving a telephone message to report directly to my Director, I hurried up to his office. 'I want you to meet Colonel Post, who wants some advice about bombing some special targets. They are important so give him all the help you can.' Post gathered up large quantities of photographs which were spread about the office, and we went down together to my office where he explained what was wanted. The story he had to tell was a very interesting one. He was chief assistant to Duncan Sandys, the Prime Minister's son-in-law, who had been specially appointed to form a small section to investigate the reports on enemy retaliation with secret weapons, and to make recommendations on how the problem was to be dealt with, if it was a serious one. The photographs alone made me think it was serious enough, for they showed large factory buildings, peculiar constructions, and very high blast walls built in large circles. In addition there were what appeared to be firing points for what must be special projectiles, and to cap it all there could be clearly seen a long cigar-shaped object near one of the firing points. Post explained that he reckoned that the object was definitely a rocket and Germany's long-sought 'secret weapon'.

It was a particularly bright bit of thinking on Post's part that had led up to the taking of those amazing photographs. Apparently although the reports received from Europe all showed that Germany was preparing some secret weapon to retaliate against the bombing, the reports were very vague and confusing. However, after studying the problem it seemed likely that any weapon launched against England would be aimed at London, the largest and most vulnerable target by far. To reach London it was probable that the weapon would have to have a range of between 150 and 200 miles. Germany would need to have a suitable area for trying out these weapons in secret, as security would be the most important factor. Where could such an area be?

Post considered it most likely that the trials would take place in the Baltic, over water, and examination of the Baltic coastline showed that the ideal spot for launching would be the island of Rugen. The projectiles could be launched from there and plots kept on the landing points from stations suitably placed along the coast.

Recent publications based on study of formerly secret documents concerning retaliatory weapons suggest that Colonel Post was not solely responsible for the breakthrough in identifying the secret weapons site (which was in fact on the island of Usedom, some 20 miles to the south-east of Rugen): it was ULTRA decrypts from Bletchley Park that provided the first clues. Sandys and Post were not 'ULTRA-cleared', so would not have known of the latest information derived from messages sent on Enigma machines by special units on the Baltic. This traffic – described as originating from 'Allied agents' – had alerted Air Intelligence (in the person of Professor R.V. Jones) to the rocket threat, and based on this information a watching brief was kept on Usedom. When the probable existence of a German rocket was communicated to the chiefs of staff in mid-April 1943, it was decided to set up a committee to oversee the investigations into it, headed by Duncan Sandys, Joint Parliamentary Secretary at the Ministry of Supply. Sandys drafted in his old Oxford friend Kenneth Post, who approached B Ops 1 and John Collier:

> A special photographic mission was sent to Rugen [Usedom], and development of the prints, which were excellent, showed all this peculiar activity on the island at a point called Peenemünde. It now looked as if some progress could be made in solving this difficult but so important problem. What, Post wanted to know, was the target like from a bombing point of view?
>
> Post thought it would be a good idea if I was part co-opted onto his committee to advise generally on the many bombing problems that would arise. I was only too ready, for I was intensely interested, and my Director agreed – so I found myself attending many meetings of the 'Duncan Sandys Committee' and these meetings became more and more interesting as time went on.

In the first draft of his memoir John Collier makes it clear that he was not in on ULTRA either, but that he saw some of its end product: 'All the secret reports from all over Europe were brought to the attention of [the Sandys] Committee, and although I was not officially on the SIS [Secret Intelligence Service] list I nevertheless used to hear a great number of them.' However, nobody was yet sure about what all this added up to:

> In spite of the photographs there were very many sceptics and 'experts' at these meetings who stated that the operation of a rocket over a distance of 200 miles was fantastic and impossible. Reports were coming in thick and fast, for priority had been turned on to the obtaining of these reports, and Allied agents were active everywhere. Even so, accurate reports were still extremely difficult to obtain. Peenemünde was very heavily guarded and our agents stood little chance of getting inside.
>
> Peculiar constructions were starting to appear in the Pas de Calais, some fifty miles inland, just where it was expected that the enemy would set up his 'firing points' for secret weapons. In addition, a small number of very heavy and large concrete constructions were being built in the area, including on the Cherbourg Peninsula. The concrete structures

[such as 'Kraftwerk Nordwest' (masquerading as a power station) at Watten, near Éperlecques in the Pas-de-Calais] were obviously designed to be completely bomb-proof, and the worrying information was received that their roofs were to be anything up to twenty feet thick. Not one of these large constructions resembled another, and [the puzzle of] their purpose could not be solved, although they looked dangerous enough. Bombing attacks were laid on to delay their completion, and if possible break them up completely.

These mysterious projects were employing thousands of French workers (as well as slave labourers, many of them Soviet PoWs), but unfortunately they were not a very useful source of information as they simply did not know what they were building. On 27 August 1943, 224 B-17s of the US Eighth Air Force bombed the Watten bunker while its reinforced concrete was still hardening, and four more raids in the next ten days destroyed most of the north side of the vast building. These raids prompted the Germans to begin an alternative semi-subterranean bunker in a former quarry at Wizernes, topped by a massive concrete dome and known now as 'La Coupole'. This was attacked without success, but was finally undermined by Tallboys in early July 1944; however, the dome itself remains intact today.

Much later it was realized that these monstrous structures were for storing rockets and manufacturing their liquid oxygen fuel. Collier noted in his first draft that '…none of them were alike and… at no time did they have any part of their constructions pointing towards London, but they were constructed "East to West"…'

In a Minute headed 'German Rocket projector', dated 29 June 1943, Wing Commander J. Collier, with his intimate knowledge of Barnes Wallis's prototype 'earthquake bombs', saw these as the only means to destroy the underground facilities that he then assumed would be used to launch the rocket. In fact, these would turn out to be the launch sites for the V3 'super gun':

The deep penetration bomb invented by Mr Wallis for the destruction of mine shafts appears to have considerable possibilities for the attack of the rocket projector sites. If a number of these bombs could be aimed reasonably close to the shaft containing the projector it appears likely that the walls of the shaft would collapse burying and probably damaging the projector and possibly killing the crew.

I understand that you have suggested that a small number of the deep penetration bombs should be manufactured for trial purposes and I suggest that Mr Wallis should be consulted concerning the possibilities of using this type of bomb against the rocket projector sites, as it may be advisable to order a large number of these bombs at this stage if it is considered suitable for use against this type of target.

Later, on 10 August 1943, B Ops 1 minuted in broader terms that the deep penetration bomb 'would appear to be the only type of weapon capable of destroying targets of massive concrete construction. It is considered that the development should proceed forward on the highest priority.'

Thus it would appear that although it eventually transpired that the rocket was ballistic – launched vertically – and did not need a directional ramp, this early championing of Wallis's earthquake bombs by John Collier and B Ops 1 did much to get them into production and operation.

Photographic reconnaissance of Peenemünde continued but had to be carried out cautiously, with RAF planes covering a wide area and seeming to happen to pass over the island to avoid alerting the Germans that their secret installation had been spotted. The photos were studied through stereoscopic viewers at the RAF Central Interpretation Unit at Medmenham in Buckinghamshire, where John Collier was a regular visitor:

Medmenham was a very large organisation whose interests covered all important enemy industries and activities. They had separate sections for shipping, aircraft industries, oil, radar etc, and in addition they gave detailed reports on the effectiveness of every bombing attack. They played an essential role in the provision of information, without which the bomber offensive could not have been effective. One section was a particular delight to me, where they made scale models of important targets – the models were dead accurate to the smallest details, even every tree and telegraph pole being illustrated on the larger scale models. I longed to take one or two home for my son to play with...

Professor R.V. Jones had spotted the first rocket by re-examining photographs taken on 2 June 1943: he saw 'a whitish cylinder about 35 feet long and five feet in diameter with a blunt nose [i.e. without its warhead] and fins at the other end', lying on a railway truck at Peenemünde. A crack Medmenham interpreter, Constance Babington Smith, was also briefed to study all the existing Peenemünde aerial photos and confirmed the presence of rockets from a recce of 23 June 1943; she also spotted 'four little tail-less aeroplanes' that proved to be prototype Me163 rocket-powered fighters. It was decided that Peenemünde should be heavily bombed to disrupt or delay the development of both of these weapons, but the attack would have to wait till the longer nights of late summer:

> It seemed likely that Germany was developing several types of weapon for the attack on England, amongst which it was thought that long range guns would feature [V3] – Germany had always shown a fondness for these weapons, the long range shelling of Paris in the First World War was proof of this – and one of the large concrete constructions had ominous slits in it, again pointing towards London. There were stories of electric guns, radio-controlled projectiles, rockets, bacterial warfare, and many other reports – some doubtless sent out by the enemy to confuse our Intelligence – but nevertheless the Germans led by Hitler and his mob of gangsters were obviously quite capable of anything, and the more dastardly the more likely!

In the first draft of his memoir Collier wrote:

> I was detailed to prepare a draft plan of attack on P, and we agreed that it was absolutely vital that only one attack should be made and that this attack must be 100% successful, as once surprise had been lost the value of further attacks would be very greatly reduced whilst the hazards would be almost too great.

In his revised text 'I' is expanded to 'we', making it clear that starting from his draft such a major raid could only evolve into its final shape by collaboration between B Ops 1, Bomber Command and the USAAF.

Nevertheless, a map in the B Ops 1 files, showing a route across occupied Denmark to Peenemünde may well be John Collier's work, along with a 'Tactical Appreciation on Possible Attack on Peenemünde', dated 25 June 1943. The raid was an exceptional one:

> …The enemy still appeared unaware of our interest in Peenemünde, and it looked as if surprise could be achieved.
>
> Bad weather delayed the attack, but Bomber Command picked a [very good] night and attacked with nearly one thousand aircraft [Operation HYDRA, 17/18 August 1943, the same day as the Schweinfurt Raid (see 'Combined Bomber Offensive' in Chapter Six) which along with a feint by Mosquitos towards Berlin distracted the Luftwaffe's defences; Pathfinders used the new H2S on-board radar system to guide the 596 RAF bombers]. This was one of the heaviest raids of the war, and was against a small target, but the concentration of the bombing was excellent and although some of the larger buildings escaped with minor damage, loss of enemy expert personnel was severe and reports were later received that essential specialist personnel were killed in the raid and that development of the rocket was delayed for months. Months was all that we had hoped for, as the Invasion was due in the near future.

Much of the rocket development work was moved from Peenemünde after the August 1943 bombing. Test firing went on at Blizna, in Poland; experimental work was done in caves in Austria; and production began at a sinister underground facility at Nordhausen, tunnelled beneath the Harz Mountains. In London, anticipation of an attack by rockets – from mid-1943 – involved preparing deep shelters as underground 'citadels' for key government departments.

In late October 1943 detailed information on a new threat came from a courageous French agent who passed on technical drawings and map references for a network of smaller launch sites in the Pas-de-Calais. They were identified by 'ski'-shaped (when seen from above) concrete buildings, possibly for storage of 'rockets'. At the same time, ULTRA decrypts described the radar tracking of a weapon on a test route eastwards along the Baltic coast from near Peenemünde. A photo reconnaissance over Northern

France on 3 November 1943 confirmed the existence of numerous 'ski sites', all oriented towards London.

The study of German secret weapons had recently been taken out of the hands of the Sandys Committee, and an investigation into the whole problem was chaired by Sir Stafford Cripps of the Ministry of Supply. Meanwhile, information-gathering was co-ordinated by a subcommittee (code-name CROSSBOW) of the Joint Intelligence Committee at the Air Ministry.

The announcement by photographic interpreters that they had identified the smaller launch sites came at a meeting of the Cripps Committee on 8 November 1943 in the Cabinet War Room and caused a sensation: so far nineteen had been identified, all pointing to London. By the end of the month ninety-five had been spotted in the Pas-de-Calais and several more near Cherbourg aimed at Plymouth or Bristol.

What sort of weapon were they intended for? The ski-shaped storage buildings were probably too constricted to admit a full-size rocket. It had to be something smaller, that could perhaps be catapulted off a metal ramp.

Constance Babington Smith at Medmenham was again asked to study the back catalogue of photographs of Peenemünde to try to identify a pilotless aircraft of some sort. She finally spotted 'an absurd little object', a cross-shaped aircraft, its stubby wings about 20 feet wide, sitting in the open air at Peenemünde on the same set of photos from June 1943 in which she had found the rocket-powered fighters. Further scrutiny revealed four launching rails at the research site identical to the ones seen in France (minus the ski-shaped storage facilities). Another recce was carried out over Peenemünde on 28 November 1943 and on one of these images Babington Smith spotted the same little cruciform device mounted on a launch rail, ready to go.

It was finally made clear that there were at least two secret weapons: a rocket (which ULTRA revealed was under control of the Wehrmacht), and a flying bomb (a rival project run by the Luftwaffe):

Initial bombing attacks on the small enemy 'projectile sites' in the Pas de Calais were carried out... by the American Medium Bomber Groups and the Light Bomber Group [2 Group], led by their dashing and colourful Air Officer Commanding – Air Vice Marshal [Basil] Embry – who personally led many of the attacks and insisted that all his Staff also flew, for he considered that this led to the best type of Staff work. A pity more Staffs are not guided along similar channels…

The bombing attacks met with considerable success, for the targets could be located and they were not heavily defended to begin with. The enemy soon began heavily camouflaging and defending them, and attacks became more and more hazardous. Fighter bombers threw in their weight. The heavy bombers were called in to assist, and to attack when weather was unsuitable in other areas. I took details of the problem down to [Bomber] Command, and again was told by ignorant and more junior officers that 'the whole business was an enemy ARP measure, to divert bombers from attacking Germany, and that the Air Ministry were fools to fall for it'. For the sake of 'good relations' one often had to suffer fools gladly, and anyway they had no say in final decisions, but at times one found it difficult to remain polite.

The threat to England steadily became more serious, as it was expected that the enemy would be able to operate a limited number of projectiles in spite of our bombing of the launching sites. Search was made elsewhere to interfere with their programme.

A new Directorate of Ops (Special Operations) – or, as Collier called it, the 'Anti-Rockets Directorate' – was put in charge of attacks on launch and production sites and prepared defensive measures. The Directorate was run by Air Commodore Claude Pelly, but its presiding genius was his heavily-overworked assistant Wing Commander Walter Lamb, who had become a great friend of John Collier's. According to Collier, Lamb's manifold considerations included

where they were produced, how they were powered and with what fuels, what warhead had they, what were the effects going to be if and when they fell in England, how could warning be given of their approach, how could they be diverted or destroyed in the air, would it be better to bomb the factories where they were made?

In the first draft of his memoir Collier expressed heartfelt sympathy for the plight of Walter Lamb, who was working any night until about 2 in the morning dealing with the countless problems which were arising over this new menace. The matter had now become of widespread significance and had been accepted as a serious threat. Poor old Walter. Every time some new big shot was informed about [the rocket], as they had to be, they wanted to start from the beginning and to know all about it. They then looked at the photographs and picked on the most obvious things and said had this been thought of? How Walter or Pelly ever managed to keep their sanity over the next few months is of credit to them as they had considerable justification to shoot many of the high level visitors who would make fatuous suggestions, waste their time and generally make themselves a nuisance. Everyone who had no responsibility and really nothing to do with the problem wanted to be 'in the know'.

Despite these distractions, there was no let-up in the bombing campaign. Heavy attacks (code-named NOBALL) on the 'ski' sites by the USAAF began in early December 1943. Results, unfortunately, were not promising:

The enemy constructions in the Pas de Calais continued with the same relentlessness as the bombing attacks. It was difficult to tell which race was winning, but the enemy became more and more cunning and it was becoming increasingly difficult for our experts to find the 'launching ramps' of the small sites, let alone for the pilots to destroy them.

The exact form of the weapon to be launched from the ramps remained a secret until a fairly short time before they [entered the fray]. Experts had got a very accurate idea of the launching sites and how they operated, but the enemy were clever at disguising the nature of the weapons. Security [for the Germans] ...presented little problem, for the concentration camps were, in many cases, turned into factories for the production of secret weapons. Control of labour was directly under Himmler's SS, and there was no hope of an operative escaping with any information. Work could be extorted to the maximum under the threat of whippings and death. It was indeed pleasing to see photographs of an excellent attack made by the Eighth [USAAF] against one such 'factory' [Buchenwald]. Precision bombing had destroyed the SS barracks and the factory buildings, without a single bomb falling on the prisoners' living quarters. Casualties among prisoners should have been slight for it was the enemy practice to herd them together outside during air raids under heavy guard for fear of them escaping. The prisoners could be clearly seen in the photographs. Shortly after this attack the Germans announced that Communist and Socialist leaders had been killed 'in a dastardly attack on a German prison camp'. Little imagination is needed to visualise the SS delighted with this opportunity to retaliate on these unfortunates, while having the chance of blaming the Allies.

In February 1944 the Combined Chiefs of Staff gave CROSSBOW priority over all other targets except the German fighter industry, and in April it was given top priority. However, despite thousands of sorties flown, heavy bombing had limited success against the many small launch sites. The switch to the lighter Mosquito and P-47 Thunderbolt made the attacks much more effective and economical, and by May 1944, when the priority of Operation OVERLORD was asserted over CROSSBOW, twenty-four sites had been destroyed and fifty-eight seriously damaged.

Yet this great bomber offensive had all been more or less in vain. It turned out that the Germans had simply left the 'ski' sites as decoys, while they created a new simpler system of pre-fabricated launch ramps concealed near farm buildings. Work on the concrete bases for these began in January 1944, using slave labour to avoid the security risk from French workers, and so little information leaked out before D-Day.

Another sharp-eyed photo interpreter at Medmenham had in fact spotted one of these new launch sites in April 1944, which led to a frantic review of all previous photos of northern France. By June sixty-eight modified sites had been discovered, but few were destroyed or even damaged by aerial attacks. The CROSSBOW Committee and all who were party to it now knew that London was as vulnerable as ever to attack by waves of secret weapons.

Inside Knowledge

As 1944 moved to its summer climax with the invasion of Europe, the burden of dealing with this imprecise though very real threat seems to have added to

John Collier's restlessness in B Ops 1, and the claustrophobic life of offices and bunkers. Above all, perhaps he really wanted to fly again and be a part of the great epic of OVERLORD. Also he would soon be a father again. He wrote to his parents in Suffolk:

> ...Elizabeth is still 'expecting' and getting a little impatient... Our work has been pretty intensive until the last few days... I may be going around the Squadrons for a visit tomorrow. It may mean that I may be away when Elizabeth does her 'stuff', but unfortunately I have no alternative.
>
> I went to visit some American planning headquarters today, and had fried chicken and ice cream for lunch! Pretty good, what? It seems my hopes for a new job have fallen to the ground. I feel that I have been in the Air Ministry quite long enough, but unless you can get someone to particularly ask for you it appears that no one will take any action at all. Still I suppose I should not complain as it is one of the best jobs in the Air Ministry. Still I would like a change.

It was only on 11 May 1944, less than a month before D-Day, that a prototype flying bomb crashed in neutral Sweden and two Air Ministry intelligence officers flew out to examine the wreckage. They confirmed that it was powered by ordinary aviation fuel. D-Day finally arrived (after Richard Reeves Collier, born in April 1944), and the riveting news distracted John Collier from his routine tasks and serious worries about retaliation weapons, as he wrote home:

> ...Yes, we are living in stirring times – I only wish I was in with the boys, it is awful watching & safely at a distance to this epic battle – I do feel however that we have helped the army as much as we can by working for them from our office – The army really are fighting magnificently – I have every confidence in them... It is interesting as I am in a position to hear the latest 'gen' & I find it almost impossible to do any work –
>
> Dad, thanks for wishing me the best for my new & 'important' job, but I am afraid I have to admit that there is little chance of either! – I do

not seem wanted except where I am & can't find anyone to particularly ask for me – so here I stay for the time until something turns up – I would like to go to France, but little or no chance –

The Allied armies were ashore in Normandy, but there was still no sign of the long-anticipated German secret weapons:

The idiom 'ignorance is bliss' was particularly true of the threatened… rocket attacks. With my 'inside knowledge' the enemy preparations for retaliation were a considerable worry, for I was living with my wife and infant [Richard; Mark, now 3 years old, was with his Bishop grandparents in Sussex] in a most ricketty house in Chelsea, near enough to Whitehall to be a primary aiming point for the enemy! My family knew nothing of this worry, nor did the many hundreds of City workers that I passed daily hurrying to and from their jobs. I used to sit in the Underground and think 'Now what would you people think and do if I told you rockets and all sorts of other unpleasant things may arrive any day in London – let alone possible atomic explosives…' What the devil could be done if they did arrive, for little or no warning could be given.

My wife found it difficult to understand my vague reasons for moving her out into the country, when I thought the threat was becoming serious. I sent her down to Sussex [to Marchants, the unrequisitioned part of Benedict House], near Battle, for I quite incorrectly thought that all the enemy missiles would pass almost unhindered to London – for frankly I saw little prospect of stopping them. Substantial evidence had been received that the first attacks would be with a pilotless jet-propelled plane, despatched from the sites in the Pas de Calais. A trainload of these weapons had been seen and the first attack was expected shortly.

By this time I had got very bored on my own in London, and as the enemy preparations had been delayed and delayed I had brought my family back… With the news of the trainload of pilotless aircraft, I hurriedly packed off the family down to relatives at Farnborough, just South East of London. Again I reckoned incorrectly that the projectiles would pass over on their way to London, although I did appreciate that Farnborough was right in the 'line of fire'.

I was staying the night with my family at Farnborough when I heard a peculiar roar, and looking out of the window I saw a small aircraft with a long flame squirting from its tail. So it had come!

In the first draft of his memoir, Collier sensed the significance of the moment:

...I was witnessing the first attack of its kind on London. Although one should not feel any sort of satisfaction, I must admit that I felt pleased that those who had scoffed so loudly and had called the German preparations 'air raid shelters' had been proved so totally wrong. The justification for the bombing of the sites in France was now 100%. This bombing had undoubtedly delayed the German attack at least six months.

The Armour-Plated Pram

On 13/14 June 1944, just eight days after the Normandy landings, ten flying bombs – or, as they soon became known by the population of London, 'doodlebugs' or 'buzz-bombs' – were launched, of which only three made it across the Channel. One landed in Bethnal Green, killing six people, but was reported by the BBC as a 'raider'. It seemed like a damp squib. However, two days later 244 were launched from 55 mobile ramps and 73 of them hit London, causing some panic and considerable damage. The next day Hitler visited France to confer with his commanders and enthused about the *Vergeltungswaffen* – retaliatory weapons – bringing the decisive blow: 'Hit London! Hit London!' he ranted. The flying bomb was now designated the V1 by the Germans, and soon their propaganda was claiming that London was a wasteland. That was a gross exaggeration, of course, although there were some horrific incidents: on 18 June a V1 hit the Guards Chapel during Sunday service, killing 121 in the congregation. By 21 June 1,000 flying bombs had been despatched.

Defensive measures had already been organized on a large scale, with every available barrage balloon arranged in a curtain across the south-eastern approaches to the city. Anti-aircraft batteries had been massed on the Channel coast and along the expected line of flight to London. It was hoped that radar would give early warning.

However, when defences proved inadequate, the need to hit the launch sites with heavier weapons became clear. Again they were given top priority 'except urgent requirements of battle'. The buzz-bombs, and especially the sinister moment as the engine cut out and they fell from the sky, were creating a state of high anxiety in the population.

John Collier felt the V1 attacks to be a personal as well as a professional challenge:

> In a bus or train one has time to study one's fellow-humans, and it used to make me realise the immense responsibility the few senior commanders and politicians had towards their countrymen. Even I felt the weight considerably, for here they all were, having suffered years of hardship, Blitz and mental strain, sitting patiently and trustfully waiting for whatever was to come... the possibilities, in spite of the successful invasion (to date), were ominous. The Allied bridgehead in Normandy appeared stagnant, and the weight of the buzz-bomb attacks were increasing steadily...
>
> It was not long before I discovered just how I had miscalculated again where the buzz-bombs would fall, and while I was in comparative safety in Chelsea, they were falling thick and fast in the southern districts of London, and in Farnborough. Again there was no point in sending my family down to Sussex, for the introduction of the proximity fuse for anti-aircraft fire had increased the effectiveness [of the defences] beyond all expectations, and batteries – with the able aid of fighters – were bringing down large numbers in the Battle area. So back to Chelsea came my family – it did have the advantage that we would all be in trouble together.

At Farnborough, baby Richard's pram had been 'armour-plated' with old baking tins as a precaution against ack-ack shrapnel and he survived the worst that could be thrown at him...

At short range, over the roofs of Central London, rockets were used against flying bombs. Collier wrote that the noise from the anti-aircraft rocket barrage (from Z-battery multiple-launchers) was

> really fantastic when it passed some two hundred feet over the top of your head. I think... the anti-aircraft fire was to begin with a far greater nuisance than the buzz bomb. My boss, Syd Bufton, who lived in one of the top storeys of Dolphin Square used to arrive in a pretty bad temper when he had had several hundred of these rockets bursting over his head during the night.

By mid-July 1944 about 2,500 V1s had hit England, but the south-east was now almost as dangerous as the capital as so many were falling short. The key factor in this was disinformation by MI5. All the German spies in Britain were controlled by them and used as double agents, and their carefully-concocted radio messages persuaded their Abwehr spymasters that instead of dropping on Kent, the majority of V1s were hitting the city. However, enough were still getting through to cause a drop in morale:

> Damage from 'buzz-bomb' attacks had reached fairly serious proportions. Arthur [Morley] was suddenly instructed to report to the Under Secretary of State for Air, Sir Archibald Sinclair, and go with him to inspect buzz-bomb damage. It appeared that the Prime Minister had become irritated at the effectiveness of the enemy weapon and had written a rather terse note to the Air Ministry, enquiring if an inspection of the buzz-bomb damage had been made and why the enemy were achieving such [psychological] results with such a comparatively small scale of attack, whilst Bomber Command's offensive on such a grand scale had not yet achieved decisive results. 'Pray, why was this?' This Note naturally caused considerable panic and a very senior member of the Air Ministry immediately set forth to inspect the damage with a small party of Air Ministry officials, including Arthur.
>
> The party set out in fine style in the Rolls... and the Senior Member turned to his fellow officials and enquired where they should inspect first. Arthur was just beginning to explain that most of the damage was

south of the Thames, when there was a very loud 'crump' and all found themselves precipitated onto the floor of the car. A buzz-bomb had landed just down the road!

All were a little shaken by this unexpected arrival of evidence of the enemy's malignance. Arthur brightly suggested that they should inspect the site where the buzz-bomb had just fallen. The Senior Member said 'Gentlemen, shall we inspect that now or later?' A member of the party replied 'After due consideration, Sir, I think later.' To the evident relief of all, the driver was instructed 'Drive on my man' (and get the hell out of here?).

Proceeding on the tour of inspection the party arrived at a gas works that had been damaged by enemy attack, and… made to enter by the main gate. In front of the gate stood the imposing figure of the gas works doorman. 'Stop,' he cried to the party, 'Where do you think you're going?' Explanations were given that they had come to inspect the damage. 'Can't help that, you can't go in there without a pass' said the worthy. 'My man I am —————' said the Senior Member. 'And these are my officers,' he added, turning to the many gold-braided officers lined up behind him. 'Can't help that – got to see your identity cards.'

The Senior Member and the officers had no alternative, and after much turning out of pockets and production of all sorts of ration books, chequebooks, letters etc… the doorman was finally satisfied when the Senior Member showed his identity card and the party was allowed to enter the gas works.

In order to satisfy the Prime Minister that the bombing of Germany was really on a scale incomparable to the buzz-bomb attacks on England, the Directorate were instructed to prepare a suitable report. Being about the most junior member it fell to my lot to undertake this rather onerous task in draft. I was given great assistance by statistical experts, and we were able to produce a quite imposing and convincing account. Photographs of the most stricken buzz-bomb hit areas of London, and photos of typical damage in Germany, spoke for themselves. The blast area of our 12,000lb [HC, rather than Tallboy] bomb showed up particularly well…

In his first draft Collier stressed this contrast:

> There really was no comparison when you saw these photographs together. It was hardly possible to spot the individual places damaged in London as a result of the buzz-bomb attacks. Where they had fallen there were little white spots where houses had collapsed. But this really had no significance when you looked at the large German cities which were completely devastated.

In the memoir he concluded:

> Much as I admired the heroism of the British public in their stand against enemy bombing and secret weapon attacks, I am more than glad they were not asked to stand up to attacks on the scale of the Combined Bomber Offensive. The test would have been of a different category.

As the V1 attacks continued through the summer, on 21 July 1944 a Joint Crossbow Target Priorities Committee was set up comprising staff from the Air Ministry and the US Strategic Air Force to co-ordinate and focus attacks in France. They ordered strikes on the big concrete bunkers such as Watten, Wizernes and Siracourt with Tallboys, and targeted the Volkswagen factory at Fallersleben that was thought to be making V1s. John Collier recalled explosive encounters with the flying bomb's launch propellant:

> …It seemed very likely that the fuel for operating the rocket [V1] would be hydrogen peroxide – apparently no one to date in England had thought of this mixture as suitable for anything but producing artificial blondes… However, it was agreed that a condensed form could be produced for trial immediately. The story I heard was that the trial had been entirely successful and hydrogen peroxide was not only a concentrated fuel but was also an explosive, for a small bottle had been left in the factory office and had been detonated by the hot sun, and the manager had returned to find his office a shambles.
> Our economic experts at once examined all the possible enemy production centres of hydrogen peroxide – the list they produced was

formidable, and it was obvious that the whole of the bomber effort could be absorbed in attacking those objectives alone, and if so the present Bomber Offensive would have to be abandoned. This, of course, was unacceptable, for in any case there was no guarantee that the fuel was essential to enemy plans.

Minutes for the 2nd Meeting of the Joint Crossbow Working Committee – operating in parallel with the Priorities Committee – marked 'TOP SECRET', have been preserved in the papers of Sydney Bufton at the Churchill Archive in Cambridge (and, with other meetings, in The National Archives). The Chairman of the Working Committee was Wing Commander Lamb; the secretary was Captain W.W. Rostow; and also attending regularly was Wing Commander Collier.

The Working Committee discussed various critical and urgent matters. It had been confirmed that air-launched flying bombs existed, and it was now known that the so far undeployed 'heavy rocket' – code-named 'Big Ben' – used liquid oxygen as fuel. Numerous sources of liquid oxygen in France and Belgium were to be bombed; smaller ones to be attacked by the SOE. To stop potential supplies from Germany, a Third Ring of Rail Interdiction might be required, targeting bridges.

Intelligence were getting close to the production centres for the rocket [V2], and the Working Committee requested 'cover and interpretation' from photo reconnaissance for two 'probable high priority plants': Siemens at Arnstadt, and the Dora works in the Nordhausen/Weimar area. Reports had come in of an 'aerial torpedo' being made in an underground factory there 'quite possibly at Buchenwald', with an estimated 8,000 PoWs as slave labour. Peenemünde, still used as an experimental station, was also producing rockets so it was bombed again three times by the USAAF in July and August 1944.

Then the Allied armies broke out of Normandy and the V-weapon problem seemed to have been solved. The last buzz-bomb was launched from France on 1 September 1944:

With the sweeping advance of the Allies, and the capture of the Pas de Calais, London was given a more than welcome relief. The rocket threat seemed to have diminished to a negligible quantity. It looked as if our bombing and troubles [with perfecting] the rocket had delayed production until it was too late to operate the weapon. Photographs of Peenemünde had shown large craters near the firing points for the experimental rockets, and it looked as if the enemy was still having considerable difficulty in controlling the weapons. Enemy-occupied areas within two hundred miles of London had been recaptured – with the exception of a small area in the Scheldt [estuary] of the River Rhine, and an area around the Hague. Even so such possible firing locations were at the extreme estimated range of the rocket, and it appeared very unlikely that the enemy would take any further action in their development.

It seemed that the much-feared rocket had turned out to be a dud. In the first draft of his memoir, John Collier sensed a dangerous complacency elsewhere in the corridors of power:

AC Pelly's anti-rocket committee were no longer popular. Here we were at the gates of Germany and yet the rocket had not arrived. The staff were all considering what job they were to do next. The number of interested visitors had dropped to zero, and although this must have been an immense relief to the Directorate there is no doubt that they were just a little disappointed that no rocket had actually arrived. Just one little one in the country would have satisfied them…

Fate was being tempted:

Even so the Air Ministry took a very cautious view, and were extremely annoyed and dismayed when Duncan Sandys informed the House of Commons and the world in general [7 September 1944] that the threat of enemy reprisal weapons was at an end ['The Battle of London is over']. We all considered that the statement was quite unnecessary and was most dangerous; in fact Walter [Lamb] informed me that they had done their best in the Air Ministry to influence against such a declaration. Duncan Sandys's statement made world headlines alright, and evacuees began to pour back into London.

As the days had gone by the intense interest shown by everyone in the Air Ministry, and those that could get entry into the Directorate for counter measures to enemy secret weapons, died. No longer did Walter have to burn the midnight oil to prepare appreciations and replies for the Cabinet and the Chiefs of Staff, no longer did the telephone ring for those who 'wanted the latest gen' – in fact, as Walter put it 'We are almost out of business, perhaps now I can get that long leave I'm due…' He had been attempting for months to find time to get over to Ireland to see his wife – now at last his hopes ran high.

[The day after the Sandys announcement, Walter] dropped into our office to say that both he and his Director were off for a short break, and that as I had worked with him to some extent he had recommended that if any difficult problem arose his Staff would refer it to me.

'Walter, I am thoroughly out of the picture now, and would not have the faintest idea what to do if a rocket arrived,' I protested.

'Oh, that's alright, you would not have to do anything, and anyway that won't happen.'

Shortly after, he popped his head round the office door: 'Well, Joe, I'm off.'

I watched Walter on his way down the corridor, and as he reached the stairs there was a very loud 'crump' and the building shook.

I shouted after him 'Hi, Walter, there's one of your damn rockets!', but by then he had disappeared.

A few hours later I saw him back in the Air Ministry again ['By God, you were right, that was a rocket' he quotes 'a very tired' Lamb in his first draft]. Poor Walter had lost his leave, but I thanked my lucky stars he had not got away.

Those Bloody Rockets

The first rocket, designated V2 by the Germans, landed on Chiswick on 8 September 1944, the day after Duncan Sandys' statement to the press. It killed several people. The era of the ballistic missile had begun.

By now it was more or less known what was coming. Intelligence regarding the precise nature of the rocket had remained patchy until the Polish Underground found fragments from a test firing near the secret factory at Blizna, west of Warsaw. These arrived in London at the end of July 1944.

Around this time key data was obtained on the much-feared weapon after another crash:

An experimental rocket fired from Peenemünde which landed in Sweden was the first concrete evidence of the enemy's intentions. It was not difficult for experts to build a model based on the bits and pieces picked up in Sweden, and this confirmed earlier beliefs, except the warhead appeared much smaller, for original estimates were that it weighed many tons, while now it would be likely to be under 200lb. An excellent piece of news, provided it did not contain any new type of explosive or bacteria [such as anthrax] – our thoughts often returned to 'this heavy water business' as we termed it.

The Germans' apocalyptic propaganda about laying waste to England had raised fears that the rockets would turn out to be atomic weapons. Collier and his fellow-planners in B Ops 1 were not to know that the Americans, deeply committed to the Manhattan Project and with resources far greater than those of the Third Reich, held the only atomic ace.

Although the warhead was an unknown quantity, the wreckage in Sweden showed that the rocket was 46 feet long with a range of 200 miles. Its mysterious fuel was reckoned to be mainly liquid oxygen. The electronic and radio-guidance systems were remarkably complex.

It was also clear from intelligence reports that the rocket could be launched from a simple stand of concrete or even a strengthened asphalt road, with its transporter trailer doubling as a launch support. The radio-control units would be mobile, too. Photographic interpretation was for once impotent: no V2 launch sites were ever identified, and trailers and rockets could simply be concealed beneath trees. Even Bletchley Park was bamboozled by the new key of the Enigma machine used by the rocketeers. Liquid oxygen plants in France and Belgium were targeted, but although the subterranean factory at Nordhausen had been identified, it was reckoned to be impervious to attack.

To read the Joint Crossbow Working Committee's reports from August 1944 is to sense a fatalistic acceptance that the rocket would be unstoppable. London would just have to endure whatever came out of a blue sky:

The first rockets were put down to gas mains and works exploding. Going back that night the city was full of rumours as to what the noises had been, but 'explosion at a gas works' held the day... The persistence of gas works explosions eventually got the public worried and doubtful, but there would be no official announcement for the enemy would be desperately anxious to know the success of the initial attacks and whether they had fallen in London.

No warning could be given, and Londoners had once more to heroically 'grin and bear it' – and the rocket was no mean thing to put up with, for it had a terror factor for some people in that it arrived with no warning. Personally I preferred it that way, for if one is to be killed knowing about it beforehand does not help, but my poor old landlady did not see it in the same light, and she would sit and cower in the cellar all day. She steadily got more and more shaky. No, she said, she could stand them buzz-bombs, but them rockets fair gave her the quivers. There was nothing that would persuade her to take no notice of them, for she was a very brave soul who had been all through the many enemy bombings of London without complaint or fear, but the rockets did indirectly cause her death for she died of a heart attack before London was given peace again. I lost a real friend, for no one was kinder or more considerate, and when I had moved my family for the umpteenth time – this time down to Cornwall when the rockets got a bit too thick – she took on the job of looking after me, and would produce a first class hot meal at whatever time of night I returned from work, although often she was dead tired from lack of sleep. I regret that I shall never be able to repay her, for she was a real 'mother' to me through those difficult times.

To those who have not experienced 'The Rocket', it really is... incredible to hear the loud explosion, followed by a noise that sounded like thousands of bricks tumbling down; the latter noise is caused, I am told, by the vibration of the [supersonic] rocket travelling through the air. I remember one Sunday walking through Hyde Park with my son [Mark], then three years old, when two rockets landed in the distance in quick succession – without thinking I remarked 'Listen to those bloody rockets!' The next morning another rocket arrived, and my infant son came tearing down the stairs: 'Mummy, mummy, there's another of those bloody rockets!' After a wigging from my wife, I concluded that rockets or no rockets you just can't be too careful with children...

Beth and the boys were sent down to Gentle Jane, near Padstow in Cornwall, for safety, as Collier informed his parents: 'Elizabeth & family will stay there for a short time and then come up here – if all is quiet – but we have had a few "bangs in the night" – not at all serious but "makes you think"...'

A little later he wrote home again: '...the family are still down on the farm & as far as I know well & hearty – I am still here & little prospect of a move – If the bomb & rocket threat has gone by the end of the month I shall move the family back to London... We shall see!'

Twenty V2 rockets had landed in England in the first week of the new campaign, ten of them in London. Little damage was done, but they thoroughly unnerved people. Some deep shelters were opened to the public and large numbers of children were evacuated once more. The news blackout, which lasted into November 1944, only increased the general anxiety.

An elaborate early-warning system was devised: coastal radar would identify an incoming rocket and alert Fighter Control, who at the push of a button would launch warning maroons all over London. Collier was not impressed:

The total warning for the public would be in the neighbourhood of three minutes at the most. This was a pretty poor look-out when you thought that the warhead might have... an atomised explosive. But at least it was something. This elaborate system, which must have cost millions to lay, was never used as it was never possible to recognise the flight of the rocket on the radar screen. Maybe it was just as well, as the precautions one would take would be negligible in three minutes, and no doubt many dozens of people would have broken their necks dashing down stairs and the public nerves generally would have been more shattered by the maroons than by the rockets.

Meanwhile, as B Ops 1 were trying to think up ways to neutralize the rocket threats, the Americans came up with something like a retaliatory weapon of their own:

Colonel Dick Hughes bustled into our office one morning with a 'Say, you boys don't know anything about retaliatory weapons, we've just designed something that goes off with a far bigger bang than the Rocket – give the Jerries a real headache, and only took a few days to design and perfect... Interested?'

He went on to explain that a couple of American air force officers had thought up the idea of filling old Fortress aircraft with explosive, fitting them with remote radio control, and then flying them over Germany and crashing them into any important target or town. The Fortress stripped of all but the essentials could carry some ten tons of explosive, and this would be five times the warhead of the Rocket! ...trials had shown the possibilities and the Americans had so many old Fortresses to spare that they would willingly have given them away. The plan was to assemble numbers of these 'robot aircraft' in France and fly them into the Ruhr area under control of a master aircraft. One of the tricky problems was that the Fortresses had to be flown off the ground by a skeleton crew, and when the master control aircraft had taken over the crew then parachuted out.

A trial attack was arranged against the (captured) ferro-concrete bunker at Watten in the Pas-de-Calais and six Fortresses laden with high explosive took off from a base in south-east England, with chaotic results. Another plane took Joe Kennedy, the eldest brother of John and Bobby, with it when it crashed shortly after launch in Suffolk. Nevertheless, there seemed to be potential for using this homegrown 'flying bomb' against larger targets, such as Germany's much-battered cities. A remote-controlled attack was made on the German island of Heligoland in the North Sea, but Germany itself was spared this extra ordeal and the whole erratic robot aircraft programme (code-named APHRODITE) was called off in January 1945.

B Ops 1 was also applying its energies to the problem of how to counter the mass-production of secret weapons – chiefly V2 rockets, but also jet aircraft – in the underground Mittelwerk in the former Niedersachswerfer quarry, near Nordhausen in the Harz Mountains. The factory was assumed to be safe from Allied bombers, and the Germans had an 'almost unlimited' supply of slave labour from the infamous Dora camp to work them. Even the biggest conventional bomb available to the Allies, the Grand Slam, would be ineffectual.

John Collier stated the problem that B Ops 1 faced at Nordhausen:

We studied all forms of attack – bowling bombs into the entrance, suffocation of the workers by special vapour fuels (we were not quite sure whether or not this violated the Hague Convention), disruption of rail communications – in fact, anything and everything, however ridiculous, but the conclusion reached was that the Allied Armies had better buck up and advance, if we did not want serious trouble in a few months' time.

An Appreciation written by Sir Roy Fedden, Special Scientific Advisor to the Ministry of Aircraft Production, who carried out a wide survey of German technical development immediately after the enemy collapse, shows that the threat was extremely serious, and as the Foreword by Air Chief Marshal Sir Keith Park states 'How near we came to losing the War will be better understood by reading this short account by Sir Roy Fedden...'

Certainly our Intelligence were very aware of the enemy activities and we were supplied in Bomber Operations with excellent photographs and models in great detail of the numerous new underground workings of the enemy. Just how the information was obtained, let alone the target found and photographed, will remain one of the big mysteries of the War to me, and will always have my most sincere admiration. I know women proved excellent 'detectives' and the WAAF at Medmenham were invaluable. One of their star turns... Flight Officer Babington Smith, ...was awarded the MBE for her excellent work – it certainly was a treat to listen to her explaining so lucidly the model of a major underground factory, employing thousands of workers producing rockets and jet engines.

There was little we could do on the Air side to interfere with the enemy plans – but they had left things too late, and the Allied armies swept into Germany before any of this last and desperate gamble by the enemy could affect the issue. The last rocket firing areas were captured and war-weary London could really look to the future with some confidence and security at last.

Bletchley Park was, of course, the mysterious source of much of the detailed information on the underground factory at Nordhausen that so puzzled and impressed John Collier; a secret which would not be revealed to the world for another forty or so years.

The Germans had continued to launch rockets from The Hague and the Hook of Holland towards both London and Antwerp in the early months of 1945, as well as some long-range V1s (which could also be air-launched from converted Heinkels). There was a failed attempt to jam the V2's guidance system by RAF planes fitted with electronic equipment while patrolling the Dutch coast. Then a disastrously-misconceived attack by RAF medium bombers on a wooded area on the edge of The Hague from which rockets were being launched resulted in the deaths of about 500 Dutch civilians in a nearby suburb.

In the first draft of his memoir John Collier agonized over the damage being done to London and the virtual impossibility of targeting the V2:

...it appeared that London would be subjected for several months to this very unpleasant experience, which was becoming increasingly serious with the improved accuracy of the firing of the rockets. There is no doubt that the Germans were now achieving creditable results and the daily plotting, which showed accumulative results, in the War Room of the Air Ministry, had the appearance of an attack of chicken pox. A certain amount of bombing was undertaken against the [liquid oxygen] fuel production centres which were chiefly in Holland and Belgium, but this was really an impossible task as this chemical could be so easily produced, although it was hard to transport... It was considered that by far the best means of reducing the rocket firing was by attacking the lines of communication by which the rockets must be brought up, rather than the firing points themselves... which consisted of a square concrete slab on to which a specially designed trolley carrying the rocket was backed. The trolley automatically tilted the rocket on to the firing position, after which other specially designed trolleys drove up and topped up the rocket with the necessary propulsion liquid. The firing was carried out electrically from a built-in trench adjoining. So really there was little or nothing to hit...

Better results were achieved by bombing trains bringing up fresh supplies of rockets to Holland, but relief only came when the Germans were forced to withdraw. The British Rhine offensive in March 1945 spelled the imminent end of the threat and the last V2 hit London on 27 March, falling on Orpington.

Despite the mess made of large parts of the capital, the whole Nazi reprisal weapons programme was, in effect, a failure, though at the time it was a terrifying ordeal for London's citizens. The total tonnage of explosives was only the equivalent of that of a single Allied raid by conventional bombers. Also it has been estimated that the development of all secret weapons cost Germany three times more than the United States (who were ultimately the real beneficiaries of Wernher von Braun's technical brilliance as a rocket engineer) spent on creating the atomic bomb. As the government scientific adviser Lord Cherwell noted to Churchill:

When it is remembered that each rocket carries a 1000hp turbine, at least two gyros working servo motors to control vanes in the jet and on the fins, two radio receivers, three transmitters etc, and all for the sake of bringing the same warhead to London as does the the flying bomb, Hitler would, I think, be justified in sending to a concentration camp whoever advised him to persist in such a project.

Chapter Ten

The Siegfried Dams

The Neglected Objective

In the early winter of 1944 the Allies were poised to invade Germany itself, having forced the enemy back across France to the formidable defensive system of the Westwall or Siegfried Line. At this time Wing Commander John Collier was coming to the end of his posting in Whitehall and was looking forward to coming up for air, but before his release he was able to make another significant personal contribution to the conduct of the war. It was one that, when he was writing his memoir in 1946, remained shrouded in the secrecy of military planning and the fog of war:

I had now been at the Air Ministry for nearly two years, the normal term of imprisonment, and my successor Wing Commander Hugh Everitt was taking over from me. One of the first things to do when taking over a job is to get to know all the 'contacts', and Hugh had gone over to the Interpretation Unit at Medmenham to have a look over the place and to collect suitable illustrative photographs for a Folder he was preparing on all the types of targets suitable for attack by the Specialist Squadrons using the 'Wallis weapons'. Hugh had had a very successful day and had brought back some excellent photographs of enemy dams, river barrages, viaducts etc.

One photograph that particularly intrigued me was of a large dam, well-defended and [a reservoir] full of water. I could not immediately recognise it, and was surprised for we had studied all German dams pretty carefully and I reckoned I knew them all by heart. I said 'Hugh, you might check up with Medmenham where this dam is.'

Later he came over with the information, which seemed most surprising – the dam was situated just inside the German frontier, near the Siegfried Line. The dam we knew nothing about, except its position; it was not targetted and apparently no one had shown any interest in it to date.

I became more and more interested, and determined to find out all I could as to how and why the dam was there, and whether it had any significance at the present time. I was well aware that the Americans were planning a big push from Aachen straight across to Cologne. They apparently intended to win the war on their own with this push and had abandoned a concerted drive [to the Ruhr Valley] with the British armies who [seemed to be] well bogged down in the flooded areas to the North. Anyway, that was what I had been told, and it was borne out by the fact that the Americans had for weeks been carrying out a most intensive barrage against the German positions – in fact it was one of the heaviest barrages of the War, and threatened to exceed the supply of ammunition...

A simple study of the map showed that the American armies would have to pass over the River [Rur (or Roer), in the Eifel region, not to be confused with the industrial Ruhr, further east], a short distance inside the enemy lines. The position of the dam was upstream of the likely crossing, and it was patently obvious that water released from the dam could flood the whole area over which the American armies intended to advance. Experience had shown the damage that could be caused by the sudden release of large volumes of water: the Mohne and Eder dam breaks were not easily forgotten. The more I thought about the problem the more agitated I became – Why had we not been asked to destroy the dam? Why had no mention of it reached our ears? The dam was obviously of little economic importance – could its importance lie in its strategic value? The [Rur/Roer] River ran almost directly North to South behind the Siegfried Line. I could not think of a better defensive weapon! The very fact that it was heavily defended and full of water when the Allies were so close showed that the enemy attached considerable importance to it. But, of course, I must be stupid to get worked up about the matter for the Americans must be fully aware of any danger on their line of advance, and a large object such as this dam could not possibly pass unnoticed, in spite of the fact that it was many miles upstream of their advance. Well, I thought, Hugh can hold the fort for me for a few days and I will scrape around and find out what I can.

On all matters of dams one automatically went straight to see [Barnes] Wallis – he was the 'Sage' and wise counsellor on all such matters. In fact, we used to consult him on many matters only of indirect interest to him, for we valued his opinion so highly. As usual, I disturbed him on a weekend. I felt the matter could not wait, for at any time the Americans might advance across the river: a telephone call and he said yes, he would come up to the Air Ministry the next morning – Sunday ['Wallis, in his usual driving manner, once he had shown any interest, was not inclined to let matters lie idle…' Collier wrote admiringly in his first draft]. He had a 'scramble' telephone and I was able to give him some details of the problem, and explained that we had no details of the dam available, and only had the one vertical photograph. He said he might be able to find some details in the reference library of the Technical Institute [Institution of Civil Engineers], who had their headquarters in a building near the Air Ministry. He would arrange for the library to be open on Sunday morning, and we could have a look through the books together. True to his word Wallis turned up on the Sunday morning and we spent many hours going through the many technical books. I was, of course, no help, but Wallis at last found what he wanted. The problem was not easy, for I could only give him the names of the local towns and villages after which it was likely the dam had been named. The problem was complicated even more by the fact that although a dam was found referred to in the technical journal, named after the district we were interested in, it did not answer to the description of the dam we had photographed. Wallis tumbled to it: 'Why shouldn't there be two dams?' The only answer was to have the whole area photographed, and I agreed to let him see the results as soon as possible.

Photographic cover of the [Rur/Roer] and of the district of the dam showed that there were in fact three dams, all of which could effect the flooding of the lower reaches of the river [a tributary of the Meuse/ Maas]. The dam Wallis had found in the technical journals [the concrete Urft Dam of 1905] was upstream of the dam I had asked him to study [the Schwammenauel Dam, completed in 1939] – both these dams were very large, and together had a capacity nearly equalling the Mohne dam – the third dam [the Heimbach Dam] was some way downstream, and was too small to be of much importance. What a master weapon the enemy held. I had visions of the American army being swept away as it advanced in confidence after a cunning retreat of the enemy. Or were my visions an exaggeration?

The implications were sufficiently serious, I considered, to worry my Director with them, and I poured out all the information and possibilities as I saw them. [Bufton] agreed that it would be wise to have an immediate check with SHAEF Headquarters in Paris, to see if they were happy about things. Arthur [Morley] put in a phone call to Paris and passed on our information [via 'our Army liaison section working with SHAEF, and although we could not speak over the open wire and stress the urgency, we drew attention to these targets and considered that once this had been done the persons concerned would immediately appreciate the danger...' – from Collier's first draft]. Well, anyway, I now felt that things were alright. Probably they were fully aware anyway of the threat...

The Americans continued their pounding, and the advance still did not take place. SHAEF representatives came over to attend one of our Target Committee Meetings at which my Director and an American Colonel – Maxwell or Hughes – were Chairman at alternate meetings. I took the opportunity to pump them for information about whether the dams had been considered, and if so what was to be done, for we still had had no requests to attack them – although with defences so strong, low level attack would be suicidal. No, they thought everything was OK, there was no particular need to worry, they would check again when they got back...

Collier's first draft expresses his frustration more pungently:

...there was no intention to change the plan. This had to satisfy us, but the more I studied the position in the War Room, and the plan of attack of the Americans, the more convinced I was that it was impossible to

plan any attack across the [Rur/Roer] before the dams were destroyed.
...it was obvious that no one was taking us seriously, or bothering to
recognise the seriousness of the position...

The appeal might have to go to the top:

>...I aired my views strongly to Arthur, who agreed. Arthur had now
>been appointed Deputy Director as a Group Captain, and as he was
>going to Paris for a conference he said he could press the matter again,
>if necessary with the highest authority he could find.
>
>Arthur was as good as his word. On his return he had told me that
>he had found no satisfaction at the lower levels, and had only received
>evasive answers and more or less told to mind his own business. Finally
>he had gone to see Air Chief Marshal Tedder, and put the possibilities
>to him personally. The Deputy Supreme Commander had respect
>for Arthur's opinion, for Arthur later joined his Staff. Action soon
>followed...

Again, Collier's first draft evokes more emphatically the frustration he and
Morley felt:

>Arthur, with his usual determination, tackled the problem when he
>arrived at SHAEF in Paris. He went and saw the officers concerned,
>and banged on the table and told them they would be personally
>responsible and probably be Court Martialled if nothing was done.
>As it was apparent to him that they had no intention of admitting
>that it had not been noticed before, which would involve changing
>the whole plan of attack, he went in to see ACM Tedder, and put the
>case before him personally. ...Tedder immediately recognised the
>significance of the dams, and promised that he would have the matter
>fully investigated. I was not surprised therefore when, a few days later,
>urgent requests arrived for BC to destroy immediately both the [Urft
>and Schwammenauel] dams. I found it difficult to refrain from saying
>'I told you so'.

Collier and B Ops 1 now contemplated a perhaps impossible task:

> ...the enemy had lowered the levels sufficiently to render the dams
> invulnerable, but at the same time remaining an effective flood weapon.
> Latest cover [photographic reconnaissance] showed that the lower
> dam [Schwammenauel], which was of 'earth construction' (rubble
> faced with brick and a concrete core), had had excavations made on
> the face of the dam. I could see these clearly in the photograph, and
> put up a suggestion that a normal bombing attack with delay fuses
> might set off any destructive charges placed by the enemy. Bombing
> attacks were made, but without result. The upper dam [Urft] was of a
> similar construction to the Mohne dam, and the enemy by lowering the
> level had rendered it invulnerable to attack with Upkeep [the bouncing
> bomb], if defences had permitted it – to all other forms of attack this
> dam was invulnerable. And so it was necessary to tell the [First and
> Ninth US] Armies that air attack would not be effective, and they must
> solve the problem themselves. It might have been better if they had
> thought about it earlier?

What John Collier did not make clear in his 1946 memoir was that the attacks
on the Rur/Roer dams were made by 617 and 9 Squadrons, with whom he
was still closely liaising at B Ops 1 [see 'Tait and *Tirpitz*' in Chapter Eight],
even though these were his last weeks at the Ministry. A secret draft plan
for an attack by Tallboys in Collier's name is preserved in the Directorate
files at The National Archives. The first raid, on 8 December 1944, was
in daylight – a sign of the impotence of the Luftwaffe – and was led by
the two specialist squadrons armed with Tallboys, followed in by over 200
Lancasters dropping conventional 1,000lb bombs. The concrete Urft Dam
was the primary target, with the more massive Schwammenauel Dam as the
alternative, and the intention was to breach the spillway at the Urft rather
than the dam wall itself. However, the operation was hampered by 10/10
cloud cover and had to be called off after only half the aircraft had bombed.
Three days later, on 11 December, an almost identical force tried again,
doing some damage to the wall, but this time not only was there still thick

cloud cover but the forewarned Germans had lowered the water level. Two more attacks were mooted for 13 and 14 December but not followed up.

So the Siegfried Line dams survived, but the US army had narrowly avoided disaster:

Whether it was the threat from the dams that caused General Bradley's attack to be cancelled, I don't know, but cancelled it was – and just as his Army was poised to strike. An American infantry officer gave me a very graphic account of the whole preparation for the advance, and how in the early morning destined for the advance he was right in the forward area with his men, waiting for the signal. Getting into their position for the big advance had proved a very tough problem, for the Germans were a tenacious and determined enemy. He noticed that the mobile guns that were to give the infantry backing were starting up and moving to the rear of the lines. He asked them what the hell they were doing, for he said 'they were always too ready to back out when it got hot'. 'Orders to retire by wireless – advance is cancelled!' The American officer was amazed, for they had been preparing for weeks and were all set to go.

It is not certain whether this advance – of unspecified date and location, but logically just before the first attack by 617 Squadron on 8 December – was actually aiming to cross the Rur/Roer. XIX Corps of General Hodges' Ninth Army had already occupied the floodplain to the west (Operation QUEEN), some way downstream from the dams, and had almost reached the Rur/Roer at the end of November. This advance had been halted by German reinforcements, but any downriver forces in the valley would still have been at risk from a sudden release of water from the Rurstausee.

The bombing attacks of 8 and 11 December were followed by a thrust from the US VII Corps who, having battled grimly through the forest, reached the Rur/Roer on 14 December 1944; their position near Düren was closer to the dams than that of XIX Corps. The situation was shaping up as John Collier had envisaged:

A secret report was received that the Germans intended to release water from the dams as a defence measure [or to cut off and trap US forces once they reached the east bank of the Rur/Roer], also that the lower dam [Schwammenauel] had been built specifically as part of the Siegfried defences [completed in 1939] – it was not surprising that we had no technical details of it! Further information stated that 'flood warning' practice was being carried out in towns on the [Rur/Roer]. We had arranged for a special study of the flood possibilities to be made, for in any case the rivers were very swollen as the result of continuous rain, and the estimate was that Düren, a small town in the line of advance for the American armies would be flooded by up to ten feet of water! It was even thought that the bursting of the dams might result in flooding of the British lines, some hundred and fifty miles downstream [on the Maas/Meuse].

It was decided that the capture of the dams was of first importance, and a 'thrust' was made in their direction [13/14 December 1944], but the country was very hilly and difficult going. Shortly after the thrust had started von Runstedt [*sic*] launched his unexpected [Ardennes] offensive, which surprised everyone and achieved such initial success that everyone was extremely worried, for the situation looked very dangerous for the Allies. I asked my American officer friend what his opinion was on why the German offensive had failed, for he had been mixed up well in the fighting – 'One of the chief factors was that von Runstedt's Panzer tanks ran out of gas, and he had been unable to capture any!' Only one man's opinion, but what a grand vindication for the bombing of enemy oil!

The eventual capture of the dams was effected [in February 1945], but not before the Germans had blown up the lower one of the two large dams, and released water which flooded the countryside. But now everyone was prepared, and only great inconvenience was caused. If the attack had gone forward as originally planned...?

The Siegfried Line Campaign, an official US army history by Charles B. MacDonald, gives much more background to the winter military preparations in the Eifel region and the puzzle of the neglected objective of the Rur/Roer dams. He claims that individual US army intelligence officers had spotted the potential danger of the dams – the Schwammenauel and the Urft – if breached by the Germans during an American advance, as early as October 1944, but their destruction had not been made an objective (which was an Air Force matter). Dams elsewhere were bombed that month, using Tallboys, including the Sorpe earth dam which the Dambusters' bouncing bombs had failed to break: on 15 October 1944 it withstood 617 and 9 Squadrons' Tallboys.

Part of the decision-making problem was that the Rur/Roer dams themselves were in the US VII Corps' territory, while the valley to the north that they could potentially flood was in the US XIX Corps' zone. Water levels rose as the winter wore on and the threat therefore became greater, but as they were not on his direct line of advance General Collins of VII Corps had no particular interest in their destruction.

The autumn and winter fighting on this front, much of it in the dense Hürtgen Forest, would be some of the bitterest of the campaign, but after the US army's painful progress was temporarily knocked back by the German counter-offensive in the Ardennes, the advance into Germany continued across the Rur/Roer, thankfully uninterrupted by a wall of water.

Collier does not mention it in his memoir, but the Americans are supposed to have wanted to thank him for his diligence concerning the dams with a medal or award, which was apparently refused by the RAF for reasons of protocol.

* * *

According to his Pilot's Log Book, John Collier flew to Paris in January 1945 in a de Havilland Dragon Rapide with his director, Air Commodore Bufton, Deputy Director Group Captain Morley and their American colleague Colonel Maxwell. This was well after the cancellation of the American advance on the Rur/Roer front, but before the defeat of the Germans' surprise Ardennes Offensive, 'The Battle of the Bulge', and the capture of the dams.

A few pages of preparatory notes for his memoir include a list of items headed 'Trip to Paris', including brief impressions of the war-damaged and wintry French landscape below: 'Bomb craters / empty roads / no life...'

They were 'not met' at the airfield, but drove into Paris to SHAEF headquarters, which was in a requisitioned hotel. There is no mention of the Rur/Roer dams; instead this was a 'Railway Meeting' at the HQ of General Carl Spaatz, now the USAAF commander-in-chief. They were well looked after: he notes gratefully 'American steaks / Menu cards / Cigars / Brandy' but also 'final sleep in clothes' before 'Return flight for meeting on underground factories', presumably regarding the V2 works at Nordhausen.

The first draft of his memoir reveals more about this rather dream-like jaunt, confirming that it was not related to the dams issue, and provides a nice retrospective anecdote on the increasingly desperate hunt for information on the German long-range rocket:

I had been attending a conference in Paris under the chairmanship of the Deputy Supreme Commander ACM Tedder, to prepare a useful plan for bombing communications in preparation for a further advance to the Rhine itself. After the conference, which of course had been a combined American and British show, I was invited by Dick Hughes, the American Chief Intelligence Officer, to come to General Spaatz's Headquarters for a drink. Dick Hughes was a most loveable character who was extremely efficient at his job. He used to act as chief link between the British Bomber Staffs and the American Bomber Command, and was General Spaatz's righthand man on all Intelligence matters. He had rather a bad stutter, but it was as much as one dared do to ever help him out over a word as he would persevere to the end... Dick had been in the British Army for a number of years and had married an American and taken out naturalisation papers... His humour and knowledge of our outlook, at the same time being an American, made him the perfect liaison officer and his influence could be felt in all matters concerning bombing policy.

General Spaatz's Headquarters was situated in the old Luftwaffe HQ outside Paris. They had occupied lock stock and barrel a most beautiful house belonging to an Argentine who had vacated in a great hurry, leaving all his precious possessions… in perfect condition. The Germans, who had left in a similar hurry, had also, strangely enough, left everything intact, and so we were able to sit down to dinner in this lovely mansion and have a wonderfully cooked meal, cooked as only a Frenchman can, and drink… French wines out of beautifully cut glass. This, I might say, struck a pretty strong contrast to the cocoa and cheese I was used to as an English dinner at home… Completely full of brandy and Corona cigar smoke I spent the night, fully dressed, stretched out on the sofa in Dick's room.

That evening I heard a most interesting story from an American scientific professor, who had just returned from a long visit to Russia. He had gone there with a party of British scientists to follow up the Russian advance into Poland so that he could inspect the rocket-testing grounds [at Blizna] in the West of Poland. The Russian advance had been held up for some time and they had spent a most interesting month at a Russian Divisional HQ waiting to move forward.

[When they finally reached the site they found that]…the Germans… with their usual thoroughness, had removed every piece of useful information concerning the rocket. Apparently their long trip and wait was to be in vain, and they walked disconsolately round this area for a few days until they finally decided to give up and return to England. Happening to look up in a tree, one of them noticed some pieces of paper which were caught in the branches, apparently blown there by the wind. On retrieving the paper he found it was a quarter sheet of foolscap containing… an early report of the rockets under test. This… was just what they had been looking for, but in itself was of insufficient value. Why had anybody… taken the trouble to tear the paper up into these sizes, which were so convenient for use during one's 'daily habits'? Without further ado they went over and inspected the German latrines, which, due to the low temperature, were in a good state of preservation, and … lowered down on the end of a rope the Professor courageously sorted amongst the waste and retrieved many quarter-sheets in relatively good condition… Piecing the papers together they were able to obtain complete results of the earlier firing trials… Their visit was not in vain.

Shortly after the trip to Paris, John Collier's two years with B Ops 1 in the Air Ministry were finally over, and he would soon be off to a new theatre. In the first draft of his memoir he wrote his valediction, not to war, but to the rarified life he had enjoyed for a while inside its intellectual machinery:

> In February 1945 my time had come to leave Bomber Ops – the war in the Far East was still on and there was work to be done there – and although I left with regret I also left with the knowledge that the work of the Air Forces in Europe was almost complete. I had seen, and had a small part in, the build-up of the Combined Bomber Offensive, which had played so vital a part in the winning of the War, had prepared the way for the Invasion, and made it possible, and supported the armies in all vital offensives; I had dabbled in the Secret Services and watched the gallant efforts… of the French Resistance movements; I had been in at the ground floor of our first knowledge of the German secret weapon development, and had seen it finally neutralised, although I too had suffered from its effects; I had enjoyed a comradeship in a small staff which I should not have believed possible. In fact, looking back, I can never experience the same interests, excitements, sense of achievement and power as I did in the two years at Whitehall. Is it any wonder that I felt that it was here that I found my real adventure during the War?

At the conclusion of his 1946 memoir he reflected further on the climax of the armed struggle and the whole experience of 'running the war' from Whitehall:

> The Siegfried Line had been broken – the German armies were retreating in confusion across the Rhine. Hitler had stated that the final decisive battle would be fought west and not east of the Rhine, and it looked as if this moment of decision had been reached for the German armies were fleeing across the river and seemed chiefly interested in their own escape. The incessant bombing attacks on enemy communications gave them little opportunity to organise – her main arteries, both water and rail, had been severed. The Dortmund-Ems and Mittelland Canal remained dry after Bomber Command had

blown away the banks – repairs and bombings followed one another in quick succession, but Bomber Command always 'trumped' the enemy [using the high-intensity OBOE Box bombing technique] and traffic remained at a standstill. The Bielefeld Viaduct was a shambles after attack with the Wallis monster bomb [Grand Slam]. In fact the Ruhr became virtually isolated with the destruction of sixteen out of eighteen viaducts or bridges, the blocking of twenty out of twenty-five marshalling yards and the cessation of all Rhine traffic.

The enemy situation was desperate, and I was lucky to leave Bomber Operations with the knowledge that I had seen all but the final 'death blow'. The Combined Bomber Offensive had virtually completed its task.

For two years I had experienced a 'comradeship' which I thought was only possible under action; I had seen plans and decisions from their embryo stage to their final execution that won or lost wars. The horrors of war had been daily imprinted on my mind, for the tragic sight of pallid children living and playing on the unswept platforms of the Underground, the piles of rubble that were once happy households, had not failed to leave a lasting impression. When you are directly involved in the unavoidable destruction of enemy population, first by physically dropping the bombs, and then by planning mass executions [by bombing], it is indeed a good thing to see daily the type of misery you are of necessity moulding. I left Bomber Operations with the knowledge that the trust put in the few had not been abused and that the lives of the many thousands of British and American aircrew killed in execution of the Combined Bomber Offensive were not lost in vain, but in a glorious victory which had saved the lives of countless numbers of their fellow-beings in all the Armed Forces and civilian life of all the Allied nations.

John Collier's opposite number at the War Office, Patrick Browne, cordial relations with whom had eased many inter-service planning problems (notably when B Ops 1 wanted to involve the heavy bomber force in Operation OVERLORD [see 'OBOE Box' in Chapter Six]), wrote in farewell and was generous in his praise:

Dear Joe,

I am terribly sorry you are going, and feel I must let you know how extraordinarily grateful I am to you for all the help you have given us. You are our first contact... & the whole of the really remarkable co–operation between our Directorates (from the Directors downwards) started with you & owes itself to you. The War Office relations with your Directorate are infinitely better & closer than with any other branch of the Air Ministry, which is really most extraordinary when you think that in the past strategic bombing was the thing about which the RAF & the Army quarrelled most violently & over which their relations were at their worst. I do hope you realise what an amazing piece of work you have done, and also realise that we know it over here. It has been pretty frustrating for all of us at times, but I honestly think (looking back over the past two years) that we have done quite a lot of good between us all; I am quite certain that, as far as any share the War Office has had in the good work, we could not possibly have done anything without the critical contact with you & your almost daily help ever since. For myself I have never worked more easily & more confidently with anyone than I have with B Ops 1 over the last two years.

Keep up the good work when you are CAS!

The very best of luck to you

yours ever Patrick Browne

The Auschwitz Report

John Collier's war in Europe was over by the time the Rur/Roer dams were finally secured in February 1945, at the precise time that he was flying off to a new campaign in the Far East. Exotic and invigorating though that prospect must have seemed after his cloistered years in Whitehall, he knew that, as well as being away from his family for some time to come, he would miss out on the satisfaction of witnessing the final push.

If he had still been in the Air Ministry in May 1945 he would no doubt have accompanied his boss Syd Bufton and colleagues on a sobering tour by air over a defeated and ruined Germany in the first week or so after VE Day. John Strachey described vividly, in a War Commentary for the BBC, passing over a wrecked Cologne, the dried-up Dortmund-Ems Canal, the great gap in the Bielefeld Viaduct, and the shattered Leuna synthetic oil plant; 'one of the main battlefields of this war', with greater ack-ack defences than Berlin. In Kiel docks a large red object proved to be the *Admiral Scheer* which had eluded 83 Squadron on the first day of the war, finally dealt with and lying bottom-up. Returning via Amsterdam, their Dutch pilot circled a suburban house four times until eventually a woman and a child ran out: his wife and son, who he had not seen for five years.

John Collier had been involved in a remarkable variety of projects, operations and investigations at B Ops 1, most of them now part of the general history of the war, but a few aspects of his work and experience remain mysterious. In his preparatory notes for his memoir of the Air Ministry years he listed a few intriguing 'Odd Items' that he did not go on to explore in detail. They seem to include projects that did not get off the ground and were left out for that reason. Some may remain 'hush-hush' or simply baffling or tangential, but others can be identified and explained, and one is of the grimmest significance.

The list includes these tantalizingly brief notes:

Lockey Committee / German Home Life / Display in Houses of Parliament / Lord Cherwell / Visits to Group HQ 5 / American Intelligence Nat Pincas / Party at Wings Club / COPC Pine Trees / Moonshine / Charles off the roof / Missing Romanian professor.

Almost as an afterthought he has written: 'Request to bomb Jews'. This could perhaps have been phrased more delicately, but it actually concerns the vexed and highly emotive question of whether or not to bomb Auschwitz. Collier adds a few more, unfortunately unamplified, notes under another stark heading: 'Bombing of Jews':

Request from Chief Rabbi to Churchill sent to B Ops / Describe target – method of despatch of Jews / Rumanian policy towards Jews / Madame Autentique / Weekly digest – Jews in Russia / Hopeless position / Bombing refused

Reports of the annihilation of European Jews had been reaching the Allies since 1942, when Jan Karski of the Polish Underground escaped to the West, bringing information on the liquidation of the Warsaw Ghetto and the mass killings in Eastern Europe that were not yet known collectively as the Holocaust. Karski met Anthony Eden, the Foreign Secretary, in London, and Roosevelt in Washington, but at that time official opinion seems to have been that his reports were exaggerated.

It is also claimed that Bletchley Park had been breaking the Reichsbahn Enigma codes from February 1941, and recipients of ULTRA decrypts (such as Churchill) should have been aware of the unusual train movements involved in transporting millions of people to the death camps.

When Rudolf Vrba and Alfred Wetzler escaped from Auschwitz in April 1944 they brought with them detailed plans of the camp and the gas chambers, and a good estimate of the vast numbers of people killed there: 1,750,000. Their report made it to the Allies via Budapest and Switzerland, and this time information from it was broadcast by the BBC and published in the *New York Times*, both in June 1944. There was no more room for doubt or prevarication.

On 6 July 1944 the Jewish Agency in Jerusalem, chaired by David Ben Gurion, which had just a month before been officially averse to bombing Auschwitz ['The view of the board is that we should not ask the Allies to bomb places where there are Jews'], changed its policy and requested that the Allies attack the camp and its railway connections. They were spurred on by the knowledge that the Jews of Hungary were about to be transported to the death camp.

Churchill now asked the Air Ministry – that is, B Ops 1 – to examine the feasibility of a bombing raid. For unspecified 'operational reasons', presumably a mixture of the difficulty of reaching deep into Poland from Britain and the fear of inaccuracy in bombing, it was decided at the highest level not to go ahead with an attack by the RAF.

One source states that the Air Ministry suggested passing the problem over to the Americans. Auschwitz had been within range of the US Fifteenth Air Force, based in Italy, since early May '44, and aerial reconnaissance of the site had been carried out in early April (just a few days before Vrba and Wetzler escaped), but the photo analysts were looking for synthetic oil plants rather than prison camps, which were not on the all-important list of priorities. Industrial plant at Auschwitz-Birkenau was bombed several times by the USAAF, including a mass raid on the vast Buna synthetic oil refineries by 452 bombers of the Fifteenth Air Force on 7 July 1944, the day after the Jewish Agency put in its urgent request to bomb the camp itself. The grim process of extermination continued unabated.

The full Vrba-Wetzler Report on Auschwitz was published by the US War Refugee Board on 25 November 1944, and the camp at Auschwitz-Birkenau was at last liberated by shocked and traumatized Red Army soldiers on 27 January 1945.

Yet who was Madame Autentique, and what role did she play in bringing information about Auschwitz to the Allies? Other references in the list can be explained but she remains a wartime mystery. In further notes Collier expanded upon some of the other 'Odd Items':

Moonshine
Prime Minister's Pet – small incendiary weapon / Pressure from Cherwell – How it was to be used / How it was to be dropped / Millions made / Why it was no use / How it would interfere with B Policy / Finally put off

[This dud weapon should not be confused with 'Moonshine' radar jamming equipment, introduced by the RAF from 6 August 1942.]

Modane Dam
Great discussion – 2 vital railways / Describe dam – 2000 feet up / Life in the valley – small villages, factories, bridges, Resistance / How dam would be broken – Specialist Sqdns / Counting of casualties / Difficult decision – life at a blow / Final decision / moral effect – relations with French

The Modane Dam is in the French Alps. Was it another chance to use Upkeep, as an alternative to bowling Highballs down the Modane tunnel, or was it a possible Tallboy target?

Other 'Odd Items' can be more confidently explained. The Lockey Committee provides funds from Oxford University for attendance at scientific conferences, symposia, etc abroad. Lord Cherwell was Churchill's Chief Scientific Adviser Professor Lindemann, a man who held considerable sway in No. 10. Irwin Nat Pincus was involved in the Marshall Plan.

However, the 'COPC Pine Trees' are baffling and the Romanian professor is still 'missing'. 'Charles off the roof' stays a puzzle, although perhaps he was Squadron Leader Verity. Hopefully he had a soft landing.

Time on our Side

At the end of an outline for the memoir on which he was about to embark in 1946, John Collier summed up the Combined Bomber Offensive:

Final Results
GAF [German Air Force/Luftwaffe] destroyed & invasion made possible

Major Factors
Oil / Transportation – enemy immobilised / Rocket plans disrupted / Over 50 German cities totally destroyed

Cost
Bomber Command – 50,000 killed / 15,000 seriously injured

His first draft ended with an appreciation of the Allies' luck:

The Germans in a last desperate attempt to turn the fortunes of War, had put first priority on to the production of their jet aircraft and rockets, although it was felt that the [Luftwaffe] was a beaten force there nevertheless was a justifiable fear in our higher commands as to whether or not they would be able to develop a serious jet fighter force in time. The development of their underground factories had been watched and studied for many months, but their great depth... rendered them practically invulnerable to any form of bomber attack, although every possible means of attack had been studied. It was fully appreciated that if we ever had to turn our bomber forces to deal with this threat they would have little effect. The only real hope was that we would win the War in time.

Sir Roy Fedden, Special Technical Advisor to the [Ministry of Aircraft Production] in an appreciation 'Time was on our side', shows how really serious the threat was of secret weapons and jet fighters. German scientists had been given a free head in order to produce some war-winner, and their development of aircraft and high-speed flying was fantastic, when considered by [then current] standards. The German factory at Kahla [in Thuringia] alone was capable of producing over one thousand jet aircraft a month, and there were many such factories. Apart from the original flying bomb, the V2 rocket and the jet-propelled aircraft, many other astounding weapons had been perfected, such as anti-aircraft missiles in the form of self-homing flying bombs that were capable of speeds up to 600mph [the small Taifun rocket, developed at Peenemünde, to be fired in batches of thirty, never saw action due to problems with propulsion]. These would have been a serious menace to our bomber formations.

Sir Roy Fedden reports that 'V2 attacks were to be supplemented by long range incendiary rockets fired from bombproof emplacements, and underground rocket guns [V3] with barrels of unprecedented length were being constructed on the invasion coast for bombardment of London'. The latter were the large concrete constructions which we had so religiously bombed without having the slightest idea how they intended to operate, but we had enough sense to realise that their construction must never be completed.

With unlimited slave labour and invulnerable subterranean factories the Germans might well have turned the scales at the last moment, particularly if they had developed atomised explosive, which they had come so near to doing. 'But the Germans failed' [concluded Fedden] 'and the brilliant efforts and tireless labours of countless scientists and technicians were frittered away by misdirection' – and this, in addition to our bomber offensive specially laid on to counter their developments won the day for us by a narrow margin.

An Honourable Mention

A tantalizing document survives in the War Office records in The National Archives, headed 'NEW YEAR HONOURS (V.E.LIST) 1946 – NON-OPERATIONAL COMMANDS'. At No. 118 in the 'Summaries of Recommendations O.B.E' is:

Wing Commander J.D.D.COLLIER (39037) Directorate of Bomber Operations, Air Ministry. Wing Commander Collier has served in this Directorate on Air Staff duties from January 1943, until January 1945, when he was posted to Combined Operations (India). From the time of his appointment to this Directorate he has been largely responsible for the operational aspects of planning and target selection and in this work his extensive operational experience with Bomber Command, allied to his sound judgment have proved of great value. His duties have involved the detailed examination of targets, including the appraisal of their vulnerability to air attack; a close liaison with the United States Air Forces and with the Representations of the other Services in the discussion of, and rendering of advice on, bombing problems, and the question of bombing policy generally. It was largely as a result of this officer's initiative, enthusiasm and drive that the high-level mining technique, which has proved most successful, was evolved and introduced to operations.

In the event, this strong recommendation (made when Collier was in the Far East) seems to have failed. However, perhaps if the precise nature of the targets concerned had been spelled out, his particular case would have received more attention further up the Whitehall chain. Already 'sprayed with gongs', the sure knowledge that many lives had been saved by his personal involvement in planning – especially, perhaps, those of RAF air crew on formerly hazardous mining sorties – was John Collier's real reward for his two years at B Ops 1.

Part III

The Wider World

Chapter Eleven

India and Japan

Combined Ops, Delhi

A BOAC Sunderland flying boat lifted off from Poole Harbour on 8 February 1945 on an epic journey to India. It touched down in French Morocco, Cairo, Iraq and Bahrain, and arrived in Karachi three days later. John Collier was on board, posted from B Ops 1 to the Directorate of Combined Operations HQ, Delhi, as deputy director with the rank of group captain (acting). On 12 February 1945 he continued by BOAC Ensign from Karachi to Delhi.

Collier's immediate superior in Delhi was Brigadier Bernard Fergusson, Director of Combined Operations for South East Asia from 1945–6, who wrote about this experience (and other campaigns) in *The Watery Maze: The Story of Combined Operations*. Fergusson was celebrated for commanding a Chindit brigade deep behind enemy lines in Burma, and equally famed for his monocle: when it broke in the jungle the RAF had organized an air-drop to the Chindits with spares.

In April 1944 Lord Louis Mountbatten had moved the Headquarters of SACSEA [Supreme Allied Command South East Asia] wholesale to Kandy in Ceylon, retaining a smaller staff in New Delhi as Rear HQ. The location of his headquarters, comprising about 10,000 people and well away from the main inland drama of the Burma campaign, is partly explained by the naval man Mountbatten's penchant for amphibious operations.

After General Bill Slim's epic victories on the Indian frontier at Kohima and Imphal, Combined Ops (essentially amphibious, but with air support) were devised to augment 14th Army's advance in the winter dry season of 1944/45.

The long Arakan coast of Burma made the Japanese vulnerable (in theory) to surprise interventions from the sea, although the rough terrain of crocodile-infested mangrove swamps and creeks – 'chaungs' – leading into dense mountain jungle, would make penetration from the coast very difficult. Despite Mountbatten's grand ambitions, in reality Combined Ops in South East Asia had to make do with few resources, and were limited to retaking islands and their airfields as forward supply bases for 14th Army.

However, despite the material restrictions, a succession of daring plans was being hatched. On 23 February 1945 a key planning conference of fifty senior officers, with the 'Supremo' in the chair and all the SACSEA military chiefs present, was held in Calcutta (and which John Collier's Pilot's Log Book suggests he attended). The meeting worked out details of the proposed Combined Ops assault on Rangoon – Operation DRACULA – and a subsequent invasion of Malaya with Operation ROGER, aimed at Phuket, halfway between Rangoon and Singapore.

DRACULA had first been mooted in the summer of 1944 and on 5 August 1944 Mountbatten had flown to London to propose it to Churchill and the chiefs of staff. Though the PM had his own madcap scheme for an attack on Sumatra, the transfer of troops to India for the operation was initially promised, then as the situation in Western Europe remained unresolved, cancelled.

Mountbatten's obsession with DRACULA was such that (before it was put on hold) he wanted to co-opt 14th Army for the amphibious operation. Slim's subsequent land campaign in Burma, beginning in December 1944, in which 14th Army out-thought and doggedly out-fought the Japanese, starkly points up the absurdity of this whim of Mountbatten's.

* * *

Resources for Combined Ops were limited by the Allied concentration on ending the war in Europe, and the American island-hopping thrust across the Pacific towards Japan for which British ships were seconded from the Indian Ocean. There were also fundamental differences between the Allies on strategy in the region that weakened Mountbatten's position at the top planning tables: the American preference was for an overland advance into China from Burma, assisting Chiang Kai Shek against the Japanese, rather than a push south to Singapore.

Mountbatten's plans were limited to the islands off the Arakan coast, and Akyab, with its key port and airfield, was retaken after the Japanese evacuated on New Year's Eve, 1944. An amphibious assault was then launched from Akyab to the mainland on 12 January 1945 by the Indian 25th Division, in a failed attempt to cut off Japanese forces retreating from Arakan. This was followed by a second landing on 21 January which blocked the single track along the coast, but the desperate Japanese cut a new jungle path inland and slipped past the blockade.

Another amphibious force landed on Ramree Island, to the south of Akyab, also on 21 January 1945. The bloody fight for Ramree, in which Japanese who were not killed in battle were eaten by crocodiles in the swamps where they had taken refuge, was still going on when Group Captain John Collier flew to Akyab in early February 1945.

* * *

In the first two months of 1945 Bill Slim put his master plan, Operation EXTENDED CAPITAL, into effect. The Japanese were deceived into thinking that the main crossing of the Irrawaddy and the key battle for Burma would take place in the east. However, Slim was secretly infiltrating an entire corps to the west and south – supplied by air – to the rear of Mandalay and the main Japanese forces. His strategic target of Meiktila was attacked on 1 March and taken after four days of desperate fighting when the last defenders committed suicide. The Japanese withdrew from North and Central Burma after losing Mandalay.

It was an urgent matter to conclude the Burma Campaign before the monsoon began in early May 1945. The 14th Army launched a motorized 'blitzkrieg' south from Meiktila towards Rangoon, in deteriorating weather, and it was now that Mountbatten's amphibious adventure was revived, at Slim's own suggestion, as insurance against the advance getting bogged down.

Operation DRACULA began in late April when a seaborne force of six convoys, together with a formidable naval escort flotilla that included four aircraft carriers and two battleships, sailed from Akyab and Ramree. The amphibious force was limited in size by lack of landing craft, comprising just two brigades of the 26th Indian Division. Twelve bomber squadrons were involved – which must have been, at least in part, John Collier's responsibility – and Rangoon was bombed on the day before the naval force arrived off the coast on 2 May 1945. The landings were preceded by a Gurkha paratroop battalion who dropped on Elephant Point at the mouth of the Rangoon River (only to be accidentally bombed by the RAF).

A pilot flying over the city had earlier spotted a message spelled out in large letters on the roof of the gaol by PoWs: 'JAPS GONE', and when the 26th Indian Division brigades entered Rangoon on 3 May they found that the city had indeed been abandoned by the enemy. The amphibious force had made it to Rangoon four days before the hard-fighting 17th Indian Division, who had advanced rapidly overland from Mandalay but been held up by a desperate last stand by the Japanese north of the capital. The next day the monsoon broke – two weeks early – and all air supply was cancelled for the rainy season.

* * *

There was some reason for 14th Army to feel hard done by after Operation DRACULA. Mountbatten (later, of course, Earl Mountbatten of Burma) had stolen the headlines and got a large measure of the glory with the great prize of Rangoon. Seemingly oblivious of all the blood, toil, tears and sweat expended by the 'Forgotten Army', the Supremo wrote to his wife Edwina: 'I can't tell you how thrilling the race to Rangoon has been...' Later writers have sympathized with Slim and excoriated the self-promoting Mountbatten, but the Supremo was undoubtedly a popular figure with the men (as Churchill well knew), and the endgame in Burma could have been very different if the Japanese had held on: the two-pronged attack on a defended Rangoon could have turned out to have been a strategic masterstroke.

Despite the celebrations at Kandy, there was still a war to be waged. The Andaman and Nicobar islands, with their key airfields, were subsequently retaken; and a few days after the reoccupation of Rangoon, on 9 May 1945, the war in Europe was over.

SACSEA and Combined Ops were emboldened and Operation ROGER was replaced by the more ambitious ZIPPER (intended to be Mountbatten's 'apotheosis as Supreme Commander', according to his official biographer), aimed at the Port Dickson/Port Swettenham area on the west coast of Malaya, about 300 miles from Singapore. It was scheduled for the second half of August, then postponed to 9 September 1945 because of supply problems.

Then on 6 August 1945 the atomic bomb was dropped on Hiroshima, and on the 9th a second bomb destroyed Nagasaki. On 14 August 1945 Japan surrendered unconditionally.

Operation ZIPPER was reconfigured as a peacetime troop movement operation to take back control of Malaya. It went ahead on its own pre-planned D-Day, 9 September 1945, while John Collier was flying home for a month's leave. It involved 300 ships, plus naval escort, 140 landing craft and 65,000 troops. All went well at Port Dickson, but if the Japanese had still been in the field the poorly-reconnoitred Port Swettenham landings, where tanks foundered in soft mud and mangrove swamps, could have been a disaster.

In Singapore on 12 September 1945 Mountbatten, with Bill Slim at his side, received the formal surrender of all the Japanese forces in South East Asia.

Closing the Station

On 24 October 1945 Group Captain John Collier flew from Delhi via Colombo to RAF Kankesanturai – his new posting – where he would be station commander. 'KKS' was a base on the northernmost tip of the island of Ceylon, on the Jaffna Peninsula, from which 160 Squadron, flying Liberators and Lancasters, had been supplying troops in Burma, performing reconnaissance and mine-laying. With the peace, 160 took on a transport role, particularly to the Cocos Islands, far off in the eastern Indian Ocean, a staging post on the air route between India and Australia. Records of 160 Squadron for 1946 at Kankesanturai detail the slow process of demobilization, preparation for the bomber squadron's return to the UK in June 1946, and the closure of the RAF station. Time was mainly spent on training, lectures, sports, etc:

January: The airmen understand the difficulties of repat and demob, and although they have but one ambition – to get back to 'Civvy St' – their moral is high as can be expected under the circumstances.

February: Demob forms are being read out to the airmen by officers i/c billets, who also note any complaints or grouses so that they can be forwarded through the proper channels. It is to be noted, however, that there are few complaints, and the airmen are contented and happy, this being due to the strenuous efforts of the Station Commander Group Captain Collier DSO DFC and Bar, and to the splendid team-work shown by all ranks.

This apparently tranquil state of affairs at KKS was not experienced elsewhere in India, Ceylon and Singapore, where there had been a series of mutinies among RAF conscripts over the issue of delayed demob, and also objecting to formal parades in 'best blue', kit inspections, poor food quality, etc. The first was at Drigh Road, Karachi, in mid-January 1946, and although it was dealt with leniently, pressure from the top brass to set an example led to the contentious court martial of one of its leading lights, Arthur Attwood.

Despite about 50,000 men being willingly and communally involved across the SACSEA area, another scapegoat was found in Singapore. On 13 March 1946 the *Straits Times* reported that an RAF General Court Martial had sentenced Aircraftman Norris Cymbalist, a radar operator at RAF Base HQ, Singapore, to ten years' 'penal servitude and discharge with ignominy' for incitement to mutiny and insubordination.

Public outrage in Britain led John Collier's old friend from B Ops 1, Under Secretary of State for Air John Strachey, to halve the sentence, and finally in November 1947 Cymbalist was released from Wakefield Prison after serving twenty-one months. Attwood, whose RAF friends and supporters in London campaigned more effectively at an early stage, was released much sooner.

In February and March 1946 Collier visited Negombo, a base close to Colombo, where there had been a mutiny/strike on 23 January by men of No.23 Staging Post. He is known to have chaired a Court of Enquiry at some point, and it is most likely to have been to do with the issues raised by the mutinies: essentially the slow pace of demobilization, but also poor administration, lack of sports facilities and entertainments. One source states that a Court of Enquiry meeting in February 1946 found that the mutinies were not directed at officers or the institution of the RAF. Without legal knowledge himself, Collier cast around for help in the ranks and found AC2 Joseph Ede, a trained lawyer, who became a friend and for many years was the Collier family solicitor. (In retirement John Collier retained large quantities of paperwork connected with the Court of Enquiry, but at some point it was all thrown away.)

Further mutinies in Indian air and naval units in February 1946 were worrying for the Attlee government, whose plans for Indian independence gathered speed thereafter.

John Collier, too, contemplated his position in a letter home:

I returned on Sunday after spending a very good week at Kandy. The AOC asked me to stay at his house, and he gave me a good time for three days. I visited one or two tea and coffee plantations. That is the life. They live very well indeed and seem to do a minimum of work. The real old Victorian ideas of a Gentleman's life…

This Station will be closing up shortly – a matter of a few months – I don't know of my future – I am hoping but unlikely to get what I want – we shall see – no good worrying about it. One snag is that from April 1st the new pay code comes into effect, and all the high overseas rates of pay are discontinued – we all go onto English rates of pay – What with going down one rank, losing my command pay and going onto English rates, my income will be exactly half what it was! I shall have to change my ideas a bit! Still it was nice while it lasted…

We had a visit from ACM Slessor, you may remember he was my Group Commander in 5 Gp. He was very nice and I was glad to see him again. He is the third ACM we have had here in five weeks! I don't think that there are many more in the RAF!!

Mountbatten and his South East Asia Command had moved from Kandy to liberated Singapore in September 1945. A British Military Administration (BMA) was installed there that did little to improve a chaotic situation where food shortages combined with disease and lack of essential services. The BMA became a byword for corruption – popularly known as the 'Black Market Administration' – and wartime collaborators and profiteers continued to thrive. This messy state of affairs continued until 1 April 1946 when Singapore became a Crown Colony and a proper civil administration was set up.

John Collier made a brief visit to Singapore in late April 1946 that may have been an occasion, famous in his family, when civil servants were 'sent packing' (and it could be an alternative venue for the Court of Enquiry over which he presided). Perhaps delayed demob was again the contentious issue; and it may be significant that Collier flew there via Negombo.

The return of 160's aircraft, air crew and most other personnel to the UK from Kankesanturai was completed on 23 June 1946, but John Collier faced the prospect of heading in the opposite direction:

Well I know the worst! No home leave & posting further East – Ye Gods am I browned off – Closing the Station has been bad enough but to know I now go further from my family is the limit! I did think, although I did not say anything, that I would get home on leave or a course, but no – I am to be thrown into 'The Wing Commander Pool' for disposal as any W/C – My G/C finishes on the 15th – I don't know what day I leave here but I am getting out as fast as I can – I've had it! …I have asked to go to Japan or Hong Kong, but as everything recently has 'turned against me' I expect it will end up in Malaya or some God damned spot –

John Collier was now in the same state of frustration as the enlisted men waiting for demob a few months earlier. Playing with his pet mongoose Joey helped pass the time, and working on his memoir of his years at the Air Ministry had the benefit of keeping the station commander awake during the hot and steamy tropical afternoons while the rest of the camp snoozed. Finally he was notified of his probable next posting:

Just a rapid line to let you know I am due off for Singapore tomorrow night via Flying Boat – I hope final destination is Japan – will let you know as I go along – Good news, our overseas tour is to be reduced to 2½ years as from October – I have therefore only a year to go.

In July 1946 a Sunderland took him from Koggala, on Ceylon, to Singapore, and in his rough notes for his memoir, John included brief mention of Raffles Hotel, bicycle rickshaws and a programme of official talks in Singapore. He was also put a bit more in the picture:

…My future job is very vague – It seems likely to be O/C the airfield at IWAKUNI which is SW of Hiroshima, the atomised city – …It is by the sea & therefore one can swim, but I hear life there is more than rugged – no amusements, no drink (almost), no women (completely), no accommodation (almost), so I am prepared for the worst –

He wrote home again from on board a ship to Hong Kong: '…it really rather amuses me this wandering around the world with only the verbal instruction – "You are posted to Japan, old boy – get there when you can!"'

Some rough notes on Hong Kong are tantalizing: '…describe cool blonde / tummy trouble & prickly heat / visit to night club…'

A Dakota took him from Hong Kong to Shanghai, then on to Iwakuni, Japan.

After Hiroshima

Following the surrender, a military government had been set up in Japan by the US army under General MacArthur. The British Commonwealth Occupation Force (BCOF) joined in and was responsible for five Western Prefectures, including Hiroshima, and Shikoku Island – with a total population of about 20 million – and was charged with demilitarization and the disposal of munitions. The BCOF's headquarters was at Kure, a former Japanese naval base, while the multi-national air forces, BCAIR, were at Iwakuni and included the RAF's 11 and 17 Squadrons flying Spitfires. Group Captain John Collier wrote home on his arrival on 6 August 1946:

Well here I am at Iwakuni, Japan – my new Station. It is a big place of over 2000 personnel. I am to be Station Cmdr...

It used to be a large Jap naval air station & it had been well bombed & is in a pretty mucky state, but it is now getting into shape a bit – although there is still considerable work to be done – We are near to the sea & have our own yacht club & motor boats.

We are situated on the inland sea – Japan was very pretty to fly over... lots of mountains covered with trees – masses & masses of islands –

Japan of course is well developed in comparison with India & Ceylon & houses are of quite good construction...

We have Jap girls to wait on us & act as bat women – a bit disconcerting at first as they wander in & out whether or not one is adequately clothed – Japs don't worry much when men & women bathe together nude, without any sign of embarrassment.

There will be a lot of work to do here & it will be difficult with a Headquarters on the doorstep – however I like the place, it has great possibilities...

In a further manuscript memoir, written in retirement, to which he gave the title 'In Those Days – a light-hearted look at service life overseas', John Collier described his first night at RAF Iwakuni. Sleep was disrupted around midnight by 'the most unearthly and blood-curdling noises ever heard by man'. He went off to investigate and found a naked, skeletal figure waving his arms and legs wildly but pinned down on a bunk by a very fat flight lieutenant, while a much smaller officer looked on:

As I was in pyjamas and with no apparent authority, I felt it necessary to announce as firmly as possible that I was the new Station Commander, and wanted to know 'What the hell was going on?'

'We are trying to get him to go to bed,' I was informed, 'but he will make this dreadful noise.'

'Well,' I retorted 'I am not surprised, with someone of your weight sitting on him! Get off him immediately!'

The officer did so and as a result the ghastly figure leapt off the bed and stood there naked amongst us, but still continued to howl.

'Who is he?' I enquired of the smaller man.

'He is the camp Senior Medical Officer.'

'And you are?'

'The camp Junior Medical Officer.'

'What is the matter with him?'

'I think he is suffering from the DTs.'

Collier ordered him to be locked up in the guard room, but the junior medical officer pleaded that that would ruin his career. An injection was out of the question; it could be dangerous. In desperation he ordered the large flight lieutenant to hold the raving man's arms behind his back, and ordered the junior medical officer to punch him on the chin. The ineffectual punch only succeeded in hitting his nose, which began to bleed. The flight lieutenant let go of him:

Then suddenly the Senior Medical Officer 'took off' – arms and legs flying, he shot out of the bunk room and was last seen flying as fast as his legs would carry him, quite naked, down the corridor and away out into the black night.

Things were fairly rough in those days, but I did not fancy my Station Medical Officer as a delirium tremens case, so immediate suspension and first boat home was the obvious solution...

As well as being the main BCAIR base, Iwakuni was the Royal Air Force HQ for Japan, under Air Commodore Cyril 'Boy' Bouchier, and as well as its Spitfire squadrons housed a variety of units: a hospital, an RAF transport squadron, a New Zealand fighter squadron, an Australian airfield construction unit, an Indian signals unit, a Transit unit and an Air Sea Rescue Wing. The base administration – and Group Captain Collier – therefore had a lot on their plate.

An excessive number of disciplinary matters were inherited from his predecessor, and the first thing he did was cancel all but the most serious cases. He circulated the Admin that no further minor charges were to be issued, with everything to be dealt with on the spot by extra duties. The over-zealous military police were ordered to confine their activities to outside the camp.

Having the RAF 'top brass' for Japan on site was 'really a pain… and to the average airman only an additional irritant, and more and more saluting'. Most of the men were conscripts, itching to go home and increasingly reluctant to go through the formal motions of service life.

The 'No Fraternisation' rule was often breached, and the Australians on the base did things entirely their own way and were running a lucrative import business on the side.

The only real danger was from the geology of Japan. In the middle of one night 'quite a healthy quake' set the buildings swaying, roads cracking and 'as all the buildings on the large camp, including the hospital, were of wood, fire was a very real risk'. Collier got to the camp electricity substation, only to find that the Japanese night staff had fled. Summoning his courage, and totally ignorant of the plant, he pulled a number of large and heavy switches and plunged the camp into darkness and safety.

Another burden was VIP visits. Collier described the chaos attending the arrival of Lord Tedder, Chief of the Air Staff, and his wife, at Iwakuni. Normally the station commander would do the honours of meeting the plane, but AC Bouchier 'wanted all the glory for himself':

The 'great day' arrived and just before midday I was startled to receive an urgent message from air traffic control that the Air Chief's aircraft, a flying boat coming in from Hong Kong, was actually in circuit and about to land – a further message from the slipway was to the effect that there was no officer there to meet the incoming party. Ye Gods – where was the AOC?

He dashed off down the single-track road through paddyfields in his battered Jeep and got to the slipway just in time to greet Tedder, who preferred not to wait for Bouchier. So Collier and the Air Chief headed back up the narrow road in the old Jeep. Coming towards them was a dust cloud, which heralded the AOC's delayed convoy. They pulled off onto some hard ground as the military police outriders passed and the large, brightly-polished official cars drew level:

I enquired from Tedder whether he would wish to now join up with the AOC and party – A firm negative was the reply... So there it was! The AOC's car could not turn about, so it was necessary for them to proceed right down to the slipway... I proceeded in the opposite direction with my passenger...

Tedder then joined the men for lunch in the canteen, chatting freely and at length, and letting the unhappy AOC stew.

* * *

There were few opportunities to take a break from duties, but John and his New Zealand counterpart Squadron Leader 'Willy' de Willmoff decided to see what lay beyond their immediate neighbourhood (which was less than 20 miles from devastated Hiroshima). They were advised not to travel in remote areas, where there might still be animosity towards the Allies, and to inform the police of their movements. In fact, the local chief of police insisted on accompanying them in case of trouble, and endured Willy's hair-raising night-time driving through hill country up to the North Coast. The next morning the relieved policeman was found swimming in the hot springs, naked but for his peaked cap. The return journey by day showed them just how perilous the mountain roads were.

Collier wrote home about another expedition in October:

Your letter of the 29th arrived today – Quite quick – but quite a lot of mail has been lost recently due to three air crashes on the route & maybe my letters have been lost...

We have had a stream of 'VIP' visitors – Admirals, Generals, five MPs, Air Marshals, Brigadiers, Captains RN etc etc – they all seem to want to look around the airfield and I always have to do it – They say they have come to study conditions & get complaints – so they get a pretty good earful from me as there are a number of important things which have been thoroughly muddled – We are supplied for food amenities etc by the Army & they have different standards, way below ours!

Due to the visitors etc I have not got away at all for about a month & I & one of the Squadron Commanders decided at very short notice to clear right off the station – We just bundled guns, beer, cans of food, blankets etc in the back of his car... & just drove around the British area of Japan for three days – We covered 400 miles of the roughest & remotest parts of Japan, but some of the most lovely scenery you can imagine... But the outstanding points were the awful roads, main roads are little better than cart tracks, the cultivation of every inch of ground, the excellent little houses of even the poorest country peasant – built of light timber & paper mostly with a good glazed tile roof – they are very picturesque against the bright green of the paddy fields – There were telephones & electricity almost everywhere – the Japs have modernised in the most amazing way – the workmanship is terrible & shoddy & is continually breaking down, but mostly it works – The Jap Police are the 'big cheeses' – the population fairly toe the line to them – The Police all look useless but they are quite tough actually – much bowing & scraping!!

...The population is generally 'friendly'... When we had a puncture we found that they were generally helpful & certainly got us out of an awkward position as we lacked a vital tool!

...We stayed each night in a Jap hotel – We provided our own food & I cooked it on a Jap charcoal fire – We slept on proper Jap mattress beds on the floor – very warm & comfortable – We were served for our meals – when I had cooked it! – by waiting girls as usual in their best kimonos – the girls then sing & dance Jap songs for you afterwards – not bad but the singing is terrible, one long rasping noise – A dance I did, plus towel on head, plus sword etc seemed to give considerable amusement to the whole hotel staff who insisted on a repeat!! The hot Saki drink helped a bit.

Collier had an operation to remove his appendix in mid-March 1947, and wrote a letter home from hospital on 5 April. By this time British forces were beginning to withdraw from Japan, leaving the Australians in charge of the BCOF zone for the next five years, and in May 1947 he returned home on the troopship *Dilwara*.

John Collier had been away for over two years in the Far East, but his RAF Service Record shows that he was allowed just four days' leave on his return. His son Mark remembers the strange sensation when 'this large brown man in sandals' arrived at their front door...

Chapter Twelve

Flying Home

The Jet Age

After about five months in a Personnel Holding Unit, Wing Commander John Collier was posted to the RAF Staff College at Bracknell on 20 October 1947, where he was an instructor for the following three years.

His RAF service for the next decade would be largely spent in the United Kingdom and Western Europe, and avoided direct involvement in the major events of the first years of the Cold War: the Berlin Airlift and the Korean War. In wartime Collier's promotion had been remarkably rapid, but his relative youth – he was 30 years old when he came home from Japan – acted as something of a brake on progress, as it did for most officers of his generation in the peacetime service. However, he was clearly enjoying the opportunity to fly once more. A Confidential Report, covering the period January 1947 to 1 February 1948, listed the types of aeroplanes flown – Proctor, Harvard, Argus, Liberator, Auster, Corsair, Dakota, Anson – and flying time (a total of 1,358 hours since he had entered the RAF in 1936). He stated his Preference for Next Employment as 'Flying'.

While he was away in the Far East, Beth had settled in Portsmouth and their third son Peter Mortimer Collier was born there in 1948. It was thus convenient that from January 1950 John Collier was appointed Wing Commander Admin, RAF Thorney Island, an airfield sited between Chichester and Portsmouth that was used for flying training. He is said to have kept the somewhat over-eager military police off the base (as he had done at RAF Iwakuni) while in charge at Thorney, and also set up a pig farm.

A new age of aviation had begun at the very end of the war, with the introduction of the first jet planes in Britain and Germany, and John Collier now had to learn to fly a quite different machine. His Pilot's Log for 15

February 1950 has 'First flight in Meteor (jet) as 2nd pilot/pupil: dual instruction local'; then on 5 May 1950 'first solo flight in Meteor'.

From January 1953 he followed a one-year course at various advanced flying schools, training initially in a Vickers Varsity, then the Meteor VII, an advanced training version of the jet fighter. In an intensive period from May to December 1953 he recorded flights as either pilot or 2nd pilot in Vampire fighters, Valettas, the Canberra jet bomber (introduced in 1951), Lincolns and Hastings.

On 8 January 1954, after eighteen years in the RAF, he obtained a Certificate of Qualification as first pilot: 'COLLIER Rank: Wg Cdr (iii) Certified that the above named has qualified as a pilot (day) \ & night / on Vampire, Meteor landplanes / Canberra. Unit RAF Flying College.'

Having mastered all these new machines, all his subsequent RAF postings were – perhaps predictably – staff jobs. From April 1954 Collier was at Headquarters, Bomber Command, in High Wycombe, then from June 1955 he was appointed Deputy Director of Operations (Reconnaissance), Air Ministry, London, again as an acting group captain.

While he was back in Whitehall the Suez Crisis blew up after Israel (with British and French collusion) attacked Egypt on 29 October 1956. Nasser had nationalized the Suez Canal on 26 July and various military options had been discussed in London and Paris over the next three months, during which time the canal continued to function normally.

When Egypt refused to evacuate the Canal Zone after an ultimatum on 30 October, Operation MUSKETEER began the following day with RAF jets bombing Egyptian airfields and destroying most of the Soviet-supplied air force on the ground. On 5 November paratroopers landed near Port Said, followed on the 6th by marines, and on the 7th by a cease-fire. Diplomatic and financial pressure by the US, sabre-rattling by the USSR, censure at the UN and public outcry in Britain forced a humiliating withdrawal that cost Prime Minister Anthony Eden his job. Labour leader Hugh Gaitskell said in the Commons that this was 'an act of disastrous folly whose tragic consequences we shall regret for years'.

The first action of this ill-starred adventure was a photo reconnaissance by Canberra jet bombers based on Cyprus, quickly followed by the raids. This must have involved John Collier in his reconnaissance role, but he made no mention of it in any of his writings. It was not something to dwell on. His son Mark remembers him having to stay overnight at the Air Ministry, sleeping on a camp bed, and 'not being at all happy' with the whole affair.

It was probably quite a relief to spend a month at 4 Flying Training School, Worksop, in early 1957.

Norway and NATO

The awkwardness of Suez was followed by a congenial posting to Norway, from March 1957, as Assistant Chief of Staff, Allied Air Forces Northern Europe. Collier is said to have been offered a posting in the United States, which seems to have been to do with rocketry, and would probably have involved a rise in rank to air commodore. He was, however, also contemplating retirement from the RAF, and Beth was opposed to a move to America. He was asked to think about the US posting while in Norway.

AFNORTH's headquarters was at Kolsas, near Oslo, and sited partly inside a mountain. Its sphere included Scandinavia and Germany north of the Elbe. The C-in-C was usually a British admiral or general, the chief of staff usually a German vice-admiral, and the Air Force Commander Northern Europe was always a USAAF lieutenant general.

Beth and their two youngest sons, Richard and Peter, came to live in Oslo, where she took lessons in Norwegian at the university. It was perhaps their happiest time as a service family. A visiting niece, Maureen Henderson, wrote home that: 'Uncle John is mad about Norway and does not want to come back to England at all.' She reported cocktail parties, boating expeditions, seeing the sights in Oslo and a trek to a remote mountain hut.

However, this was a Cold War idyll. While at Kolsas Collier completed a NATO Senior Officers Special Weapons Course in 1958 that was something to do with nuclear weapons and which prompted him to write a letter home to his widowed mother full of anxieties about their potential for wreaking mass destruction. Britain had tested its first hydrogen bomb at Christmas Island in the Pacific in May 1957, and the first US-engineered Thor intercontinental ballistic missiles were supplied to Britain in September 1958. A Defence White Paper presented by none other than Duncan Sandys in April 1957 had signalled a major shift for the RAF from an aircraft to a missile force.

In Norway John and Beth (whose instincts had been strongly pacifist for some time) were still debating whether to take up the offer of a staff job in the USA. Perhaps this close encounter with the ultimate deterrent at the Special Weapons School – and Beth's convictions – finally brought John to the critical decision to leave the service in the winter of 1958–9 after twenty-two years.

His Record of Service concludes: '3/1/59 – 1 Personnel Holding Unit/ Record Office / Supernumerary pending terminal leave (Disemb 5/1/59). / 9/3/59 – Placed on the Retired List retaining the rank of Group Captain'.

John was tempted to remain in Norway after leaving the Royal Air Force, and apparently Fred Olsen Lines offered him a directorship, but instead the Colliers came home. He pondered various options, and missed out on a few promising business ventures, even contemplating taking on the old family home in Devon, Foxhams, using his gratuity from the RAF, with a plan to deal in agricultural machinery from there. However, finally he returned to his pre-war civilian role, working for a land and estate agency in Ringwood, Hampshire. He and Beth settled nearby at Moortown, then moved to Ford Cottage, Blashford. John Collier retired again in 1981 and subsequently devoted much of his time to charitable work for Barnardo's, for which he received a Distinguished Voluntary Service Award in 1996.

Forty Years On

After decades spent in the shadow of the more glamorous Spitfires and Hurricanes of Fighter Command, interest in Bomber Command began to revive in the early 1980s, stimulated by the growing campaign for public recognition of the 'Bomber Boys'. A proposal for a statue honouring Sir Arthur Harris after his death in April 1984 inevitably rekindled public argument over the morality of area bombing, and in particular the fire-bombing of Dresden in 1945. The statue was unveiled in 1992 outside the RAF church St Clement Danes, but had to be guarded for some months to prevent attempts to damage or deface it.

The death of his bugbear Harris seems to have stimulated John Collier's old boss in B Ops 1, Sydney Bufton, who had retired in 1961 with the rank of air vice-marshal, to plan a book about the Air Ministry's part in planning the Combined Bomber Offensive. This was partly to counteract the general tendency, as he saw it, to see everything bombing-related in the war as purely the work of Harris and Bomber Command.

While researching his landmark book *Bomber Command* Max Hastings consulted Bufton, and their correspondence is now preserved in the Churchill Archive in Cambridge. This reveals how strongly Bufton felt that Harris had obstructed the progress of the air campaign with his 'private war of city-bashing', but at the same time he took issue with Hastings' suggestion that Harris could have been sacked; who else, he argued, was there?

Bufton also began a correspondence with John Collier, perhaps needing moral support for his own book project as well as hoping to tap the memories of a former close collaborator. His first, sent from 1 Castle Keep, Reigate, is dated 2 July 1984:

Dear Joe,

...we must get together some time to discuss writing a bit of history...I am planning to write up the achievements of Bomber Ops; I've already written reams about it, but unfortunately for other people's books!

Some of the items which should be covered are:- Incendiary scheme; Hooded flares; massed use of flares; marker bomb; Pathfinder Force; emergency landing grounds; high-level mining; Oboe 'box' technique for canals, Caen break-out etc; our joint plans for bombing surveys, foiled by Winston; and bombing policies generally. It's a big task and any little tit-bits and reminiscences... would be gratefully received.

I've got a rough thumb-nail account of high-level mining and your long wait at Bomber Command to see Bert Harris, but any extras would be welcome and especially what Bert said...

I shall never forget the long sessions in my office when we all sat around tearing the problem to pieces and then finally re-assembling the bits in the form of an answer for 10.00 hrs tomorrow.

…We are all in reasonably good shape and Sue joins me in sending you and Elizabeth our warmest good wishes and the hope that we can meet up and have a thrash over old times in the not-too-distant future.

Yours sincerely

Syd Bufton

John Collier replied on 9 July 1984, from Ford Cottage, Blashford, Hampshire:

Dear Syd

…I am glad to hear that you are really thinking of writing about Bomber Ops, for it does seem right that some other view than only Bomber Command should be heard – Strange, but I still feel quite strongly about the matter – What a pity it is that Arthur [Morley] is no longer with us, for he could really have helped, particularly if he could have produced the files that I understand he dumped at the bottom of his well!

Personally I was hoping that you would cover broad policy matters and items that were seen as effecting the air war – there were a number of special occasions well worth recording. I would be happy to help. I think perhaps it best if I just jot down any item which, from my point of view, proved of great interest at the time…

Yours ever, Joe C

Bufton replied by return of post, outlining the concept of a book that sounds very like John Collier's memoir of forty years earlier:

Dear Joe,

…I have roughed out some sort of pattern for a book on the Combined Bomber Offensive. The headings below give you some idea; each will be a thumb-nail sketch of events, more or less complete in itself, and not necessarily all in chronological order. Hopefully, they will all blend, in the end, into a comprehensible pattern.

Target Finding Force idea.

Hooded flares.

Flare Scheme.
Renault Factory attack (using flare scheme).
Incendiary Technique.
Marker Bomb (Morley; Essen raid; Boscombe Down trials).
Directives (Strategic ones; 14th Feb '42 Incendiary + T.F.F.).
Americans arrive (Berliner; Hughes; fighter escort essential).
CBO Plan (Cabell; Economic Analysts; Oliver Lawrence etc).
USAF raids; Schweinfurt etc.
Mohne Dam; Barnes Wallis; Upkeep.
V-Weapons; discovery; attack on.
Pre-invasion bombing plans; Zucherman [*sic*].
Oil Offensive (should have started 3 months earlier).
Strategic Bombing Survey(s).

In addition we should weave in high-level mining; the 'Oboe-Box' method of destroying the canal banks with 1000lbrs, and the German army positions around Caen, and so on. The 1000lb craters were I believe 50ft in diameter and when drawn to scale on a sheet of Perspex by Dr Cunningham with a Gaussian distribution [a bell-shaped graph of probability, falling away from a central peak] of 150 Lancs x 14 1000lbrs = 2100 craters it could be demonstrated by throwing the sheet onto the map that the banks could be breached every time. Bert Harris bought it.

Re the oil offensive, they were down to 5% of aviation fuel by September '44, then the weather folded October – December; if we had started on oil in March instead of July (thanks to Zucherman [*sic*]) the war could have been over in 1944 or Jan 45.

Anyway Joe, any ideas you have would be more than welcome. Could you also please refresh my memory on your dates in B. Ops and your prior time in Bomber Command.

…with all best wishes
Syd Bufton

Collier replied to Bufton on 6 October 1984:

Dear Syd,

I have both your letters of last July before me, and much to my shame they have remained unanswered – I have always been waiting a suitable 'break' or quiet period, but I now believe that such conditions do not exist, and now Elizabeth and I are to go off to Canada in early November. I think that perhaps an 'interim' reply, together with apologies may be the answer for the moment.

As far as I was concerned, my two years at the Air Ministry is recalled by me as being a form of 'battle' with Headquarters Bomber Command to achieve acceptance by them of important proposals for the progression of the war in the air. Their role appeared to be to resist any proposals or suggestions originating from the Air Ministry. It is to me little wonder that the general public believed and still do that Bomber Command entirely conducted the 'air offensive', and it was the Air Ministry who were the 'stumbling block'. My earnest hope is that your book will, in some way, rectify such an illusion.

I found that if I was able to get as far as an interview with Bert Harris, the 'day was won' – he would listen and finally agree – what drove me mad was getting past the block of Staff Officers on the way to him – [AVM] Robert Saundby [Deputy Commander-in-Chief Bomber Command] being my particular problem – he had a delight in his sarcasm – On one occasion I had your instructions to get Bert Harris's agreement, and had to insist that Saundby took the Air Ministry Plan out of his 'bottom boot draw[er]' in his desk, where he had placed it without reading it, with the words 'ah yes! very interesting, very interesting!'

I do not think I can add to your detailed knowledge of anything to do with Path Finder Force, various trials of weapons, and policy decisions over Directives, for I was on the bottom rung of the ladder, but the delays in convincing Bomber Command to take action were often expensive, in my opinion, to the war effort. Even tactical decisions took far too long to action – there was always this reluctance to do anything that was outside Bomber Command's (self-appointed?) role of mass destruction of the German war effort. There was even a reluctance to accept any tactical information (from Americans or elsewhere) which could be of considerable importance.

Some examples:-

You mention the High level Mining. From my personal knowledge this proposal was resisted by Bomber Command and the Navy for many months – I put the idea at a meeting at the Air Ministry in the summer of 1943, but was told particularly by a Naval representative that it was not technically acceptable (in spite of a contrary opinion by the Admiralty Mines Dept). Very many months later, after an impassioned plea by an officer from my old Squadron, who was very concerned about the heavy losses in mining, I was able to arrange direct with B Ops 1 Bomber Command (Wg Cdr Smales) who had been in the same Squadron as myself, to undertake trials to test practicability – he came back with a positive answer, and managed to introduce the technique to the Command.

There were on occasion excellent tactical targets for Bomber Command, but the delays normally meant that the targets dispersed – I well remember some 40 troop trains at a marshalling yard in South France, gathered together because of a blocked Modane Tunnel into Italy – they sat there for days, and when [the yards were] eventually bombed had dispersed.

Bomber Command, of course, needed to resist outside calls that could lead to a weakening of the communal effort, and that was understandable, but their attitude, I considered, was carried to extreme – again Bert publically declaring that the only way to help the Invasion [of France] was to simultaneously bomb Berlin!

I well remember taking the first photos of the V2 down to Bomber Command, and was informed I think by Bert himself that the 'Air Ministry were easily fooled', and that it was probably a dummy laid out to frighten us into diversionary attacks. To be fair to Bomber Command that was also the opinion of one or two of the experts on the so-called Duncan Sandys Committee which I attended as Air Ministry representative – fortunately Colonel Post, who seemed to be specially detailed to deal with the problem, did not agree, nor did Bomber Operations, Air Ministry!

A phase of the war which was of great interest to me was before the 'battle of the bulge'. You may recall the [Schwammenauel] Dam – this had been 'mined' by the Germans with the intention of flooding the approaches around [Cologne] – Barnes Wallis was marvellous over this and took me to the British Museum? [British Library] on a Sunday to look up the German records of the construction of the Dam, which were in detail there in a technical book (in German). In this book it actually said (as I remember) that the dam was built as part of the defences of that area. You will remember that Arthur Morley was sent to Paris to explain the implications of this to Tedder, and at the 11th hour... the whole American offensive around [Cologne] was called off, and additional divisions brought up from Cherbourg, which played such a decisive part in the battle of the bulge. Little of this matter has ever come to light, to the best of my belief, but the whole course of the war was effected.

Another aspect of Bomber Ops which I found very interesting was the role with SOE. We used to hold regular meetings in B Ops 1 with representatives of Ministry of Economic Warfare and SOE to try and provide suitable targets for SOE to link with the general Bomber Offensive. This tied in with targets selected for attack by [617 Squadron] in France and I used to fly up to discuss practicability of these with Cheshire, so that when they were presented to Bomber Command they would not be ruled out – it seemed to work!

I imagine that the problem you face is 'where to start and where to finish', or given enough time volumes could be written – but I do think the role of the Air Staff should be better understood by the public, and my hope is that you will achieve this...

I actually was in B Ops for only two years, from February 43 to February 45, but it was to me an unforgettable experience.

...Yours Joe C

A brief note to Syd Bufton followed on 20 May 1985:

Dear Syd,

I feel that I should have written long ago, to follow up the ideas put forward in your letters of July last. I think that I can help best by having the 'stimulation' of a discussion together to recall 'old times' in Bomber Ops…

Yours Joe C

In this letter Collier reiterated his account of the difficulties of getting his idea for high-level mining accepted; a copy of his June 1943 paper was enclosed [see Appendix]. Syd Bufton replied a week later:

Dear Joe,

It was most interesting to get your ideas on high-level mining. I am not clear why the Admiralty ruled the idea 'out of court' other than possibly from habit! The whole idea was a natural and it was scandalous that there was so much opposition and so much delay.

The use of overlays and visual demonstration as a means of making people see the light was notable. The same principle won the day for the use of the 'Oboe box' and 1000lbrs for the Dortmund-Ems & Mitteland [*sic*] Canals and the concentrated German defence positions around Caen. I went down to 22 Army Group Headquarters at Portsmouth and convinced Freddie de Guingand with a War Office defence layout and one of our overlays with little or no trouble at all.

Bomber Ops made tremendous contributions to Bomber Command's success, eg:-

a) the incendiary attack technique

b) the Pathfinder Force

c) the hooded flare and massed use of flares (all above pre-Bert Harris)

d) high-level mining technique

e) the Oboe-box high density attack for specific targets like canal banks and ground defence concentrations

f) probably a lot more, one way and another I had hoped to have drafted a chapter or two to discuss with you before this but other things have intervened. However I think your idea of a discussion to recall old times would be the best way of getting started…

Yours ever, Syd

Sadly it seems that John Collier and Syd Bufton never did manage to get together to talk over old times in B Ops 1, and the projected book was never completed beyond a wide-ranging synopsis and a first chapter. The manuscript that Air Vice-Marshal Bufton left behind when he died in 1993 covers just the creation of the Pathfinder Force, the achievement of which he was most proud and for which he remains celebrated today. The story of his career, *Forming the Pathfinders* by Hugh Melinksy, was published in 2010.

In about 1990 Bufton was interviewed on tape by a fellow RAF veteran Anthony Furse (author of a biography of Sir Wilfred Freeman), and the transcripts of this uninhibited conversation are preserved at the Churchill Archive.

Bufton again railed against Harris, who he described as 'a sort of pompous, great sort of Duke of Wellington chap and he'd go down and say what are the targets, what's the weather, what's this and then he'd say Hamburg or Nuremburg and then he would walk out and leave it to the staff to work out the details…' In the first draft for his own memoir, John Collier described Harris selecting

…without discussion, walking up to a large map on the wall and pointing and barking out the name of the target for that night. His Staff who had failed to see exactly where he had pointed or clearly hear what he had said were left with a quandary as to whether it was Friedrichshaven or Frankfurt, but were much too frightened to ask him what he had said.

Bufton listed some of the achievements of B Ops, in the process somewhat condensing the saga of John Collier's attempt to have high-level mining adopted:

…we did various other major things like mining. The Admiralty wanted us to mine all the submarine bases and so on… and they insisted on doing it at 500 feet and the place was stuffed with flak ships and

our losses on mining were 5%... Joe Collier, one of my operational
Wing Commanders, started working on this and trying to persuade
the Admiralty, the liaison officer of Bomber Command, to go for high
level mining, so that by dropping the mines from 10,000 feet you got
just as good or better result... after a hell of a lot of argument with
de Mowbray, the naval liaison officer agreed and they dropped the
casualties [to] a tenth. It went down from 5% to half a per cent.

All the best ideas, Bufton concluded, came from B Ops, not Harris's own
staff 'because they were afraid'. The monument to 'Bomber' Harris at St
Clement Danes was not yet erected when the interview was conducted, but
Bufton sensed that that would be the end of the story: 'Once you get a statue
there you're never ever going to move it.'

The Old Crowd

'Memories in time fade, but some characters remain in one's mind even
many years later...', wrote John Collier, many years after the war. It was a
melancholy reflection: by 1945 he was the 'great survivor' of 83 Squadron's
'old crowd', and when he went to a reunion at RAF Scampton in later life he
found only three or four faces that he recognized.

For a while in 1943 and 1944 John shared this distinction with Guy
Gibson, until Guy grew restless with his role as the peripatetic war hero,
raising morale on both sides of the Atlantic, and fatally engineered his
return to front-line operations. When he wrote *Enemy Coast Ahead*, Gibson
tempted fate when he recalled that very first anticlimactic sortie to find the
Admiral Scheer on the day war broke out. He had straggled home late and
reported his arrival at Scampton:

The first thing I saw when I went into the Mess was a look of surprise
on the boys' faces as they drank their cans of beer. 'We thought you had
been shot down,' they said. 'A wireless operator in Z Zebra saw you go
down vertically into the sea. What happened?' I told them I didn't know
what the hell they were talking about and went to bed. Looking back
it is funny to think that out of all those boys there, with one exception

[that is, John Collier], I was the only one who never was to go vertically down towards the sea or the land.

In March 1941, having recovered from his crash, Collier moved on from 83 Squadron to 44 Squadron, but in years to come his greatest affections remained with this his first operational unit and the 'old crowd' of young men in 83 with whom he had trained, partied and flown through flak and searchlights and foul weather. Many years later his nostalgia and emotion were palpable when recalling:

...the wonderful comradeship among men who had been together for a considerable time, years, and then laughs, the moments of tension, the dangers – lightly dealt with – and the partings, so often for ever – The ground crew... men who really gave you the support and encouragement needed, who really did their very best for you – and even flew, some of them, as airgunners...

One just remembers some mixed highlights... Harrison getting married in the morning, and missing that night... I had lent him my car, and we had tied flowers to it for the wedding – I felt bad taking the flowers off the next morning... Jackie Withers asleep in the cook's chair – he did not bother to go to bed after a night raid, he just slept by the kitchen range! Tony Bridgman and his whisky – there were objections when he had whisky out of the bottle on the breakfast table, so he had it out of the teapot to oblige... Sam Threapleton and his damn budgies which he kept in a cage in his office – he got so upset when we put a cat in the cage (having taken out the budgies). Guy Gibson and his devotion to Tony Bridgman... he had reason to admire that personality who seemed to 'have the edge on us all' – certainly all the airmen in his Flight thought the world of him too... The pair of Australians, Rossie and Mulligan, who went everywhere together – they certainly put life into the Squadron, and gave us no end of laughs... they even got shot down together on the same night, by Dortmund-Ems. Ross nearly fell blazing into our aircraft when he was shot down – Mull now lives in Australia, having survived, thank goodness... My best man at my wedding, Pitcairn Hill, if ever there was a fine man, there was he... a sturdy Scot, the kindest of dearest of fellows, could have had his 'cap' for Scotland, I am sure... he came to see me in hospital just after winning his DSO, and shortly after he went 'missing' at Dunkirk, bombing the barges... Probably he was too devoted to duty to know when he should give in... for myself, I would stand the Hampden almost on its nose and dive furiously towards the earth, when I thought that the anti-aircraft had the measure of me – a bit nerve-racking for the rest of the aircrew, but an effective measure of evasion to which I consider I owe my life on more than one occasion.

There is no doubt in my mind that the early days of the war were the only ones when there was an opportunity for adventure without risk. One was completely confident that one would survive anything, and it makes me shudder to look back and realise just how badly we were briefed and how haphazard our approach, but what was lost on these counts was made up by a certain dash and individuality, difficult to emulate later in the war when the dangers were greater and the hand of authority heavier.

Anyway, the moments to remember of the early days surely were the laughs together over bacon and eggs, in the early mornings after the sortie...

Obituaries for Joe

Beth Collier died in 1998 and John Collier in 2000. Press obituaries contained the inevitable errors and omissions, but nevertheless gave a strong impression of a remarkable warrior. The first appeared in *The Times*, 21 November 2000:

GROUP CAPTAIN 'JOE' COLLIER

Bomber pilot and planner of high-precision air operations

AFTER flying 63 missions with Bomber Command, during which he won the DSO and two DFCs in some of the desperate early raids on Germany, in late 1942 'Joe' Collier (as he was known throughout the RAF) joined a select band at the Air Ministry whose job it was to plan precision operations. This brought him into contact with the personalities associated with the most famous of all precision bombing squadrons, No.617 of dambusting fame.

Collier became a close friend of those celebrated VCs Guy Gibson and Leonard Cheshire. He also frequently liaised with Barnes Wallis, the apostle of precision bombing and the creator of some of Bomber Command's most effective weapons: the 'bouncing bomb' which broke the Moehne Dam; the 12,000lb 'Tallboy' which caused severe delays to V2 production at Peenemünde and wrecked the V3 programme at Mimoyecques before its giant guns could be fired at London; and the 22,000lb 'Grand Slam', the heaviest bomb ever to be used operationally by the RAF. As a selector of targets for 617 Squadron, Collier was often involved in the intensive technical discussions between its commanders, Wallis and 5 Group's scientifically minded AOC Sir Ralph Cochrane, on the most effective ways of deploying Wallis's remarkable creations.

John David Drought Collier was born in Plymouth in the second year of the First World War. He was educated at St Petroc's School, Bude, and Tetton Hall, Staffordshire, after which he went into land agency, serving a pupillage of two years on Lord Leigh's estate. He saw earlier than most young men of his generation that war with Hitler's Germany was inevitable, and in 1936 joined the RAF and was commissioned in Bomber Command.

In 1937 he was posted to 83 Squadron, flying Hampdens. Soon after the outbreak of war he took part with No 83 in some of the early 'armed reconnaissance' missions in search of German shipping in the North Sea. (At this stage in the war, with Neville Chamberlain Prime Minister, the RAF was not allowed to bomb Germany itself, for fear of damaging private property.)

After the fall of France the squadron was deployed in bombing targets on land and Collier won his first DFC for an attack on an oil refinery at Bordeaux in August 1940. In 1941 he was posted to 44 Squadron, also flying Hampdens, and was awarded a Bar to his DFC later that year.

In December 1941 he was given command of 420 Squadron, RCAF, another Hampden unit. Then with the Hampden by that stage becoming rapidly obsolescent, with its short range, low service ceiling and small bombload, it was gratifying, in March 1942, to be posted in command of 97 Squadron, operating the newly-introduced four-engined Lancaster.

No 97 was able to undertake much more ambitious operations, flying far more deeply into Germany than any of the Hampden squadrons with which Collier had served. One of his early missions was as part of the RAF's first thousand-bomber raid, against Cologne on the night of May 30, 1942, which signalled to the German authorities the growing might of Bomber Command. Subsequent raids he led were against Bremen and Hamburg, during which he was mentioned in dispatches. He was awarded the DSO after his last raid, that on the German diesel engine plant at Augsburg in August 1942.

By this time the Air Ministry was looking for an experienced bomber officer to join its small team of specialist mission planners. One of the names on the ministry's list was that of Guy Gibson, whom Collier had known well since the early days of the war.

But Gibson wanted to keep on flying (he was to win the VC in May 1943 on the Ruhr dams raid, before being killed the following year over Holland) while Collier was keen to be at the centre of planning operations. He was to remain at the Air Ministry for the remainder of the war, planning SOE missions as well as bombing raids.

In November 1945 he was posted to Ceylon to command the air station at Kankesanturai, from where he went on to Japan in the following year to command the RAF unit at Iwakuni. Among his subsequent appointments were a period instructing at the staff college and a spell at Air Staff HQ Bomber Command. His final posting, in 1957, was as Assistant Chief of Staff at the Nato air headquarters in Norway, based at Kolsas.

Collier retired in 1959 and went back to his old profession, land and estate agency, working with a well-established firm in the New Forest area. He was also active with Barnardo's and received a Distinguished Voluntary Service Award in 1996.

His wife, Elizabeth, predeceased him, but he is survived by three sons.

Group Captain John 'Joe' Collier, DSO, DFC and Bar, wartime bomber pilot, was born on November 10, 1916. He died on November 9, aged 83.

An obituary was published by the *Daily Telegraph* on 22 November 2000:

Group Captain J D D 'Joe' Collier

Bomber pilot who completed 63 perilous sorties on German-occupied Europe and planned the Dambusters raid

GROUP CAPTAIN J D D 'JOE' COLLIER, who has died aged 83, took part as a bomber pilot in no less than 63 attacks on heavily defended targets in Germany and occupied Europe, and in 1943 used his experience to help prepare the celebrated 'Dambusters' raid.

In 1940, as RAF Fighter Command fought the Battle of Britain, Collier was a flight lieutenant in 83 Squadron, flying Handley Page twin-engined Hampdens, and at the forefront of Bomber Command's attacks on such essential enemy communications as the Dortmund Ems canal, on which materials for the invasion of Britain were being conveyed to the coast.

A particularly hazardous operation took place on the night of August 12–13, when Collier led three Hampdens in a diversionary attack on Münster, while other members of 83 Squadron, under Roderick 'Babe' Learoyd, attacked an aqueduct.

Learoyd was awarded the VC after flying through intense flak at very low level to reach his target. Collier's supporting role, however, was hardly less perilous. Although his Hampden was hit again and again, his navigator wounded, and his rear gunner forced to jump for it, he pressed home his attack until Learoyd had completed his work. It required all his skill to coax his badly damaged aircraft home.

In the same period Collier led a low-level attack on an oil refinery at Bordeaux, for which he was awarded the first of his two DFCs. Despite intense fire from local defences, Collier managed to set the tanks ablaze, so that the enemy gun positions were also enveloped in flames.

He took part in another raid on September 15–16 1940, at the height of the invasion scare, when 15 Hampdens of 83 Squadron attacked a concentration of barges near Antwerp. As chance had it, Collier was not skippering his usual Hampden, named 'Bet' after his wife.

In the event, 'Bet', badly damaged by flak and on fire, only just managed to get home, thanks to the valiant efforts of Sergeant John Hannah, its 18-year-old wireless operator and gunner. After exhausting every fire extinguisher, Hannah, though forced to remove his face mask and suffocating in the heat, eventually beat out the flames with his logbook and hands. He was awarded the VC.

In addition to being mentioned in despatches, Collier won a Bar to his DFC for his outstanding courage and airmanship in an attack on the battle cruiser *Scharnhorst*, which, together with its twin *Gneisenau*, was subjected to unremitting day and night assault while sheltering at Brest on the French Atlantic coast.

In the New Year of 1943, Collier was posted to the directorate of bomber operations at the Air Ministry where he served with Group Captain Sydney Bufton. Together they planned the operation for the delivery of Barnes Wallis's bouncing bombs on the Mohne, Eder and Sorpe dams.

Collier was also delighted to work closely with his friend Wing Commander Guy Gibson, who had also been in No 83. Their easy and fruitful co-operation had much to do with the success of the Dambusters' raid.

John David Drought Collier was born near Plymouth on November 10 1916, the son of a businessman. After education at St Petroc's School in Bude, Cornwall, and Tettenhall College, Staffordshire, he trained as a land agent under Lord Leigh at Leamington Spa. Subsequently he was employed by John Bishop of Northam, Devon, whose daughter Elizabeth he married in 1939.

In 1936 Collier received a short-service commission and was posted to 83 Squadron at Turnhouse in Scotland, where he flew Hawker Hind biplane light bombers. In 1938 he moved with the squadron to Scampton, Lincolnshire, where it was re-equipped in No 5 Group with Hampdens, known on account of their elongated appearance as 'panhandles'.

Shortly after Neville Chamberlain's announcement that Britain was at war with Germany, 83 Squadron carried out a sweep over the North Sea. On December 21 Collier led the squadron into action as part of a force of 24 Hampdens and 18 Wellingtons attacking the pocket battleship *Deutschland*.

The operation, however, was frustrated by poor weather conditions and after failing to locate *Deutschland* off Norway, the bombers scattered and straggled home. Collier, almost out of fuel, managed to land at Acklington in Northumberland, where another Hampden crashed. Worse still, two Hampdens were mistaken for Dornier 17 bombers and shot down over the sea by Spitfires of No 602 (City of Glasgow) Squadron.

After his exploits with No 83, Collier was posted in March 1941 to No 44, another Hampden squadron, and that December received command of No 420, a Royal Canadian Air Force squadron similarly equipped. Then in 1942 he took over No 97, an Avro Lancaster four-engined bomber squadron, which he led on many dangerous missions. For maintaining the squadron 'in the highest state of efficiency', and for his 'exemplary conduct', he was awarded the DSO.

In 1944 Collier continued to further action against enemy industry and communications as chairman of a small committee which included representatives of Special Operations Executive and experts in the Ministry of Economic Warfare.

With the return of peace, Collier received a permanent commission, and in late 1945 was appointed station commander at Kankesanturai in Ceylon, and the next year at Iwakuni in Japan. He returned home in 1947 to become a member of the directing staff at the RAF Staff College, Bracknell, Berkshire. After further appointments at the Air Navigation School, HQ Bomber Command, and with Nato in Norway, he left the RAF in 1959.

Collier then resumed his pre-war career as a land agent, joining Hayward and Coundley at Ringwood in Hampshire. After retiring at 65 he devoted much of his time to voluntary work for Dr Barnardo's.

His wife survives him [in fact, Beth Collier had died in 1998]. They had three sons.

High-level Mining Technique

1. Mining operations against the Biscay ports are at present impeded by the requirements of accuracy and restrictions on the height of release of the mine. The requirements for accuracy originated from the early days of the war when precise mining of harbour channels was possible and small numbers of mines were laid, with the aim of sinking ships. Today this position has greatly altered. We are unable to lay mines in the narrow channels near the port entrances; we now lay a greatly increased number of mines, and our aim in mine laying particularly against the Biscay ports, is primarily to delay sailings by forcing the enemy to sweep a clear passage, although it is of course still hoped to cause some sinkings.

2. It is contended that if height restrictions on mine laying are removed and mine laying is undertaken from heights of 10 to 15,000 feet, new tactics can be evolved that will permit, with a reduction in hazards, the mining of the near approaches to ports and in certain cases the port area effectiveness of our present operations.

Advantages and Disadvantages of High Level Mining.

3. Our present low level mining tactics are subject to serious restrictions. Our aircraft at low heights are highly vulnerable to the light flak defences of the narrow approaches to the bases. The enemy have now become familiar with our tactics and have a highly developed watching organisation which is able to plot the track of our aircraft and the areas likely to be infected by our mines, thus simplifying their sweeping problems. High level mining would eliminate a number of these restrictions and should make it possible to mine the actual entrances to the harbours. The enemy would be unable to track our aircraft accurately and would be forced to clear a safe channel from the port entrance to the

deep water. The Admiralty estimate that this would probably involve the enemy in three times their present sweeping commitment and, in addition, reduce our own casualty rate. Thus the blockade effect would be considerably increased.

4. The chief disadvantage of high level mining is that inaccuracies in aiming are liable to result in a number of the mines falling outside the navigable channels, or possibly on the land. However, as the aim is to force the enemy to undertake sweeping operations as well as to get a percentage of the mines into the narrower channels, the loss could be well afforded. The enemy would be unable to foresee where the mines had actually fallen and would therefore have to treat the whole port area and approaches as suspect.

Description of Operations.

5. The mining operation would be undertaken from heights between 10/15,000 feet, the lowest height which would not incur serious losses, being chosen according to the strength of the defences.

6. A pre-determined aiming point would be chosen so that when the likely scatter of mines is allowed for, the main channels leading to the port will be covered.

7. The aiming point would be accurately marked by aircraft from the Path Finder Force employing Oboe or H.2.S. technique. The main force would approach along a chosen track parallel with the main channels and use a marker float as aiming point for the other mines.

8. It is calculated that an aiming error of not greater than 2,000 yards would be achieved by the main force – this error would permit the very great majority of mines to fall in useful water. This is illustrated by:-

Appendices 'A', 'B' and 'C' are charts of Lorient, Brest and St Nazaire respectively, and Appendices 'D', 'E' and 'F' are transparencies showing the expected distribution of mines aimed from 10,000 feet with an average error of 2,000 yards at the aiming point; by placing the transparencies over the charts it will be seen that the main channels in each port can be adequately and economically covered by mines from small forces of aircraft.

Type of Mine and Sea Marker to be employed.

9. Aiming carried out from a high level would undoubtedly increase the possibility of a small number of mines falling into enemy hands. The ideal mine to use is therefore the water/land mine (Mark VIA) which will be introduced in Service about August 1943. This mine is designed for release from high level and is provided with a detonator for use as a land mine if it does not fall in the water. If it is desirable to operate the scheme before August, the Admiralty state that they have a number of mine assemblies available, the design of which has been compromised, which they would be willing to use for high level mining and accept the risk of their falling into the hands of the enemy.

10. The Marine Marker Mk II is available and is considered suitable as a sea marker for use in High Level Mining Technique. This marker burns for 2 hours and is visible for 10–20 miles.

Conclusions.

11. The proposed new technique for mining operations is designed mainly for use against the Biscay ports. Here the value of mining operations is primarily the delay to sailing rather than the sinking of submarines. The new technique has, however, many possibilities for operation in defended areas such as Kiel Bay, Hamburg etc. when the mining aircraft could operate in conjunction with a bombing attack.

12. The disadvantage that a small percentage of mines will be wasted, however, is more than offset by the following advantages:-

(i)   It will be possible to mine the narrower channels now prohibited to us, without undue risk to the mining aircraft.

(ii) The present elaborate enemy mine spotting organisation is likely to be thrown into confusion, and be unable to plot the fall of the mines.

(iii) The enemy will be forced to undertake a far greater mine sweeping commitment, as all waters are likely to be suspect in the area of operation, irrespective of the strength of mining force employed.

(iv) Mining operations can be readily combined with bombing operations against ports.

B.Ops.1.
25th June 1943.

Sources and Bibliography

Manuscript Sources

John Collier's 1946 memoir of B Ops 1 *Adventure in the Air Ministry*, and assorted later writings on his years with front-line squadrons in RAF Bomber Command, and experiences in Japan in 1946/47. / Letters from John Collier to his parents. / RAF Pilot's Log Books and RAF Officers Record of Service.

Archival Sources

The National Archives at Kew: Operations Record Books – 83 Squadron [AIR27/686/2–15]; 44 Squadron [AIR27/448/5–21]; 420 (RCAF) Squadron [AIR27/1825/3–6]; 97 Squadron [AIR27/766/27–33]. Combat Report, 28/29 Aug 1942 [AIR50/200/5]. Directorate of Bomber Operations files: Sea Mining (including 'High level mining by H2S') [AIR20/4731]; Joint CROSSBOW Target Priorities Committee and Working Committee [AIR20/4754]; Tunnels (Highball tests) [AIR20/4756]; Schwamenauer & Urfttalsperre dams [AIR20/5984]; Directives to Bomber Command (including instruction not to bomb Peugeot, Montbelliard, 1943) [AIR20/6110]; Attacks on CROSSBOW (Rocket Projectile) sites [AIR40/1884]; Tallboy [AIR40/1885].
Churchill Archive, Churchill College, Cambridge: Bufton Papers [BUFT].
97 Squadron Association – online excerpts from Operations Record Books.

Bibliography

Babington Smith, Constance, *Evidence in Camera* (Chatto & Windus, 1957)
Barclay, Marion Jean, *The Brave Die Never* (1993)
Barker, Ralph, *Strike Hard, Strike Sure* (Chatto & Windus, 1963 & reprint Pen & Sword, 2003)
Beck, Pip, *Keeping Watch: A WAAF in Bomber Command* (Goodall, 1989 & Crecy, 2004)
Bending, Kevin, *Achieve Your Aim: The History of 97 (Straits Settlements) Squadron in the Second World War* (Woodfield Publishing, 2005)
Bishop, Patrick, *Bomber Boys* (Harper Press, 2007)

Campbell, Christy, *Target London* (Little Brown, 2012)

Cooper, Alan, *Beyond the Dams to the* Tirpitz (William Kimber & Co., 1983)

Fergusson, Bernard, *The Watery Maze: The Story of Combined Operations* (Collins, 1961)

Flower, Stephen, *Barnes Wallis's Bombs – Tallboy, Dambuster & Grand Slam* (Tempus, 2004)

Foot, M.R.D., *SOE – The Special Operations Executive 1940–1946* (BBC, 1984)

Gibson, Guy, *Enemy Coast Ahead Uncensored* (Crecy, 2006)

Grayling, A.C., *Among the Dead Cities* (Walker & Co., New York, 2006)

Hastings, Max, *Bomber Command* (Pan Books, 1999)

Holland, James, *Dam Busters – The Race to Smash the Dams 1943* (Bantam Press, 2012)

Low, Ronald G. & Harper, Frank E., *83 Squadron 1917–1969* (1992)

Lyall, Gavin (ed.), *Voices from the War in the Air 1939–45* (Vintage, 2007)

MacDonald, Charles B., *The Siegfried Line Campaign* (Center of Military History, US Army, Washington DC, 1990)

McLynn, Frank, *The Burma Campaign – Disaster into Triumph 1942–45* (Bodley Head, 2010)

Melinsky, Hugh, *Forming the Pathfinders: The Career of Air Vice-Marshal Sydney Bufton* (The History Press, 2010)

Morris, Richard, *Guy Gibson* (Viking, 1994)

Richards, Dennis, *The Royal Air Force 1939–1945, Vol I, The Fight At Odds* (HMSO, 1953)

Richards, Dennis & Saunders, Hilary St George, *The Royal Air Force 1939–1945, Vol II, The Fight Avails* (HMSO, 1954)

Sainty, Peter J., *Zig-Zag – The Hampdens of 420 (RCAF) Squadron RAF* (2008)

Saunders, Hilary St George, *The Royal Air Force 1939–1945, Vol III, The Fight is Won* (HMSO, 1954)

Swiebocki, Henryk (ed.), *London Has Been Informed... Reports by Auschwitz Escapees* (The Auschwitz-Birkenau State Museum, Oswiecim, 1997)

Taylor, A.J.P., *The Second World War: An Illustrated History* (Penguin, 1976)

Zaloga, Steven J., *German V-Weapon Sites 1943–45* (Osprey, 2007)

Ziegler, Philip, *Mountbatten – The Official Biography* (1985)

Ziegler, Philip, *London at War 1939–45* (Sinclair-Stevenson, 1995)

Index